The Masterworks of Literature Series

Sylvia E. Bowman, *Editor*
Indiana University

The Valley of Shadows

The Valley of Shadows

by FRANCIS GRIERSON

Edited for the Modern Reader by
Harold P. Simonson
UNIVERSITY OF WASHINGTON

COLLEGE & UNIVERSITY PRESS · *Publishers*
NEW HAVEN, CONN.

New Material, Introduction and Notes
by Harold P. Simonson

MANUFACTURED IN THE UNITED STATES OF AMERICA BY
UNITED PRINTING SERVICES, INC.
NEW HAVEN, CONNECTICUT

To Bill and Trudi

Contents

Introduction   9

A Note on the Text   23

Suggestions for Further Reading   24

Preface   27

Proem   29

I.   The Meeting-House   33

II.   The Load-Bearer   43

III.   The Log-House   52

IV.   Socrates Gives Advice   58

V.   Silas Jordan's Illness   66

VI.   The Cabin of Socrates   71

VII.   At the Post-Office   84

VIII.   My Visit to the Load-Bearer's Home   89

IX.   A Night of Mystery   99

X.   Sowing and Reaping   105

XI.   The Flight   113

XII.   The Camp-Meeting   124

XIII.   The Pioneer of the Sangamon Country   138

XIV.   The Regulators   149

XV.   Alton and the Mississippi   161

XVI.	Abraham Lincoln	166
XVII.	St. Louis: Society and the Churches	171
XVIII.	The Great Fair	178
XIX.	The Planters' House	180
XX.	The Torch-Light Procession	185
XXI.	Camp Jackson	189
XXII.	General Fremont	193
XXIII.	The Dance of Death	198
XXIV.	In the Maze	206
XXV.	Grierson's Raid	213
XXVI.	The Valley of Shadows	217

Introduction

"A strange fish" was Van Wyck Brooks' encomium to Francis Grierson. The same adjective can describe *The Valley of Shadows*, Grierson's major book. When it first appeared in 1909, readers were hard pressed to know just what kind of a book it was. Grierson had stated in his preface that it was not a novel but "recollections of scenes and episodes" of his childhood spent in Abraham Lincoln's Middle West just prior to the Civil War. But the book obviously depicted something more: something Grierson himself called "silences" which he later explained as the spiritual atmosphere of the Lincoln country—the atmosphere in which Lincoln "lived and moved, thought and worked."

Outdated as terms like, "silences" and "spiritual atmosphere" were in a new century heralding literary Realism, readers were disinclined to ignore the book. Although it may lack "startling reality," said a critic in *The Dial*, Grierson's art should "not be quarreled with." The English critic A. R. Orage, in *The Art of Reading* (1930), said Grierson's book contained "one of the rarest qualities in literature, namely, atmosphere." In recognizing this same quality, still other readers described *The Valley of Shadows* as "poetic," "haunting," "uncanny," "drenched in mysticism." From the guarded statement in the *New York Times* ("It is no ordinary book that Francis Grierson has written") to the exaltation of Shaemas O'Sheel in *The New Republic* (the book is "unsurpassed by anything since Homer and Xenophon") readers continually acknowledged Grierson's success in capturing the darkening mood perculiar to the coming of America's irrepressible conflict. Mary Austin, who also spent her childhood in Illinois, was still another person struck by the book's tonal authenticity. "Often while I have read your book," she wrote in 1911 from London, "I would lay it aside and weep

9

quietly for I knew not what. . . . It was as if something—the spirit of the land perhaps—which I had worshiped afar off, had turned back after all these years and hailed me."

Appraisals of this work underscore the fact that today the book is still regarded as quite unlike anything in American literature. So impressed was Carl Sandburg by Grierson's description of Lincoln debating Stephen A. Douglas at Alton, Illinois, that Sandburg quoted generously from it in his *Abraham Lincoln: The Prairie Years*. Roy P. Basler argued in *The Lincoln Legend* that, as an interpretation of Lincoln the mystic, Grierson's book is "by far the most entrancing of any." In *Patriotic Gore*, his study of Civil War literature, Edmund Wilson devotes lengthy attention to Grierson and to the puzzling question of why his "unique" book has been "so strangely disregarded by historians and by writers on American literature." The question Wilson raises touches the vagaries of art itself; and, rather than fully pursue them in connection with Grierson, he suggests that to go back into America's literary past is to unearth "some remarkable writers and some admirable books." "One of the very queerest of these queer cases," he adds, is Francis Grierson. Actually, what may be the most succinct appraisal of *The Valley of Shadows* is Theodore Spencer's statement, in his introduction to the 1948 edition, that the book is "a minor classic." Bernard DeVoto went a step further in his editor's note to the same edition: "I should be willing to delete [Spencer's] adjective."

I

Grierson's real name was Benjamin Henry Jesse Francis Shepard, and until 1899 he was called either "Jesse" or "Ben Shepard." With the publication of *Modern Mysticism* in the same year (he considered this book his first important one), he took his mother's maiden name, Grierson; and, from that time on he went by Francis Grierson. He was born on September 18, 1848, in the English town of Birkenhead, across the Mersey River from Liverpool. In March of the next year his parents emigrated to the United States to escape widespread economic depression which, by 1850, had sent nearly nineteen thousand English settlers to Illinois alone. His father, Joseph Shepard, built a log cabin for his family and worked hard on the prairies, but he knew almost from the start that he was ill-suited to this kind of life. Francis' mother, Emily Grierson Shepard, found frontier life no less hard and its social isolation even more depressing. Out on the prairies it was no advantage that her Scottish lineage included Sir Robert Grierson, fourteenth Laird of Lag in the fifteenth century, and Sir Robert Redgauntlet of Sir Walter Scott's novel *Redgauntlet*. Therefore, when Joseph Shepard accepted a government position in St. Louis in 1859, neither he nor Emily regretted leaving behind the log cabin and prairie sod. By 1871, with the prospect of returning to England in a few days, Emily described her many years in America as "wanderings in a wilderness." Three years after her return to "civilized life" in England, she wrote back to her cousin, General Benjamin Harrison Grierson of the Union Army, encouraging him to join them across the Atlantic.

With his parents and sister, young Grierson also left the frontier. He was eleven when they moved to St. Louis and seventeen when they moved to Chicago. Four years later, in 1869, he was in Paris. With little formal education but with a remarkable talent for the piano, he hobnobbed with royalty and artists alike. He never returned to anything remotely resembling pioneer life. In fact, he seemed to have irrevocably put aside his memories of the American frontier, and, instead, found his pleasures playing weirdly beautiful piano improvisations in palaces and salons. He made friends with literary and musical celebrities including Stéphane Mallarmé, Paul Verlaine, Arnold Bennett, John Lane, François Auber, and Samuel David. Because of his musical ability he became something of a celebrity himself. Furthermore, he conducted seances with General Jourafsky in St. Petersburg and, back in America, with Madame Blavatsky in Chittenden, Vermont, and with Spiritualists in both Chicago and San Diego. He wrote essays—fragile, impressionistic pieces resembling classical French pensées—for California's *The Golden Era* and for his own subsequent volumes bearing such wispy titles as *Essays and Pen-Pictures* (1889), *Pensées et Essais* (1889), *Modern Mysticism* (1899), and *The Celtic Temperament* (1901).

These were fabulous years for Grierson, wandering through Europe with his friend Lawrence Waldemar Tonner and playing in old, historic salons. At Baden-Baden, for example, he mixed with opera stars like Gabrielle Draus from the Paris Opera, and he also fell in with the King and Queen of Prussia; with Madame Viardot-Garcia, who was Turgenev's mistress and in whose villa

Grierson spent many evenings; and with Helene von Racowitza, the mistress of Lassalle. In St. Petersburg, he played for Alexander II; and he met Hortense Schneider, the Parisian singer, at a reception given for her by the czar. In London he gave recitals for small but distinguished audiences, such as those who gathered in the homes of Dowager Countess Dunsay or of S. C. Hall, editor of *The Art Journal*.

During these years he also travelled widely in the United States and, on one occasion, visited friends in Australia. But it was in California that a sequence of events led to his most astonishing experience, one which unfortunately is colored with charlatanry.

He and Tonner had come to San Diego in 1887 where they soon introduced themselves to a group of Spiritualists. At fever height all over the country in the late 1800's, Spiritualism had an especially active following in San Diego; and it was not long before Grierson took over. With exotic piano improvisations, spirit messages, hypnotism, or whatever, he persuaded two members of the group—William and John High—to build him a mansion to be called the "Villa Montezuma." Certain that the spirit messages came from William's deceased wife, the two brothers mortgaged their holdings and financed the house. They also furnished it with exquisite *objets*, so that, with its several turrets and stained-glass windows, it resembled some kind of feudal manor.

Amid these surroundings Grierson gave musical séances, enthralling his guests with unearthly chords and melodies. Some persons claimed to have heard drums, tambourines, and trumpets sounding all over the room; other guests reported hearing choirs of voices led by Grierson's own soprano voice soaring among the higher notes, then by his bass—"as grand and melodious as it was magnetic." The effect was "simply indescribable!" Even Sam High, who had cautioned his uncles William and John about Shepard (Grierson), reported that at first he was "contemptuous" about the whole mysterious business; but, after attending a musicale, he found the experience "one of the most wonderful" in his life.*

---

*The accounts come from H. C. Hensley, *Early San Diego*, I (unpub. MS in San Diego Public Library), pp. 498-99; Mrs. Vine Bowers, "Recollections of Jesse Shepard" (unpub. MS in Serra Junipero Historical Museum, San Diego Historical Society), p. 1; *San Diego Union* (July 20, 1913), Sec. 2, p. 1.

Late in 1888 Grierson took time to go to Paris where he arranged for the publication of *Essays and Pen-Pictures* and *Pensées et Essais*, thin volumes of essays written in San Diego and most of them previously published in *The Golden Era*. When he returned in September, 1889, he learned the disastrous fact that the High money was running out and that his own financial requests to General Grierson, his second-cousin, availed nothing. In the spring of 1890 he left San Diego as mysteriously as he had arrived, and by the summer he and Tonner were again in Europe to begin a twenty-three-year residence during which Grierson established his literary reputation.

II

When *The Valley of Shadows* appeared, Grierson was sixty-one years old; and, up to this time, he had written four books including *Modern Mysticism* and *The Celtic Temperament*. He had earlier seen at close hand how the Franco-Prussian War in 1870 brought France's Second Empire to a turbulent end. To him this event signaled the end of an era—the end of pomp and ceremony; the end of the delirious gaiety Jacques Offenbach's music inspired; and, most importantly, the end of what Grierson called the "wonderful, romantic movement." With the Third Republic came what to him was the "reign of the commonplace." Soberly, he watched the "lions of romance" depart—Hugo, Lamartine, and George Sand. In their place came "the jackals of realism," especially Emile Zola who, said Grierson, "had already begun to gnaw the bones left by Balzac."

Thirty years later, in England, Grierson witnessed the end of another era, this one ominously signaled by the death of Queen Victoria whose cortege on a cheerless January day in 1901 passed through the London streets as Grierson watched. As before, he saw the enfeeblement of aristocracy and all its appurtenances. He feared the consequences of bourgeois democracy "merging the classes into the masses" and "the aristocratic into the democratic." He thought the end of Victorianism would bring rampant materialism and social disintegration. Moreover, he grew increasingly uneasy about the international rivalries that appeared to him to be taking on frightening proportions. His outlook was also darkened by certain ideas advanced by late nineteenth-century thinkers. These ideas pertained to Darwinian science and to questions about the nature and purpose of man.

In the meantime Thomas Huxley popularized the term "agnosticism"; Max Nordau played on the theme of degeneration; Freud and Nietzsche studied human irrationality. Francis Grierson—as a deeply unsettled conservative, as a belated romantic longing for peaceful order and *noblesse oblige*—saw the end not only of an era and a century but, to him, of man's spirit.

What bedeviled Grierson was what, by the turn of the century, had become a fact of life: the scientific method. It offered no apparent place for the imagination and metaphysics; instead, its adherents presupposed that life consisted only of predictable and measurable facts. The French scientist Claude Bernard said in 1865 that, whereas empirical science had not yet reduced life to physico-chemical terms, it "shall doubtless succeed some day." That day seemed ever closer to Grierson, who decried the growing popularity of Auguste Comte's Positivism and, with it, the kind of literary Realism Hippolyte Taine preached in the famous introduction to his *Histoire de la littérature anglaise*, an essay in which he united the laws of art and the so-called scientific laws of society. In all this, Grierson saw an end to beauty and mystery, to spiritual reality and to imagination. If art were nothing more than an intellectual problem for rational understanding and social application, as Taine suggested, then for Grierson its metaphysical importance was hopelessly lost.

As the nineteenth century waned, Grierson observed that literary Realism founded upon the exactitude of fact was itself evolving into Naturalism and into an even more doctrinaire extension of pseudo-scientific principles. He abhorred the Naturalists' literary emphasis upon the conflict of social forces and, worse yet, upon the sordid, shocking, and depressive aspects of existence. With the Rougon-Macquart series of Zola highlighted by such novels as *L'Assommoir, Nana, Germinal*, and *La Terre*; with the novels of the Goncourt brothers, J. K. Huysmans, de Maupassant, and the so-called "putrid literature" of the Germinie Lacerteux school; and with the culmination of scientific Realism and Naturalism in the morbid decadence of the *fin de siècle* which proclaimed, with Jules Laforge, the "eternullity" of life—with all these came Grierson's still small but protesting voice.

Modern Mysticism, his third thin volume of essays, treated such subjects as art, beauty, nature, and wisdom—favorite subjects for a late nineteenth-century Romantic who, like Grierson, was clinging to the dying hopes of an expiring era. Grierson delicately wove these essays into a single theme—modern mysticism—by which he believed modern man could yet recover his lost sense of wonder and divine imaginings. In his fourth volume of essays, *The Celtic Temperament*, his theme shifted to more immediate problems; for he saw in contemporary England the oncoming end of philosophic idealism and, concurrently, the increasing impact of rationalism, Positivism, and Darwinianism which, to him, meant a denial of fixed species, an attack upon Christian morality, and a dehumanized scientific method. To him mankind was losing its capacity to absorb the mysteries of the supernatural. In this volume Grierson looked back to the old Celts whose temperament, he thought, enabled them to understand the nature of ultimate reality. This Celtic temperament, as he found it best expressed in François Chateaubriand, was absent in the modern age.

Grierson was a traditionalist who wanted to preserve the class distinctions favoring the élite. He also wanted to keep alive post-Kantian idealism which had achieved its definitive German statement in Hegel, its English expression with T. H. Green and F. H. Bradley, and its American form in the absolutism of Josiah Royce. Like them, Grierson asserted that behind the realm of appearances, the province of science, there exists a world of spirit. He believed that imagination when joined with intuition enables a person, especially the artist, to discover this transcendental realm. Grierson lacked the philosophical sophistication to conceptualize this kind of idealism; he constructed no complex intellectual system. His method was more the mystic's: music, poetry, contemplation, and his own uncanny manner of musical séances. A new day would come, he hoped, when once again the heart would dominate the head, when art would prevail over science, and metaphysics over empiricism.

It was fitting, then, that his chief protest should have taken the form of lyrical reminiscences. In them he would rediscover Abraham Lincoln and interpret him as an apocalyptic hero, one who had successfully contacted superphenomenal forces and, by appropriating them, had affected the destiny of men and history.

By the time Grierson was ready to write *The Valley of Shadows*, he had moved widely in social and cultural circles and, moreover, had taken his stand against many of the forces shaping a new century. His voice, however, was never command-ing; and, as he undertook to write his *chef d'oeuvre*, he with-drew almost entirely from public life. According to Van Wyck Brooks, who saw him occasionally in London at this time, Grier-son was "solitary, poor and all but forgotten." In *Scenes and Portraits* Brooks remembered Grierson as a tall man "with his worn old tweeds, his drooping moustache, pink cheeks, and crimson necktie." He continued: "The moustache was evidently dyed and he rouged his cheeks, and that he wore a wig was also apparent from the white hairs that straggled out over his ears; and later when he was caught by the rain and obliged to stay in my house I was sorry that I could not help him in the matter of cosmetics." A strange fish indeed, and a strange book too—one which, Grierson said, "took me ten years to write, and all my fortune to the *last* silver shilling. When the last page was fin-ished, the last shilling was spent."

III

To write *The Valley of Shadows* Grierson went back to the years when he had lived in Illinois amid the exciting times of camp-meetings, the Underground Railway, and the last of the Lincoln-Douglas debates. He recalled the prophecies of frontiers-men and the role the Emancipator would have. For a person so many years away from the prairies, Grierson's success was the more remarkable. In this book he gave shape to his deep child-hood memories and used them to corroborate his present atti-tude toward the spirit-world of idealism and mysticism. His recollection of those years vivified again such presentiments as he had seen as a child: prairie fires and Donati's comet, warning of strange powers moving over the land, of oncoming war, and of one (Lincoln) who would come to lead his people through the "valley of shadows." In short, Grierson recalled these events at a time when his idealism demanded a narrative.

What Grierson did so well in this book was to re-create these times of national upheaval and religious fervor. Of course the first of these issues concerned the momentous question of slav-ery and Lincoln's task in resolving it. In 1858 the Shepards lived in Alton, Illinois, where on October 15 Lincoln and Douglas held the last of their seven famous debates. Standing close to the front, young Grierson watched the two men, so strikingly different in word and manner. Years later in *The Valley of*

Shadows Grierson described that occasion when, as he remembered, Lincoln "rose from his seat, stretched his long, bony limbs upward as if to get them into working order, and stood like some solitary pine on a lonely summit, very tall, very dark, very gaunt, and very rugged, his swarthy features stamped with a sad serenity, and the instant he began to speak the ungainly mouth lost his heaviness, the half-listless eyes attained a wondrous power, and the people stood bewildered and breathless under the natural magic."

It is clear that Grierson wished to interpret his youth as a time when he not only participated in the crucial events of history but, even more importantly, intuited meaning in them. And it was especially in Abraham Lincoln that he found the symbol of American destiny. To young Grierson, the figure of Lincoln loomed awesome enough; but, by the time he wrote *The Valley of Shadows*, the hero-figure had grown to mythical proportions. But it had also grown equally large to millions of Americans to whom hero-worship was nothing new. John C. Fremont was the "Pathfinder"; Andrew Jackson, "Old Hickory"; Zachary Taylor, "Old Rough-and-Ready." Lincoln, however, was more than even the composite frontiersman; for something mystical made him appear like another Moses, another Jesus Christ.

As Basler points out in *The Lincoln Legion*, Americans thought that Lincoln, assassinated on Good Friday, may have uttered with his dying breath, "Father, forgive them, for they know not what they do." Walt Whitman made this same connection between Lincoln and Jesus in "When Lilacs Last in the Dooryard Bloom'd," as did Emerson in his eulogistic essay entitled "Abraham Lincoln." Grierson's memory of Lincoln in Illinois helped him sustain this myth in *The Valley of Shadows*, as well as in a still later work—*Abraham Lincoln, The Practical Mystic* (1918)—which hailed Lincoln as "the greatest practical mystic the world has known for nineteen hundred years."

Other boyhood incidents made these times vivid to Grierson, the author. When the family lived for a while in Macoupin County, near Palmyra, their log house served as a station on the Underground Railway. Grierson's father several times narrowly avoided serious trouble with neighbors strongly sympathetic to the Southern cause. Even more memorable was the April day in 1861 when young Grierson sat in his St. Louis schoolroom and watched the flag of Secession go up. He had earlier witnessed the torchlight parade in St. Louis on the eve of the November election in 1860, a night heavy with fatality. "On it went," he wrote, "winding, winding, in and out, the flickering lights passing like a fiery dragon as far as one could see, the whole city receiving a symbolical visitation by fire, a baptismal warning of what was coming within the short space of a year from that hour."

On May 6, less than a month after the shots against Fort Sumter were fired, young Grierson saw Southern troops assemble at Camp Jackson in St. Louis. Four days later he stood on the street as five Northern regiments marched heavily by on their way to Camp Jackson which they easily forced to surrender. In the "Camp Jackson" chapter of *The Valley of Shadows* he said that the sight was "indescribably horrible," and he repeated his father's words, "this was civil war." In June, he became a page to General Fremont whose headquarters were in St. Louis; and the following year he was close at hand as Northern troops assembled for their attack upon Vicksburg farther down the river.

Religious revivalism in the Middle West was the other issue which in its own way added significant dimensions to the times Grierson was reliving. That there was a spiritual awakening in this region prior to the outbreak of the Civil War is a fact many historians have noted. From miles around pioneers came to open camp-meetings, there to struggle with the devil and, conveniently, to find an outlet for their starved emotions. Reaction against the Enlightenment of the previous century saw worshippers once again attempting, as had their Calvinist forefathers, to detect revelations of God's power. The people looked to comets, earthquakes, storms, and prairie fires as the peculiarly awful language of God. Of Donati's comet, which mysteriously appeared in the skies in 1858, Grierson's Load-Bearer in *The Valley of Shadows* says: "Thar's a mighty power movin' over the yearth." Such signs convinced the pioneers they were to be God's chosen instruments in His ineffable plans. This was old-time religion, nowhere better described than in Grierson's chapter on "The Camp-Meeting." Appropriate to these meetings were throngs of clapping, weeping, shouting, moaning, fainting rustics—like "a coast," Grierson wrote, "strewn with the dead and dying after a great wreck."

Evocative as these accounts are, Grierson expected his reader to get beyond them into what he called "silences." In the *antebellum* days of Illinois there was, he said in his Preface, "a power emanating from the spiritual side of life, and I have done my best to depict 'silences' that belonged to the prairies, for out of those silences came the voices of preacher and prophet and a host of workers and heroes in the great War of Secession." His characterizations of Kezia Jordan, Elihu Gest, Minerva Wagner, and preacher Azariah James represent the rough-chiseled but indomitable pioneer of both fact and legend who intuited this spiritual side and found strength in it. The scenes in *The Valley of Shadows* are intended to serve, therefore, as something more than either history or autobiography. Grierson said in his proem that "nothing but the term 'mystical'" can fittingly describe them. They are Grierson's attempt to touch his reader with a sense of the supernatural and to have him affirm what Grierson himself found to be elemental and real.

Whether Grierson succeeds in bringing his reader to this point may depend upon the reader's previous experience, to say nothing of his intellectual presuppositions, and must certainly depend upon the writer's use of language. Many persons have attested to Grierson's success. Others, like Edmund Wilson, feel the power in Grierson's writing and yet become slightly uncomfortable in what Wilson calls the "realm of mist." However, the very unpredictability of the newcomer's response to the book validates Grierson's own argument that a person is more than a rational mechanism. What is clear is Grierson's intention to enlarge America's 1850's and '60's into mythical proportions. In doing so, he created a mythical Garden, peopled it with mystics and seers, brought to it the shadows of war, and everywhere imbued it with a destiny not unlike a paradise to be regained. Abraham Lincoln is the symbolic attestation of a new order of man. "What he stood for in the middle of the nineteenth century," Grierson wrote in 1918, "the English-speaking people must stand for at the beginning of the twentieth."

IV

Grierson lived to write other books consisting largely of essays. *Parisian Portraits* (1910) carries the same gentility, idealism, and belated romanticism as before. *La Vie et les Hommes* (1911) and *Some Thoughts* (1911) are little more than collections of aphorisms, but it is worth noting that Grierson considered an aphoristic style the hallmark of an accomplished writer of prose. With his next two books—*The Humour of the Underman* (1911) and *The Invincible Alliance* (1913)—comes a new tone of desperateness, bringing to the surface what in his previous writing runs as an undercurrent. Written originally for A. R. Orage's journal *The New Age*— which published such writers as H. G. Wells, George Bernard Shaw, the Chestertons, Hilaire Belloc, and Arnold Bennett—the essays in these two books contain unembellished warnings about the war soon to sweep over the Continent. And always there was Grierson's additional point: the coming conflict was between not only ignorant armies but two ways of looking at life—the scientific and the metaphysical. What he saw ahead was a civilization given over to a wholly scientific and mechanistic world-view.

Hearing the rumblings of war, he sailed with Tonner on the *Lusitania*, arriving in New York on November 30, 1913. A New York *Evening Post* reporter sent to interview him wrote that Grierson's lips were rouged, his eyes darkened: "His hair was arranged in careful disorder over his brow, his hands elaborately manicured and many rings on his fingers; he wore a softly tinted, flowing cravat." Within two weeks Arthur Farwell, the editor of *Musical America*, welcomed him back as a "musical liberator." Other articles appeared in quick succession, all calling attention to Grierson's remarkable career.

For the next several years he lectured and gave piano recitals up and down the East Coast and as far west as Wisconsin and Illinois where he appeared at the state universities. In 1918 his American lectures were published as *Illusions and Realities of the War*. He now stressed the need for Anglo-American unity as the only defense against the German "monsters, brutes, cutthroats and the like." This book also registered his shock at new American fads, of which the most repellent to him were jazz and the "barbaric" saxophone, dancing in "syncopated embrace," cigarettes and gin, materialistic science, pragmatism, the cult of efficiency, and, in general, what Harold Stearns in *America, A Re-Appraisal* described as America's "modern, Western, abundance-founded, this-worldly, anti-mystical, gay and progress-convinced attitude."

Fortunately, there was a place where Grierson found refuge. In 1920, he moved to Los Angeles where, amid orange blossoms and occultists, he lived until his death on May 29, 1927. Finding inspiration in the writings of P. D. Ouspensky, he joined other Southern Californians in the quest for what the master had called "higher consciousness." From such exploration came a bizzare little volume Grierson entitled *Psycho-Phone Messages* (1921) in which he recorded messages he had received from the dead. Interpreting these "psycho-phonic waves," he gave his readers the words of such notables as Thomas Jefferson, Benjamin Franklin, Daniel Webster, Oliver Wendell Holmes, Abraham Lincoln, and Henry Ward Beecher.

Grierson's death in 1927 came suddenly. At the suggestion of Zona Gale, a benefit piano recital had been arranged by a close group of friends who planned to give the money collected to Grierson. He had played several improvisations already; and, just as he finished an unusually long one, Egyptian in character, he slumped over the keys dead.

It is true that Francis Grierson will never be more than a minor figure in American literary history. Nevertheless, there is a place for him, a unique place no one else can take. The same must be said for his masterpiece, *The Valley of Shadows*, a book truly written for Americans. As this nation continues to come of age and to discover an ever more variegated texture to its life, Grierson's account of this blood-stained land will find its readers and they will not forget it.

Harold P. Simonson

A Note on the Text

The text of *The Valley of Shadows* reprinted here is that of the first edition, published in London and New York in 1909. The principal editorial policy of this new edition is word-by-word accuracy. The only editorial changes are in spelling and punctuation, both intended to make the book easier and more pleasant to read. One exception should be noted: the editor has thought it best to leave Grierson's writing of dialect untouched, for the simple reason that to change even inconsistent spelling in any way may be to distort nuances in sound upon which written dialect depends for its authenticity. The overall aim in matters of editorial decision was to offer an accurate text that retains the spirit and effect of the original, but one that presents the fewest hindrances to the modern reader.

Suggestions for Further Reading

The only full-length biographical and critical study of Francis Grierson is Harold P. Simonson, *Francis Grierson*, Twayne's United States Authors Series, (New York, 1966). Several shorter studies include Edmund Wilson, "The Valley of Shadows," *The New Yorker*, XXIV (Sept. 18, 1948), 101-7, expanded and reprinted in *Patriotic Gore: Studies in the Literature of the American Civil War* (New York: Oxford University Press, 1962); Theodore Spencer, Introduction to *The Valley of Shadows*, fifth edition (Boston: Houghton Mifflin Company, 1948); Van Wyck Brooks, *The Confident Years, 1885-1915* (New York: E. P. Dutton, 1952), and *Scenes and Portraits* (New York: E. P. Dutton, 1954); Edwin Björkman, "Francis Grierson, A Study in Modern Mysticism," *Forum*, XLVIII (August, 1912), 145-58, and "The Music of Francis Grierson," *Harper's Weekly*, LVIII (Feb. 14, 1914), 15. Björkman also devotes an important section to Grierson in *Voices of To-Morrow: Critical Studies of the New Spirit in Literature* (New York: Mitchell Kennerley, 1913). A biographical essay on Grierson appears in *Dictionary of American Biography* (New York, 1931), vol. 7.

Bibliographies of Grierson are given in Simonson, "Francis Grierson—A Biographical Sketch and Bibliography," *Journal of the Illinois State Historical Society*, LIV (Summer, 1961), 198-203, and in *Francis Grierson*, noted above.

THE VALLEY OF SHADOWS

RECOLLECTIONS OF THE LINCOLN
COUNTRY 1858–1863

BY

FRANCIS GRIERSON

AUTHOR OF " MODERN MYSTICISM "
AND " THE CELTIC TEMPERAMENT "

These pages—concerning Abraham Lincoln
and heroic times—are dedicated
to my sister,
Mrs. Joseph Vance

Preface

This book is not a novel, but the recollections of scenes and episodes of my early life in Illinois and Missouri, the writing of which has been a labour of love. A cosmopolitan life in the different capitals of Europe during a period of forty years has not sufficed to alienate the romance and memory of those wonderful times.

In looking back I have come to the conclusion that the power displayed by the most influential preachers and politicians of the *ante-bellum* days in Illinois was a power emanating from the spiritual side of life, and I have done my best to depict the "silences" that belonged to the prairies, for out of those silences came the voices of preacher and prophet and a host of workers and heroes in the great War of Secession.

In 1863 President Lincoln issued his famous proclamation for the emancipation of the slaves, and with it the old order passed away never to return. Indeed, the social upheaval of that year was greater than that produced by the Declaration of Independence in 1776, and no matter what happens now, the old political and social conditions can never be revived. Not only have the people changed, but the whole face of the nation has changed— the prairies are gone, and luxurious homes are to be found in the places where log-houses, primitive woods, and wild flowers were the only prominent features of the landscape for many miles together.

I have recorded my impressions of the passing of the old democracy and the old social system in the United States, and, curiously enough, I witnessed again in 1869-70, while residing in Paris, the passing of another social order—that of Napoleon and the Empire, the recollections of which I shall leave for a future volume.

F. G.

Mill House, Radclive, Buckingham.
January, 1909.

Proem

IN THE late 'Fifties the people of Illinois were being prepared for the new era by a series of scenes and incidents which nothing but the term "mystical" will fittingly describe.

Things came about not so much by preconceived method as by an impelling impulse. The appearance of "Uncle Tom's Cabin" was not a reason, but an illumination; the founding of the Republican party was not an act of political wire-pulling, but an inspiration; the great religious revivals and the appearance of two comets were not regarded as coincidences, but accepted as signs of divine preparation and warning.

The settlers were hard at work with axe and plough; yet, in spite of material pre-occupation, all felt the unnameable influence of unfolding destiny. The social cycle, which began with the Declaration of Independence, was drawing to a close, and during Buchanan's administration the collective consciousness of men—that wonderful prescience of the national soul—became aware of impending innovation and upheaval.

It was impossible to tell what a day might bring forth. The morning usually began with new hope and courage; but the evening brought back the old silences, with the old, unsolved questionings, strange presentiments, premonitions, sudden alarms. Yet over and around all a kind of sub-conscious humour welled up, which kept the mind hopeful while the heart was weary. Dressed in butter-nut jeans, and swinging idly on a gate, many a youth of the time might have been pointed out as a likely Senator, poet, general, ambassador, or even President. Never was there more romance in a new country. A great change was coming over the people of the West. They retained all the best characteristics of the Puritans and the settlers of Maryland and Virginia, with something strangely original and characteristic of

29

*the time and place, something biblical applied to the circum-
stances of the hour.*

*Swiftly and silently came the mighty influences. Thousands
laboured on in silence; thousands were acting under an imperative, spiritual impulse without knowing it; the whole country
round about Springfield was being illuminated by the genius of
one man, Abraham Lincoln, whose influence penetrated all
hearts, creeds, parties, and institutions.*

*People were attracted to this region from Kentucky, Missouri,
Indiana, the shores of the Ohio, the British Isles, France, and
Germany. Other States had their special attractions: Indiana,
Kentucky, and Missouri contained hills and forests appealing to
the eye by a large and generous variation of landscape; Iowa and
Kansas sloped upward toward the West, giving to the mind an
ever-increasing sense of hope and power. To many, Illinois
seemed the last and the least because the most level. Only a
poet could feel the charm of her prairies, only a far-seeing
statesman could predict her future greatness.*

*The prairie was a region of expectant watchfulness, and life a
perpetual contrast of work and idleness, hope and misgiving.
Across its bosom came the covered wagons with their human
freight, arriving or departing like ships between the shores of
strange, mysterious worlds.*

*The early Jesuit missionaries often spoke of the Illinois prairie
as a sea of grass and flowers. A breeze springs up from the
shores of old Kentucky, or from across the Mississippi and the
plains of Kansas, gathering force as the hours steal on, gradually
changing the aspect of Nature by an undulating motion of the
grass, until the breeze has become a gale, and behold the prairie
a rolling sea! The pennant-like blades dip before the storm in
low, rushing billows as of myriads of green birds skimming the
surface. The grassy blades bend to the rhythm of Nature's
music, and when clouds begin to fleck the far horizon with dim,
shifting vapours, shadows as of long grey wings swoop down
over the prairie, while here and there immense fleeting veils rise
and fall and sweep on towards the sky-line in a vague world of
mystery and illusion.*

*The prairies possessed a charm created by beauty instead of
awe; for besides the countless wild flowers, they had rivers,
creeks, lakes, groves, and wooded strips of country bordering the
large streams.*

Everywhere, even in the most desolate places, at all times and seasons, signs of life were manifest in the traces, flights, and sounds of animals and birds. Over the snow, when all seemed obliterated, appeared the track of the mink, fox, and chick-a-dee, while during the greater part of the year the grass, woods, and air were alive with winged creatures that came and went in a perpetual chorus of audible or inaudible song.

The prairie was an inspiration, the humble settlers an ever-increasing revelation of human patience and progress. There was a charm in their mode of living, and real romance in all the incidents and events of that wonderful time.

CHAPTER 1

The Meeting-House

ALL through the winter the meeting-house on Saul's Prairie had stood deserted and dormant, its windows rattling in the bleak winds, perhaps longing for the coming revivals and the living, vital sympathy of beings "clothed in garments divine"; but now, how different it looked on this wonderful Sunday morning, with its door and windows wide open, the flowers in bloom, and the birds perched on the tallest weeds pouring forth their song! The fleckless sky and soft, genial atmosphere had made of the desolate little meeting-house and its surroundings a place that resembled a second Garden of Eden.

How calm and beautiful was the face of Nature! The prairie here in Illinois, in the heart of Lincoln's country, had a spirit of its own, unlike that of the forest, and I had come to look upon the meeting-house as a place possessing a sort of soul, a personality which made it stand out in my imagination as being unique among all the meeting-houses I had ever seen. It must, I thought, feel the states of the weather and the moods of the people.

The settlers made their way to meeting in wagons, on horseback, and on foot; and for nearly an hour people straggled in. They came in family groups, and a moment of excitement would be followed by a period of impatient waiting. They came from the west, where a faint column of smoke rose in a zigzag in the warm, limpid atmosphere; from the north, where houses and cabins were hidden in groves or in hollows; from the south, where a forest of old oaks and elms bordered the horizon with a belt of dark green; and from the east, where the rolling prairie spread beyond the limits of vision, a far-reaching vista of grass and flowers.

I had arrived early on my pony. Our neighbours would be here, and I should see some of them for the first time.

Silas Jordan and his wife, Kezia, were among the first to arrive. He, small, thin, and shrivelled, with wiry hair and restless nerves, had a face resembling a spider's web; cross-bars of crows' feet encircled two small, ferret-like eyes, sunk deep in their sockets, out of which he peered with eager suspicion at the moving phenomena of the world. She, with that deep glow that belongs to the dusk of certain days in autumn, had jet-black hair, smoothed down till it covered the tops of her ears; her neck rose in a column from between two drooping shoulders, and her great lustrous eyes looked out on the world and the people like stars from a saffron sunset. Dark and dreamy, she seemed a living emblem of the tall, dark flowers and the willows that bordered the winding rivers and creeks of the prairies.

Then came the Busbys on a horse that "carried double," Serena Busby wearing a new pink calico dress and sun-bonnet, the colour clashing with her reddish hair and freckled face.

When these had settled in their seats there came one of those half-unearthly spells of silence and waiting not unlike those moments at a funeral just before the mourners and the minister make their appearance.

I had taken a seat inside for a while, but I slipped out again just in time to see a man come loping along on a small, shaggy horse, man and animal looking as if they had both grown up on the prairie together. It was Zack Caverly, nicknamed Socrates. Zack was indeed a Socrates of the prairie as well in looks as in speech, and the person who first called him after the immortal sage had one of those flashes of inspiration that come now and then to the scholar whose cosmopolitan experience permits him to judge men by a single phrase or a gesture. He tied his horse to a hitching-post, then stood at the door waiting to see what new faces would appear at the meeting. Here he met his old acquaintance Silas Jordan.

The talk soon turned to personalities.

"Have ye heerd who them folks is down yander in the Log-House?" began Silas, alluding to the new home of my parents.

"They air from the old kintry," Socrates answered, his round eyes blinking a manner not to be described.

"Kinder stuck up fer these diggin's, I'm thinkin'."

"I 'low they ain't like us folks," was the careless response.

"They hed a heap o' hired help whar they come from."

"The Squar tole me hisself what kyounties he hez lived in sense he come from the old kintry. He hez lived in two kyounties in Missouri en in four kyounties in Illinois, and now I reckon it's root hog or die ez fur ez these diggin's goes. It's his second trial on prairie land. He 'lows it'll be the last if things don't plough up jest ez he's sot his mind te havin' 'em. He's a-layin' in with the Abolitionists, and he voted oncet fer Abe Lincoln, en he sea he air ready te do it ag'in."

Socrates looked down the road, and exclaimed:

"Bless my stars! if thar ain't Elihu Gest! He's got a stranger with him."

When Elihu Gest hitched his horse to the fence Socrates greeted him:

"Howdy, howdy, Brother Gest. I war wonderin' what hed become o' ye. Ain't seen ye in a coon's age."

Elihu Gest was known as the "Load-Bearer." He had earned this nickname by his constant efforts to assume other people's mental and spiritual burdens. The stranger he brought with him was the preacher.

"I war jes' wonderin' ez I come along," said the Load-Bearer, "what the Know-nothin's en sech like air a-goin' te do, seein' ez how Lincoln en Douglas air dividin' the hull yearth a-twixt 'em."

"Providence created the Know-nothin's te fill up the chinks," answered Zack Caverly, "en ye know it don't noways matter *what* ye fill 'em up with."

"I 'low the chinks hez to be filled up somehow," replied the Load-Bearer, "en a log-cabin air a mighty good place te live in when a man's too pore te live in a frame house."

"Thet's it; them thar politicioners like Abe Lincoln en Steve Douglas hev quit livin' in log-cabins, en thar ain't no chinks fer the Know-nothin' party te fill," said Socrates.

He had taken out a big jack-knife and was whittling a stick.

"'Pears like thar's allers three kyinds o' everything—thar war the Whigs, the Demicrats, en the Know-nothin's, en thar air three kyinds o' folks all over this here kintry—the Methodists, the Hardshells, en them thet's saft at feedin'-time, plumb open fer vittles en dead shet agin religion. Ez I war explainin' te Squar Briggs t'other day, in the heavings thar air the sun, the moon, en the stars; thet air three kyinds agin. En whar hev ye ever see a kivered wagin 'thout hosses, critters, en yaller dogs?

The yaller dogs air steppin'-stones te the hosses, the hosses comin' in right betwixt the varmints en human bein's, which the Scriptur' sez air jest a leetle below the angels. But ye'd never guess 'thout a heap o' cute thinkin' thet a yaller dog could make hisself so kinder useful like ez wal ez pertickler. Ez fer folks gen'ly, thar air three kyinds—Yankees, niggers, en white people."

"Ye don't calc'late te reckon niggers ez folks!" ejaculated Silas Jordan.

"They air folks jes like we air," said the Load-Bearer, "en they hev souls te save. They air bein' called on, but somehow the slave-owners ain't got no ears fer the call."

"Wal," chimed in Socrates, "I ain't agin th' Abolitionists, en up te now I ain't tuck much int'rest in the argiments fer en ag'inst. I ain't called on fer te jedge noways." He looked about him and continued: "They air talkin' 'bout freein' the niggers, but some o' these here settlers ain't got spunk 'nough te choose thar partner fer a dance, ner ile 'nough in thar j'ints te bow in a ladies' chain. Mebbe arter all the niggers air a sight better off'n we uns air. They ain't got no stakes in the groun'."

At this point there was a shuffling of feet and spitting. Then his thoughts turned to the past.

"Afore Buchanan's election I hed all the fiddlin' I could do, but when Pete Cartwright come along he skeered 'em, en when the Baptists come they doused 'em in p'isen cold water, en now folks air predictin' the end o' the world by this here comet.* I'll be doggoned if I've drawed the bow oncet sence folks got skeered plumb te thar marrer-bones! T'other night when I heared sunthin' snap I warn't thinkin' o' the fiddle, en when I tuck it down the nex' day jes' te fondle it a leetle fer ole times' sake I see it war the leadin' string; en good, lastin' catgut air skase ez crowin' hens in these 'ere parts."

Silas Jordan, returning to the subject of my parents, remarked:

"I reckon them Britishers at the Log-House 'll hev te roll up en wade in if they want te git on in this here deestric'."

Just then the talk was interrupted by the appearance of the persons in question, and the crowd at the door stared in silence as they walked in. When Silas recovered his wits he continued his remarks:

*Donati's great comet.

"She's got on a store bunnit en he's got on a b'iled shirt." To which Socrates replied, without evincing the least surprise:

"Tallest man I've seed in these parts 'cept Abe Lincoln."

There was a pause, during which the two men gazed through the open door at the tall man who had passed in and taken a seat.

There was something strangely foreign and remote in the impression my parents produced at the meeting. My mother wore a black silk gown and a black bonnet with a veil; the tall, straight figure of my father appeared still taller with his long frock coat and high collar, and his serious face and Roman nose gave him something of a patriarchal look, although he was still in the prime of life. The arrival of the family from the Log-House caused a flutter of curiosity, but when it was seen that the newcomers were devout worshippers the congregation began to settle down to a spirit of religious repose.

It was a heterogeneous gathering: humorists who were unconscious of their humour, mystics who did not understand their strange, far-reaching power, sentimental dreamers who did their best to live down their emotions, old-timers and cosmopolitans with a marvellous admixture of sense and sentiment, political prophets who could foresee events by a sudden, illuminating flash and foretell them in a sudden, pithy sentence. It was a wonderful people, living in a second Canaan, in an age of social change and upheaval, in a period of political and phenomenal wonders.

A vague longing filled the hearts of the worshippers. With the doubts and misgivings of the present, there was a feeling that to-morrow would bring the realisation of all the yearnings and promises, and when the preacher rose and announced that wistful old hymn:

> "In the Christian's home in glory
> There remains a land of rest,"

an instant change was produced in the faces of the people. Silas Jordan led the singing in a high, shrill voice which descended on the meeting like a cold blast through a broken window, but Uriah Busby, always on the look-out for squalls, neutralised the rasping sounds by his full, melodious waves. His voice gave forth an unctuous security, not unmixed with a good part of Christian gallantry. In it there was something hearty and fraternal; it leavened conditions and persons, and made the strangers feel at home.

If Uriah Busby's singing gave substance to the meeting, that of Kezia Jordan gave expression to its soul. In the second line her voice rose and fell like a wave from the infinite depths, with something almost unearthly in its tones, that seemed to bring forth the yearnings of dead generations and the unfulfilled desires of her pioneer parents.

A voice had been heard from behind the thin veil that separates the two worlds.

My mother felt somewhat timid among so many strangers. As she looked down at the hymn-book in her hands, her brows, slightly elevated, gave to her face an expression of pensive reverence. Kezia Jordan had noticed two things about the newcomer: her wonderful complexion and her delicate hands. Kezia had as yet only glanced at the stranger; had she heard her speak, she would have remembered her voice as an influence going straight to the soul, touching at the heart's secrets without naming them —a voice that enveloped the listener as in a mantle of compassion, with intonations suggestive of unaffected sympathy for all in need of it.

My mother had often heard the old Methodist hymns, but now for the first time she felt the difference between the music of a trained choir and the effects produced by the singing of one or two persons inspired by the spirit of the time, hour, and place. Never had sacred song so moved her. Kezia Jordan had infused into two lines something which partook of revelation. The words of the hymn, then, were true, and not a mere juggling with sentiment. Here was an untrained singer who by an unconscious effort revealed a truth which came to the listener with the force of inexorable law, for the words, "there remains a land of rest," came as a decree as well as a promise; and my mother now realised what life in the Log-House would be for her.

A glance at the singer confirmed the impression created by her singing. There, in her strange prophetic features, shone the indelible imprints made by the lonely years in the long and silent conflict; there, in Kezia Jordan's eyes, shone the immemorial mementoes of the ages gone, while the expression of her face changed as the memories came and went like shadows of silent wings over still, clear waters.

Prayers had been offered with more or less fervour; and now with awkward demeanour the preacher stood up, his pale face and half-scared expression arousing in the minds of many of the people no little curiosity and some apprehension.

"Brethering and sistering," he began, in a rambling way, "ye hev all heared the rumours thet hez been passed from mouth te mouth pertainin' te the signs and wonders o' these here times. Folks's minds is onsettled. But me en Brother Gest hev been wrastlin' with the Sperrit all night yander at his God-fearin' home; we were wrastlin' fer a tex' fittin' this here time en meetin', en it warn't till sommairs nigh mornin' thet Brother Gest opened the Good Book, en p'intin' his finger, sez: 'I hev found it! Hallelujer!' It war Isaiah, nineteenth chapter, twentieth verse."

Here the preacher opened the Bible. He read slowly, emphasising certain words so that even the most obtuse present might catch something of the meaning.

" 'En it shell be *fer* a sign, en *fer* a witness unto the Lord of hosts in the land of Egypt: fer they shell cry unto the Lord bekase of the oppressors, en he *shell* send them a savior, en a *great* one, en he shell deliver them.' "

He stopped a moment to let the congregation muse on the text, and then proceeded:

"It looked like when he put his finger on the tex' Brother Gest war changed ez in a twinklin', en our watchin' en prayin' war over fer thet night. Brethering, with the findin' o' thet tex' our troubles war gone, en in thar place thar come te our innermost feelin's a boundin' joy sech ez on'y them thet hez faith kin know."

Here he lost himself; then like a drowning man who clutches at a straw, he seized hold of an old hackneyed text, the first that came into his mind, and continued, regardless of consequences:

"Fer ez the Scriptur' sez, 'What came ye out fer te see? A reed shaken by the wind?' I 'low most o' ye hez plenty reeds if ye're anywhars near a snipe deestric', but I reckon ye ain't troubled much by seein' 'em shake."

He began to regain confidence, and leaving reeds he grappled with the earth and the heavens in periods which carried everybody with him.

"But thar ain't a sinner here, thar ain't no Christian here to-day thet warn't plumb shuck up by thet yearth-quake t'other night thet rocked ye in yer beds like ye were bein' rocked in a skiff in the waves behind one o' them Mississippi stern-wheelers. No, brethering, the Lord hez passed the time when He shakes yer cornfields en yer haystacks by a leetle puff o' wind. He hez opened the roof o' Heaven so ye can all see what's a-comin'. He hez made it so all o' ye, 'cept them thet's blind, kin say truly, *'I hav seen it.'* Under ye the yearth hez been shuck, over ye the stars air beginnin' te shift en wander. A besom o' destruction 'll overtake them thet's on the wrong side in this here fight!"

He eyed the people up and down on each side, and then went on:

"But the tex' says, 'He shell send them a saviour, en a *great* one, en he shell deliver them.' Now it air jest ez plain ez the noonday sun thet the Lord God app'ints His own leaders, en it air jest ez plain thet His ch'ice ain't fell on no shufflin' backslider. Ye kin bet all yer land en yer cattle en yer hosses on this one preposition, en thet is ye cain't git away from fac's by no cross-argimints thet many air called but mighty few air chosen; en thet means thet on'y one man is 'p'inted te lead."

At this there was a visible change in the attitude of many of the listeners.

"What air he a-comin' to?" whispered old Lem Stephens to Uriah Busby.

It was a bold stroke; but Elihu Gest, the Load-Bearer, had won over the preacher to speak out, and he was coming to the main point as fast as an artless art and blunt but effective rhetoric would let him.

He proceeded with his sermon, now bringing the expectant people to the verge of the last period, now letting them slip back as if he were giving them a "breathing spell" to brace them for a still stronger stage in the argument. It was wonderful how this simple preacher, without education or training, managed to keep the interest of the congregation at boiling point for more than an hour before he pronounced the two magical words that would unlock the whole mystery of the discourse. Before him sat old Whigs, Know-nothings, and Democrats, Republicans, militant Abolitionists, and outspoken friends of slave-owners in the South. But the Load-Bearer was there, his eyes riveted on the speaker, every nerve strung to the utmost pitch, assuming by moral compact the actual responsibility of the sermon. If the preacher failed Elihu Gest would assume his loads; if the sermon was a triumph he would share in the preacher's triumph.

As the sermon drew to a close it became evident that by some queer, roundabout way, by some process of reasoning and persuasion that grew upon the people like a spell, they were listening, and had all along been listening, to a philippic against slavery.

At last the preacher's face lost its timorous look. With great vehemence he repeated the last part of his text:

" 'Fer they shell *cry* unto the Lord bekase of the oppressors, en he shell send them a savior, en a *great* one',"—here he struck the table a violent blow—" 'en he shell *deliver* them!' "

There was a moment of bewilderment and suspense, during which Lem Stephens was preparing for the worst. His mouth, usually compressed to a thin, straight slit, was now stiffened by a bull-dog jaw which he forced forward till the upper lip had almost disappeared; Minerva Wagner sat rigid, her mummy-like figure encased in whalebone wrapped in linsey-woolsey.

The preacher gave them no rest:

"Now right here I want ye all te ask yerselves who it air thet's a-cryin' fer deliverance. Who air it?" he shouted.

"Why, thar ain't but one people a-cryin' fer deliverance, en they air the slaves down thar in Egypt!"

The words fell like a muffled blow in the silence. Lem Stephens sat forward, breathless; Uriah Busby heaved a long sigh; fire flashed from Mrs. Wagner's grey, faded eyes; Ebenezer Hicks turned in his seat, his bushy eyebrows lowering to a threatening frown; while the face of Socrates wore a look of calm and neutral curiosity.

But hardly had the meeting realised the full force of the last words when the preacher put the final questions:

"En *who* shell deliver them? Do any o' ye know? Brethering, thar ain't but one human creatur' ekil to it, en thet air Abraham Lincoln. The Lord hez called him!"

An electrical thrill passed through the meeting. A subtle, permeating power took possession of the congregation, for the preacher had pronounced the first half of the name, Abraham, in such a way that it seemed as if the patriarch of Israel was coming once more in person to lead the people. An extraordinary influence had been evoked; a living investment of might and mystery, never at any time very distant, was now close at hand.

Ebenezer Hicks rose, and casting a fierce glance about him

hurried out; Minerva Wagner sprang from her seat like an automaton suddenly moved by some invisible force, and left the meeting, followed by her two tall, lank sons; Lem Stephens hurried after them, and with each step gave vent to his feelings by a loud thump on the bare floor with his wooden leg. When he got to the door he cast one last withering look at the preacher.

But Uriah Busby's voice rang out loud and sonorous:

> "How tedious and tasteless the hours
> When Jesus no longer I see."

The old hymn was taken up by Kezia Jordan in the next line. Once more her voice filled the meeting-house with golden waves, once more every heart beat in unison, and every soul communed in an indescribable outpouring of religious melody.

The whole congregation was singing now. With Kezia's voice a balm of Gilead came pouring over the troubled waters created by the strange, prophetic, and menacing sermon. The Load-Bearer, with hardly voice enough to speak aloud, was singing; the preacher sang even louder than he had preached; Serena Busby sang as I never heard her sing again; and while those who had left the meeting were about to depart they heard what they would never hear repeated. The opportunity to join hands with the coming power had passed, and as they set out for home they must have been haunted by the matchless magic and simplicity of the words and music, and more than ever would the coming hours seem "tedious and tasteless" to them.

CHAPTER 2

The Load-Bearer

WE HAD been four months in the Log-House, and my mother was just beginning to feel at home when one afternoon, as I was sauntering along the road near the gate, I saw a man on foot coming from the south.

As he approached I noticed that his features had a peculiar cast, his hair was rather long, his movements somewhat slow, and when he arrived in front of the gate he squared about and stopped with a sort of jerk, as if he had been dreaming but was now awake and conscious that this was the place he had come to visit. He peered at the Log-House as though awaiting some interior impulse to move him to further action; then he opened the gate, and, walking through the yard to the front door, rapped lightly.

I had followed him in, and when my mother opened the door and the stranger said, in a listless sort of way, "I jes' called to see how ye're gettin' on," I saw it was Elihu Gest, the Load-Bearer.

My mother thanked him, invited him in, and offered him a chair.

"I 'low ye're not long settled in this 'ere section," he said, taking a seat.

"Not long," she answered; "we are quite settled in the house, but on the farm my husband has so much to do he hardly knows where to begin."

She placed the kettle on the stove for coffee, and busied herself about getting the strange visitor some substantial refreshment. I thought I had never seen a face more inscrutable. He eyed my mother with grave interest, and after a silence that lasted some considerable time he said:

"If yer loads is too heavy jes' cast 'em off; the Lord is willin' en I ain't noways contrary."

Not till now did she realise that this was the man she had heard so much about; but not knowing just what to say, she gave no answer.

As he sat and stared at my mother his presence diffused a mysterious influence. My mind was busy with queries: Who sent him? What are his loads? Why does he take such an interest in my mother? And I thought she must be giving him coffee and eatables the better to enable him to support his loads, whatever they might be. She placed the coffee and other good things on the table and cordially invited the stranger to make himself at home. After pouring out a cup of coffee she sat down with folded hands, her pale face more pensive than usual, making some remarks about the weather and the good prospects for the new settlers.

Elihu Gest sat, a veritable sphinx of the prairie, wrapped in his own meditations. She almost feared that his visit might be a portent of some coming calamity, and that he had come to warn her and help her to gather force and courage for the ordeal.

Yet there was something in his look which inspired confidence and even cheerfulness, and she concluded it was good to have him sitting there. He began to sip his coffee, and at last, as if waking from a reverie, he put the question:

"How air ye feelin' in sperit?"

"The Lord has been merciful," she replied, the question having come as an immediate challenge to her religious faith and courage.

"Yer coffee is mos' appetizin'," he said, with a slight sniff.

"I am glad you like it, and I hope you are feeling rested, for you seem to have come a long way."

"They's a powerful difference a-twixt a mile and what a man's thinkin'. When yer mind is sot on one thing the distance a-twixt two places ain't much noways."

"Do you always walk?" she asked sympathetically.

"It's accordin' te how the hoss is feelin'. If the beast's anyways contrary he gives a snort, ez much ez te say, 'Mebbe I'll carry ye en mebbe I won't'; but when he snorts and kicks both te oncet thet means he'll kick the hind sights off all creation if I try te ride him. I've seen him when Joshua en his trumpet couldn't git him outen the barn door. I don't believe in workin' dumb critters when their sperits air droopin'. I'm allers more contented when I'm 'bleeged te walk; en hosses air powerful skase."

"Necessity compels us to do many things that seem impossible, but we learn to accept them as the best things for us. Won't you have some more coffee?"

"Yer coffee is mos' appetizin', it is so."

"And won't you eat something?"

"I'm much obleeged, but I don't feel no cravin' fer vittles. Accordin' te Sister Jordan, yer cakes en pies beats all she ever see."

"Mrs. Jordan is a very good woman."

"She is so; I've knowed her from away back."

There came another pause, during which the visitor looked straight before him, lost in thought. Presently he began:

"Thet comet's convicted a good many folks. Ebenezer Hicks war skeered half te death when he see it a-comin', makin' the loads mos' heavy fer his pore wife."

Then, addressing my mother, he continued:

"The night he war 'flicted, I couldn't git te sleep nohow. I sez to myself, 'Thar's an axle-tree wants ilein', en I'll be blamed if it ain't over te Ebenezer Hicks's.' I went te the barn te see how the hoss war feelin', en I sez, 'Kin ye carry me over te Ebenezer Hicks's if I saddle ye?' But Henry Clay give a kick thet sot me wonderin' how I war ever goin' te git thar."

"Many people think the end of the world is at hand," said my mother.

"They do, fer a fact."

He paused a moment, then went on:

"But them thet's skeered air folks without faith. I ain't got no call fer te take loads from folks what's skeered. Sommow I cain't carry 'em."

"The burdens of life are, indeed, hard to bear alone."

"They air so; en 'twixt you and me, marm, I'm jest a mite onsartin 'bout what it air 'flicts some folks. 'Pears like Satan skeers more folks 'n is ever won over by the Lord's goodness en mercy. Them thet's allers a-tremblin' ain't much account when it comes te strappin' the bellyband real hard; they don't never set tight in the saddle when they're called on te go plumb through a wilderness o' thistles."

After meditating again for a time, he resumed:

"But Ebenezer Hicks warn't a patchin' on Uriah Busby what lives yander at Black B'ar Creek. He war so skeered he sot to weepin' when he see me come in, en I never see a woman ez hoppin' mad ez Sereny Busby! I couldn't take no loads from Brother Busby; accordin' te my notion, he warn't settin' up under none, en jest ez soon ez I sot eyes on Sister Busby I see *she* hedn't hitched up to nothin' of any heft neither. She don't set still long enough. I 'low I war some dis'p'inted."

He laughed faintly; perhaps he wished to convey the impression that the burdens of life were not so dreadful, after all.

"I fear you had your trouble all for nothing," said my mother.

"Ye see, Brother Busby war skeered, en Sister Busby got her dander up. I never knowed a woman with red hair that war afeared of man or beast."

"Mr. Busby must have been very much frightened," remarked my mother, smiling.

"Not so skeered but what he could talk. Si Jordan had his speech tuck plumb away, en I never see Sister Jordan so flustered. But she don't say much nohow. Sereny Busby she keeps the top a-spinnin' the livelong day. But I hev seen Uriah Busby caved in more'n oncet. I knowed 'em both afore they war married. If I wanted a woman sprightly with her tongue ez well ez with her hands, I'd take Sereny Busby fer fust ch'ice; if I wanted a woman what knows a heap en sez mos' nothin', I'd take Kezia Jordan. Human natur' ain't allers the same. I 'low Sister Busby's got the most eddication."

"But education never helps much if the heart is not in the right place."

"Thet thar's what I've allers said. 'Pears like sometimes Sereny Busby's heart's jest a leetle lopsided en wants resettin', ez ye might say. But thar's a sight o' difference a-twixt one load en another. When I set with some folks what's in a heap o' trouble, I go away ez happy ez kin be, but when I hev te go away without ary a load, I feel mos' empty."

Here there was another spell of silence, but after a few sips from a third cup of coffee he continued:

"'Pears like that warn't never no heft te Sereny Busby's troubles. She don't give 'em no chance te set; en jest ez a duck's back goes agin water, her'n is set agin loads."

"The Lord has given her a cheerful mind; I think she has much to be thankful for."

"She hez, fer a fact. But I never kin tell jes' how her mind is a-workin'. She steps roun' ez spry ez kin be, hummin' fiddle tunes mos'ly; en when Brother Busby tuck te bed with thet fever what's mos' killed him, she hept on a-hummin', en some folks would a-said she war triflin', but she warn't. She give Uriah his med'cine mos' reg'lar, en mopped his head with cold water from the well, en made him appetizin' rabbit soup. The Bible sez the sperit's willin' but the flesh is weak, but I don't see no failin' in a woman thet kin hum all day like a spinnin'-top. . . . But I allers kin tell what Kezia Jordan is a-thinkin', en thar ain't no two ways 'bout it; Sister Jordan kin sing hymns so ye want te give right up en die, ye feel so happy."

"She has something wonderful in her voice when she sings," said my mother; "I felt that when I heard her sing 'in meeting.' "

"I 'low Si Jordan ain't pertickler benv'lent, but Kezia Jordan counts fer more'n one in that 'ar house."

"I fear she has had a life of much care and trouble, and perhaps that is one reason why she is so good."

"Folks is born like we fine 'em, marm. I've been nigh on thirty year wrastlin' with the sorrows o' life, en I ain't seen ary critter change his spots. A wolf don't look like a wild cat, en I never see a fox with a bob tail; en folks air like varmints: God Almighty hez marked 'em with His seal."

He looked round the room abstractedly, and then said:

"It's looks thet tells when a man's in trouble; en a heap o' tribulation keeps folks from hollerin'. Sister Jordan hez knowed trouble from away back. But thar's a tremenjous difference a-twixt her en Si Jordan. He kin talk en pray when he gits a-goin', en I've heared him when it looked like his flow o' words would swamp the hull endurin' meetin'; but when the risin' settled, thar warn't much harm done no way. But jes' let Sister Jordan sing a hymn, en ye feel like the hull yearth war sot in tune."

"That is because she is so sincere," observed my mother gravely.

"Thet's a fact. I ain't never forgot the time when I hed thet spell o'sickness en felt ez if thar war nothin' wuth a-livin' fer. What with sickness, en the defeat o' Fremont, en them desperadoes cuttin' up over in Kansas, en the goin's on o' them Demicrats in Springfield, 'peared like I never would be good fer nothin' more. All te oncet the feelin' come over me te go over te Kezia Jordan's. Thet ud be 'bout ez much ez I could do, seein' I war like a chicken what's jes' pecked its way through the shell. I hedn't got ez fur ez the kitchen door when I heared her a-singin':

> " 'Come, thou Fount of every blessin',
>   Tune my heart te sing Thy praise.'

"Thet voice o' her'n set me a-cryin', en I sot right down on the door-steps, en thanked God fer all His goodness. Arter a while, she come out fer a bucket o' water.

"Good Land!' she sez; 'I'm right glad te see ye. Go right in; ye're jest in time fer dinner; I've got some real nice prairie chicken en pum'kin pie; everything's mos' ready.'

"Soon as I went in she sez:

"Mercy on us, Elihu! I never see ye look so! Set right down, en tell me what ails ye; ye ain't been sick 'thout lettin' me know, hev ye?' "

"I like to have such a good Christian for my nearest neighbour," said my mother, with much feeling.

"I allow she warn't allers a Christian. I war over at Carlinville when she heared Pete Cartwright fer the fust time, en the meetin'-house warn't big enough te hold the people. Sister Jordan warn't moved te sing any durin' the fust hymn, but she j'ined in the second, en arter thet Brother Cartwright tuck right holt, ez ye might say, en swung 'em till their feet tetched perdition.

" 'Yo're ripe,' he sez, holdin' out his fist, 'yo're ripe, like grain waitin' fer the reaper! Ye'll be mowed down, en the grain 'll be plumb divided from the chaff, en the Christians 'll be parted from the sinners.'

"The hull meetin' began to move like wheat a-wavin' in the wind. The preacher knowed Kezia Jordan fer a nat'ral-born Christian by her singin', fer he p'inted straight, en sez:

" 'Ye're at the cross-roads, sister; ye'll hev te choose one or t'other; en the years en the months air gone fer most o' ye, en thar's on'y this here hour left fer te choose. Which will it be? Will it be the road thet leads up yander, or the one thet leads down by the dark river whar the willers air weepin' night en day?'

"This war the turnin' p'int fer a good many; but the preacher warn't satisfied yet. He rolled up en went te work in dead arnest. He tole 'bout the fust coon hunt he ever see:

" 'Sinners,' he sez, 'is jes' like the coon asleep in thet tree—

never dreamin' o' danger. But the varmint war waked all on a sudden by a thunderin' smell o' smoke, en hed te take te the branches. Someone climbs up the tree en shakes the branch whar the coon is holdin' on.' En right here Pete Cartwright slung his handkerchief over his left arm en sez, 'A leetle more, a leetle more, a l-e-e-e-tle more en the varmint's bound te drap squar' on the dogs.' He shuck his arm three times—'down, down, down,' he sez, lettin' the handkerchief drap, 'down te whar the wailin' en gnashin' air a million times more terrible 'n the sufferin's o' thet coon.' "

The Load-Bearer bent forward and his face assumed a look of tragic intensity as he continued:

"A veil o' mournin' war a-bein' pulled down over the meetin'. He war takin' the people straight te jedgment, like a flock o' sheep, with the goats a-followin', usin' no dividin' line, for he put it to 'em:

" 'Whar would ye all be if this here floor war te slide right from under ye, leavin' ye settin' on the brink, with Time on one side en Etarnity on t'other?'

"The hull meetin' war shuck te pieces, some hollerin', some too 'flicted te set up; en I see nigh on twenty plumb fainted en gone."

Elihu Gest sighed as he sat back in his chair, and proceeded in his usual way:

"When the meetin' war over I sez te Sister Jordan, 'How air ye feelin' in sperit?' En she sez, 'I've had more'n enough o' this world's goods!'

" 'I want te know!' sez I.

" 'Yes,' she sez, 'I don't never want no more.' En I see it war for everlastin'."

No one spoke for a long time.

At last he rose from his chair and moved towards the door like one in a dream, his face wearing a look of almost super-human detachment.

Then, just before passing out, he turned and said: "I'll bid ye good-day, fer the present."

This visit made the day a memorable one for me, for I saw in Elihu Gest a human wonder; he opened up a world of things and influences about which I had never dreamed. And when he had disappeared down the road to the south, the way he had come, I wondered how he was carrying his loads, what they could be, and whether my mother felt relieved of any of her burdens. But I held my peace, while she simply remarked:

"A very strange but very good man. I wonder if we shall ever see him again?"

Here was a man who did everything by signs, tokens, impressions; who was moved by some power hidden from the understanding of everyone else—a power which none could define, concerning which people had long since ceased to question. He came and went, influenced by signs in harmony with his own feelings and moods, by natural laws shut off from our understanding by the imperative rules of conventional religion and society. Things which were sealed mysteries to us were fingerposts to him, pointing the way across the prairies, in this direction or in that. Is it time to go forth? He would look up at the heavens, sense the state of Nature by the touch of the breeze, sound the humour of the hour with a plumb-line of his own, then set out to follow where it led.

The Load-Bearer's presence, his odd appearance, his descriptions and peculiar phrases, his spells of silence, his sudden enthusiasms, the paradox of humour and religious feeling displayed, brought to our home the fervour and candour of the meeting-house—honest pioneer courage and frankness, and, above all, an influence that left on me an impression never to be effaced. How far, how very far, we were from the Episcopal rector, with his chosen words, studied phrases, and polite and dignified sympathy! How far it all was from anything my parents had ever dreamed of even in so remote a country! The prairie was inhabited by a people as new and strange as the country itself.

And what a gulf there was between the customs of the old country and the customs usual in the new West! Visitors appeared unannounced and at almost any hour. To-day a neighbour would come two miles to borrow some sugar; to-morrow another would come still farther to borrow tea or coffee. All were received as if they were old and tried friends. My mother attended to the wants of those who came to borrow things for the table, while my father did his best to satisfy the men who came to borrow ploughs, spades, saws, wagons, and even horses.

For the neighbours considered my father a rich man, judging him by the horses, sheep, and cattle he owned. And when he appeared at meetings, wearing a handsome velvet waistcoat with rich blue checks—one of the waistcoats he purchased during his visit to Paris before his marriage—they thought him richer still.

Thus are appearances even more deceptive and dangerous than words, for all, without exception, are judged by the illusions produced by property and personal attire.

CHAPTER 3

The Log-House

THE Log-House was built some twenty-five years before we came to live in it, but we never knew who planted the trees and flowers. Surely it must have been a lover of Nature, for these we know by the little signs and tokens they leave behind them. Certain flowers were omitted, such as the rose, the flower of fashion and convention, the one with least suggestive influence on the heart and the affections, for it always turns the thoughts on more personal and worldly things.

There is a law of correspondence, a kind of secret code proper for each condition of life, and people become distorted and confused when this law is ignored. How often I wanted to know who planted these flowers! I thought I could guess how the woman looked—for it certainly was a woman—and I fancied I could see her arriving here from the South with her husband, the couple intent on leading a quiet life, the husband raising stock instead of wheat and corn, the wife attending to household duties and to the planting and watering of the flowers—the old familiar ones which harmonised with the prairie and the inmost instincts of the soul.

I seem to see a tall, spare woman, with a pensive face, as silent and psychic as Kezia Jordan, planting the flowers in the first warm spell of the first April, in the evenings, after supper, when the earth that had waited her coming for aeons and aeons yielded up the fragrance of that marvellous loam composed of withered grass and flowering weeds. Her husband is seated in an old rocking-chair in the kitchen getting all the music he can out of a raspy fiddle, a bloodhound lying on the floor beside him. The wife plants only those flowers that have wistful eyes and homely souls, and with every one a thought goes out that fills a void between the past and the present, as she says to herself:

"That is the way they were at home." For the silent figure, intent on digging with her own hands the holes for the seeds and young plants, is thinking of one who planted flowers of the same kind years before, far away in another part of the country. And so she works through the warm evenings, placing each thing, not according to any rule of art, but according to memory and the promptings of instinct. For the yard around the Log-House was not disfigured with walks made by measure and strewn with sand and shells. Everything grew as if by nature, and this freedom gave the place a character of its own which the slightest show of conventional art would have made impossible. The sweet-william grew in great high bunches, interlaced with branches of other shrubs, and the jimpson-weed and sumac were not far off, under which the chickens stood and cleaned their feathers, and where, on rainy days, they lent an air of gloom to the surroundings.

And now that the silent figure has planted the summer flowers, she thinks of the last and most important of all, the morning-glory. This she places at each side of the north door, where in the future it will be the only green thing on that side of the house, excepting one large locust tree. But the morning-glory! With what care she waters the plant when the ground is dry, and how she looks forward to the day when it will be full of bloom, covering each side of the door, reminding her of the old homestead and absent friends!

And thus the last planting is done, and she steps inside and sits down beside her husband, musing for awhile, as my own mother would now do before beginning some new work.

How does it happen that between people who are strangers to one another there should be a connecting link of sympathy, forged by little acts like the planting of a certain flower, at a special time, in a special place? Perhaps there is a secret and invisible agreement between certain persons and places, a definite meaning in the coming and going of certain persons we have never seen, and that nothing is wholly futile. However it may be, the flower that was planted on the north side of the house by someone years before seemed planted there as much for my special benefit as for anyone else's.

One day, after breakfast, my attention was arrested by a sight which gave me a thrill of admiration. The morning-glories were in bloom! There they were, like a living vision, revealing to me something in the kingdom of flowers I had never seen or felt before. The radiant days of summer had decked the Log-House with a mantle more beautiful than any worn by the Queen of Sheba or by Solomon when he received her. And now, as the days were growing more languid and the evenings more wistful, autumn, with her endless procession of far, faint shadows, would steal across the threshold under a canopy of infinite and indescribable colour.

How the spell of their magic changed the appearance of the house! The flowers looked out on sky and plain with meek, mauve-tinted eyes, after having absorbed all the amaranth of a cloudless night, the aureole of early morning, and a something, I know not what, that belongs to dreams and distance wafted on waves of colour from far-away places. At times the flowers imparted to the rugged logs the semblance of a funeral pyre, their beauty suggesting the mournful pomp of some martyr-queen, with pale, wondering eyes, awaiting the torch in a pallium of purple. They gave to the entrance a sort of halo that symbolised the eternal residuum of all things mortal and visible.

How impressive around the Log-House was that hour of the evening when, just after sundown, the birds, the chickens, and the turkeys began to seek a resting-place for the night! With the gradual dying away of sound and movement, everything was tinged with mourning. When at last, with the slowly fading twilight, the fluttering of wings and chirping ceased, a vague stillness evoked a feeling of mystery that spread over the house and everything around it.

Now and again the quiet was broken by the sharp whiz of insects darting here and there through the gloaming, the cry of the whip-poor-will, as it flitted between the house and the hollow, or the far, lonesome call of the hoot-owl, followed by a puff of wind, the rustling of grass and a period of nameless unrest, during which the crickets and the katy-dids began their long, languid litanies of the night.

Then, on certain evenings, a faint glow in the east would appear, and above the horizon the dawn of moonrise gradually illumined the borders of the wilderness. In a few moments more an immense crimson disc looked out on the silence from behind great sheets of blood-red clouds, presently merging into amber, with stripes of silver and gold. But these colours would soon give place to a serene glow, and from that time until daybreak all Nature was wrapped in phantasmal twilight, the Log-House looming like a spectral silhouette in the silver light, its rugged logs heaped together like something in a dream, on the borders of a world apart, haunted by gliding shadows and illusive sounds.

Inside the house, after supper, when everything was put in order for the night, the stillness was oppressive, for the quiet was not that of repose. It suggested an immense and immeasurable sadness, and my mother would sit knitting in silence, with thoughts of the far-absent ones. About ten o'clock my father would read the evening prayers from the Anglican prayer-book, with the whole family kneeling, and I wondered what efficacy written prayers could have. But whenever I heard my mother utter the words: "May the Lord in His goodness have mercy on us!" I felt an instant accession of power. The words, coming from that magical voice, unlocked the reservoirs of the infinite, and faith came rushing through the flood-gates. They brought a presence which filled the house with hope and comfort. I was satisfied without being able to explain why. There were moments when she seemed to bring a superhuman power to the threshold of the Log-House beyond which danger and despair could not enter. She had implicit faith in what she called the "Promises." "The Lord in His mercy will never permit it," she used to say when a calamity seemed inevitable; and with all her sorrows the irreparable never happened. Faith and prayer form a bulwark around the lives of some people through which no permanent misfortune ever penetrates.

Sometimes, after the evening prayers, the house became subdued to a stillness which produced the effect of someone having crept in by stealth. The flames had gone from the logs; the embers were smouldering into ashes; the light and sparkle had turned to something that resembled audible thought. This was the hour when the things which during the day gave forth no noticable sound now seemed to speak or to chant. The stroke of the old clock, with its long pendulum, went like a plummet to the depths of the soul. It brought forth that part of Nature which is hidden from our sight by a thin veil behind which we can sometimes hear the voices on the other side. The cry of the cricket was that of a tiny friend, affecting only the smallest nerves of silence, but the solemn tones of the time-piece accentuated our isolation. Some clocks are nervous and rasping, others emit a tone of hope and serenity, but the one in the Log-House had a deep, portentous tone which filled one with a sense of the hollowness of things, the futility of effort, a consciousness of days and nights continually departing, of vanishing memories, and of people passing into lonely, isolated, and everlasting dreams. A great gulf now separated us from the rest of the world, and my mother sat like one under a spell.

About midnight the stillness became an obsession. All Nature was steeped in an atmosphere of palpable quiet, teeming with dismal uncertainty and sombre forebodings. The flickering of a tallow candle added something ghostly to the room with its dark mahogany furniture, while every unfamiliar sound outside startled the members of the family who were still awake. The doleful duets of the katy-dids often came to a sudden stop, and during the hush it seemed as if anything might happen—the apparition of a phantom, or the arrival of a band of masked marauders. An owl would visit the solitary locust tree which stood between the north door and the barn, and its weird calls sent a shiver through the night. The first note had an indescribable quality, and the series of half-veiled trumpet calls that followed produced on me a sensation never to be forgotten. They sounded like nothing else in Nature, and came to me as a lament from some waif of the wilderness.

"Hear me, hear me, inhabitants of the Log-House! Is solitude now your portion?"

Again, in the dead of night, some animal would carry off a fowl, and the long-drawn-out "caws" came like the cries of a child for help, growing less and less distinct, and at last dying away in the distance as the animal passed the barn and began the descent into the hollow towards the woods. The effect on me was one of nervous apprehension. It was the mystery which added a nameless dread to a mere incident of the night.

On stormy nights in the autumn the north wind brought with it voices that moaned and sighed. Every sweep of the wind came with a chorus of lamentations that moved round and round, first on one side then on the other, and the intervals of silence between the gusts came as respites before some final disaster. The big locust, that stood alone, had an ominous whistle, while the trees and bushes at the front and back swayed under the low, swooping gusts, until the Log-House seemed once more a part of the wild and primitive forest.

At times streaks of cold light from the semi-circling moon would fall through the window on the old rag-carpet—old, because each strip had belonged to garments worn long before the carpet was put together. It needed the moonlight or the soft rays of the setting sun to bring out all its romance and mystery. Then the stripes of saffron evoked the presence of Kezia Jordan, and the darker hues memories of the Load-Bearer, Socrates, and Minerva Wagner. What romantic adventure these patches suggested! I would sit and count the pieces and compare one colour with another, for each seemed imbued with a personality of its own. Here, in the common sitting-room filled with chimeras about to vanish, each strip of cloth was a pillow for some dead thing of the past, some greeting or regret. There were strips worn when the wearer set sail from the old country, others had faced a hail of bullets at Buena Vista, passed through an Indian rising, or the first stormy meetings of the Abolitionists in Illinois. Once all these strips of cloth had stood for life and action; they wrapped a world of dreams and moods, but now they covered a rough floor in a house of logs. They humanised the interior as graves humanise a plot of earth. And never did sacred carpet of Mecca contain so much of the magic of life; for here, too, daily prayers were said on bended knee, and the carpet seemed one with the religious aspirations of the occupants, with all our hopes and fears, joys and sorrows.

How genial and home-like it was! It belonged to the order of the wild roses and flowering weeds, the corn and clover, the morning-glories, the jimpson, the sumac, and the red-winged blackbirds that soared in circles around and above the house.

If its shreds and patches suggested things of the past, the Log-House life it represented was palpitating with the present: full of human dreams and ambitions, of the voiceless sentiments that make a home in the bosom of the prairie. It invited the tired wayfarer of the lonely roads to come in and be refreshed with steaming coffee and hot biscuits, pound-cake, and dainty pies made from the products of the loamy soil; it invited all to step in and listen to words of encouragement if in trouble, and words of sympathy if in affliction; for the rag-carpet was made for the Log-House, and the Log-House was made for Man.

CHAPTER 4

Socrates Gives Advice

THE day Socrates made his first call at the Log-House I happened to be at home, instead of fishing a mile away, or wandering about in my accustomed haunts among the squirrels, birds, and rabbits. He brought Ebenezer Hicks with him.

Socrates entertained me with some simple stories of his experience as a hunter and trapper twenty or thirty years earlier: how he killed big game during the winters of the great snows, his buffalo hunts in Missouri and Iowa, his strange devices for snaring the mink, the fox, and the raccoon.

I devoured every word with eager excitement: here was the actual romance of the wild woods.

"And have you killed many bitterns and owls?" I inquired.

"I don't b'lieve in killin' things ye cain't eat or skin."

It seemed to me that this Socrates of the wilderness had something of the look of a big horned owl, with his bushy eyebrows and short scraggy beard. Over his sparsely covered head the years had cast a halo of experience and wisdom, and I began to respect this man who united in himself so much adventure and common sense. He seemed strong as a lion and harmless as a lamb, free as the winds of the prairie, yet methodical and never in doubt. He brought with him into the Log-House— where our family had gathered like a flock of sheep in a strange land—a feeling of security and a renewal of faith and courage.

"There's not much need of raising stock in this part of the country," said my father jokingly; "game is so plentiful."

"The new settlers air givin' tharselves a heap o' trouble jes' fer the fun o' ploughin' en reapin'. They snap the bow-strings. They air tryin' te kill big game with a shotgun, en the shot scatters all over the kintry. It air good 'nough fer rabbits en squirrels, but it don't stop a buck jumpin' er a b'ar from browsin'. I see a heap

58

o' hard work fer some o' these here settlers what's comin' in from the ole kintries over East. 'Tain't wisdom.

"Some folks air too good fer this world 'thout bein' plumb ready fer the nex'. Accordin' te thar reasonin', a prairie-chicken settin' on the fence air better'n two birds o' paradise over yander. The world air a sorrowin' vale, kase folks hez too many stakes in the groun'. Ez fer me, I kin shoot en trap all I kin eat, jes' plantin' 'nough corn fer hoe-cakes en a leetle fodder, en some taters en turnips en pum'kins; en I hev a sight more smoked venison en b'ar meat in winter than I kin eat ez a single man with on'y one stommick; en I 'low I kin give a traveller hoe-cakes en fried chicken all he wants to fill up on."

Socrates sat like a lump of hewn adamant, his look alone being sufficient guarantee of his ability to take care of himself without the slightest trouble or worry.

"Thar be folks that air trampin' over these prairies a-spadin' up trouble like thar warn't none te be hed by settin' down in the city en lettin' other folks bring it to 'em. Thar's a heap too much corn en wheat, a durned sight too many kyows en hosses; en the four-legged critters chaws up what the two-legged critters gathers in. It air wus nor dog eat dog, seein' ez how the four-legged critters air livin' on the fat o' the land while the pore planters air livin' on spar' ribs en hens with sinoos ez tough ez b'iled owels."

"But it makes a great difference when a man has a family to support and educate," remarked my mother, thinking of the responsibility of parents.

"I allow readin' en writin' air a good thing if ye've got any figurin' to do; but cipherin's a drefful load on the mind. Thar's Si Jordan yander; he sets figurin' o' nights, en calculatin' te see jes' how he'll come out at the end o' the year; but I allers say to myself he's like the groun'-hog, he won't come out."

"Still, it would be awkward to have to calculate with nothing but your fingers," observed my father, smiling.

"Fingers or no fingers, book-larnin' don't make a man no better than he war in a state o' natur'. Them as reads newspapers knows too much 'bout other folks's sins en not 'nough 'bout thar own. Over Decatur en Fancy Creek way they built meetin'-houses with steeples on 'em en the wimin-folks tuck te wearin' store clothes en the men-folks put on b'iled shirts. But when the comet come into view the wimin put on their ole sun-bonnets, allowin' pink calico te be more'n enough te be jedged in."

My mother, as she looked up from her knitting, thought his round grey eyes seemed bigger and rounder than ever. She noticed in his face an expression of naive irony and unconscious satire which she had not remarked before. But later there radiated from his face a sense of pity when he thought of all the hard work she would have to do. In some unaccountable way he had come into touch with the unexpressed hopes and fears of the silent man sitting before him, and the pale, passive face of his wife, who was knitting.

Then, as if struck with a sudden, new idea, he said:

"Ye kin divide the day's doin's into two passels—the happenin's en the fac's; en thar ain't but two leadin' fac's in all creation—bein' born en bein' dead. Howsomever, right in betwixt 'em thar's some purty lively happenin's a-steppin' roun' on all fours, ez when a panther takes a notion te drap on a pig's back; it's a shore thing fer the panther but a dead loss fer the owner. En it air jest ez sartin the fact air plumb again the pig, but he don't live long 'nough te know it. Thar's been a suddin burial, en the mourner kin see the fact, but he ain't never see the corpse. Anyhow, it's an argiment thet'll work itself out ez easy ez a groun'-worm arter rain, en it don't make no pertickler difference which end comes up fust, heads en tails bein' purty nigh ekil."

My father enjoyed a hearty laugh, and my mother stopped knitting and eyed Socrates as if trying to fathom the secret of his strange originality.

"It beats my time all holler," he went on, "te see folks so kind o' waverin' en onsartin. Instead o' waitin' fer the last hour they make fer it with thar heads down like a bull agin a red flag, en no tail-twistin' 'll stop 'em. Thar's skasely a settler among the new uns but what'll tell ye they air workin' te live. It air workin' te die, thet's what *I* call it."

"Thar's a good many workin' land they ain't got no title to," remarked Ebenezer Hicks.

"When I go te meetin'," said Socrates, "en hear some o' these settlers sing about readin' thar title cl'ar te mansions in the skies I allers feel like askin' 'em how they're holdin' on te the land they got; kase thar ain't but two kyinds o' settlers—them ez buys right out, and them ez squats right down, en I've allers found thet hymn air a dead favourite among the people thet set right down jes' whar thar feet begin te swell.

"What I know 'bout Bible-teachin' air plumb agin squatters takin' up land t'other side Jordan. The Lord God hez issued a writ statin' His objections. I ain't never knowed a real live Yankee thet war any good at squattin'. They come from below the Ohio, whar they hev seen the niggers do all the work. En when they come up to this kintry they sing about readin' thar title cl'ar te big slices o' land in the nex' world! I tell ye what it is, if thar's ever goin' te be war it'll be betwix' them thet wants the land fer nothin' en them thet wants it fer sunthin', if it ain't fer more'n shootin' snipe en plover. The squatters air lazy; en t'other folks, like the Squar hyar, air killin' tharselves by doin' too much.

"My ole daddy larnt me te go through this sorrowin' vale like the varmints do—easy en nat'ral like, never gallopin' when ye kin lope, en never lopin' when ye kin lay down. It's a heap easier. Thar ain't a hog but knows he kin root fer a livin' if ye give him a fair show; thar ain't a squirrel but knows how te stow away 'nough te nibble on when he wakes up en finds his blood's kinder coolin' down en things is p'intin' te zero."

After a pause he looked hard at my father, and put the question abruptly:

"What'll ye do, Squar, when ye plough up the prairie thar nex' year, en sow it with corn ez ye calc'late on doin'? How d'ye 'low ye'll git all the work done 'thout extry hands?"

It was an unexpected query that left my father without an immediate answer. He had never given the subject any serious thought.

Socrates continued without waiting for explanations:

"Ye'll hev a heap o' corn-huskin' te do, en ye suttingly ain't a-goin' te reckon on thet leetle lady with them hands o' her'n doin' much corn-huskin' en sech. 'Pears like she'll hev more'n enough te keep her a-goin' right in the house."

My mother was thinking: "The Lord's will be done. He had a reason for sending us here; some day we may know *why*."

Socrates resumed:

"Hirin' extry hands means payin' out a lot o' money; mebbe yer purse-strings air like yer latch-string, en mebbe ye got a plenty te last ye till nex' harvest time. Things ain't like they war; folks useter come twenty mile to a corn-huskin', en the doin's ud end up with eatin' en drinkin' en dancin'. Now people air too busy with thar own funerals. They useter help other people work tharselves to death; now they stay at home and dig thar own graves 'thout borrowing shovels er sendin' fer a fiddler te help 'em mourn with thar tired feet. I keep sayin' the comet may pass over 'thout drappin'; but if the politicioners, en the lawyers, en them ez sez they don't know nothin', en the hordes o' settlers thet can't tell the difference betwix' a yaller dog en a long-eared rabbit ain't a-bringin' the world to a spot stop, then Zack Caverly hez missed fire, en it'll be the fust time."

"As for that," said my father, "it certainly does look as if some great change would soon come over the country. Many are turned to religion for consolation, while others predict civil war."

"I see some cussed mean folks pretendin' te hev religion. Some on 'em air thet deceivin' I allers feel like watchin' em with a spy-glass till they git into the woods en then sendin' my old hound arter 'em te see they don't commit bigamy er hang themselves right on my diggin's."

"Wal," said Ebenezer Hicks, who had been listening attentively, "I 'low ye've tetched a festern sore when ye say some on 'em air ekil te committin' treason en blasphemy, but ez fer me I hev allers been a church member; but some folks ain't never satisfied te leave things ez they wur. It's my opinion all the trouble hez come about in the Church by them busybodies mixin' up religion with politics. Abolition hez been bone o' contention en a skewer through both wings o' the Methodists. You war thar when Azariah James preached thet sermon, windin' up by h'istin' the Abolition flag, en you too, Squar, en you heared what he said."

"Ye'll allow he hed all creation te h'ist on," remarked Socrates; "the stars en stripes te begin with, two kyinds o' lawyers en four kyinds o' preachers—all on 'em off'n whisky. T'other party ain't got no flag, but thar whisky makes 'em see the stars en they make the niggers feel the stripes."

Ebenezer Hicks, wishing to turn the conversation, simply observed:

"Over at Bloomington en Springfield the people air all fer Lincoln."

But Socrates held to the subject and went on:

"What beats my time is te know what you folks hez te do

with the nigger question anyway. Did ye ever own any slaves?"

"Nary a one."

"Wal, then, what difference does it make te you whether they work ez slaves er work ez we uns work? Looks like ye belong te them thet's pinin' away kase ye ain't got sorrers enough o' yer own te hitch to. When we all heared Azariah James preach—the on'y time the meetin'-house hez been open all summer—I see right away we'd got plumb into the middle o' the Abolition circus en someone ud turn a somerset afore he got through. Fact is, the people o' this here State air a-gettin' ready te send Abe Lincoln te Washington, en ole Buchanan's jes' keepin' the presidential cheer from warpin' till Abe comes."

"That preacher, Azariah James," said my father, "was not such a fool as some of the congregation thought he was."

"Not nigh," returned Socrates, as he rose from his seat and took his leave.

A few days after his visit my mother remarked:

"Now, I suppose, we shall not have any more visitors for a long time. There are days when I wish someone would call, and somehow I have been thinking a good deal of Mrs. Jordan lately. I should like a visit from her more than from anyone else I know just at present."

That same afternoon, as I was returning to the house from the hollow where I had been gathering hazel-nuts, I thought I could discern a stranger through the window. I entered the house and found Kezia Jordan seated in the rocking-chair.

Once more her presence opened the door to a world that transcended all the familiar forms of speech; for it was not what she said, but what she looked, that impressed me so profoundly.

Moulded and subdued by the lonely days, the monotonous weeks, the haunting hush of the silent nights, and the same thoughts and images returning again and again, she appeared as one who had conquered the world of silence. Elihu Gest partly explained himself by his explanation of others, but Kezia Jordan made few comments, and they were rarely personal. She never talked for the sake of talking. As she sat there she might have been a statue, for to-day she brought with her an inexorable detachment from worldly thoughts and influences.

The sentiments she inspired in me were like those produced by the motion of clouds on a calm, moonlight night, or the falling of leaves on a still, dreamy day of Indian summer. There were moments when her presence seemed to possess something preternatural, when she imparted to others an extraordinary and superhuman quietude. Her spirit, freed for ever from the trammels and tumults of the world, seemed heedless of the passing moments, resigned to every secret and mandate of destiny; for hers was a freedom which was not attained in a single battle— the conflict was begun by her ancestors when they landed at Plymouth Rock. In the tribulations that followed the successive generations were stripped of the superfluities of life. One by one vanities and illusions fell from the fighters like shattered muskets and tattered garments. Each generation, stripped of the tinsel, became acquainted with the folly of plaints and the futility of protests. Little by little the pioneers began to understand, and in the last generation of all there resulted a knowledge too deep for discussion and a wisdom too great for idle misgivings.

Where was the hurried visitor from foreign lands who could sound the depths of such a soul?

The influences were different when Mrs. Busby came to the Log-House. She brought with her pleasnat maxims about her bakings, her messes, and herb-medicines, and talked on and on without caring what the subject was. She created commotion and movement, and under her hands the kettle hissed and spouted.

Mrs. Jordan handled things as if they had life and feeling, and without being conscious of influencing others she brought with her a power that penetrated to the core of things. She had passed the time when her duties had to be accomplished by the aid of a strenuous use of the reasoning faculties. She had arrived at that stage when religion was not a thing of reason, but a state of perpetual feeling. Circumstances altered, conditions changed and found her the same, unaltered and unalterable.

Yet she had her day-dreams, moments of rapt meditation which bordered on forgetfulness, when the formless visions and homely realities of kitchen, meeting-house, and prairie became one, and the song of the blackbird and the chirping of the cricket seemed a part of her own life and feeling. She possessed the dominant influence of an abiding power with a total absence of self-assertion, for hers was that true power of the soul, an influence that penetrates to depths which intellect alone can never reach.

I thought the rocking-chair was made for Kezia Jordan, and

the rag-carpet too, and somehow I could never quite free my mind from the impression that the flowers about the house were hers as well.

Soon after my arrival a rap was heard at the door, and in walked Minerva Wagner, proud, lean, wrinkled, and unbending. She came within the category of those who, according to Zack Caverly, were labouring under the necessity of borrowing trouble. She had not yet recovered from the shock produced by the Abolition sermon of the preacher, Azariah James. Mrs. Wagner was our nearest neighbour to the north, and every time I glanced in that direction I would marvel at the listless, lonely life of the family in the little frame house stuck like a white speck on the brow of the prairie, ten times more lonely and isolated than the Log-House we inhabited. Whenever I saw someone moving about over there I thought of a tomb opening its doors and letting out an imprisoned ghost; for every member of the family looked and walked and talked alike, except, perhaps, old Minerva Wagner, who stood to-day facing the inexorable present—stern, relentless, unable to account for anything she saw or heard, but choking with prejudice against what she persisted in calling "the Yankee trash of Indianny and Illinoise."

After some talk about pickles and bacon and apple-butter, and some allusion to the awful state of the country, brought on by the Anti-Slavery agitation, Mrs. Wagner took her departure, and once more the room assumed the calm, peaceful aspect commensurate with Kezia Jordan's presence. My mother made tea, and the moments passed as if there were no clock ticking the time away and no regrets for the old days that would never return; and when at last Mrs. Jordan rose from her seat she looked more slender than ever in her simple dress of copperas-coloured jean; and when the clouds parted and the setting sun shone full on the windows, her spare figure cast a shadow that fell across the rag-carpet, and there, under her feet, were strips of coloured cloth, the counterpart of her own dress, and it seemed as if she had always belonged to the Log-House and ought never to leave it.

CHAPTER 5

Silas Jordan's Illness

THE solemn hush of the wilderness had its voices of bird and insect, wind, rain, and rustling grass; but from the song of birds and grasshoppers to the noiseless march of the comet was a far and terrible cry, and more than one head of a family, seeing it approach nearer and nearer to the earth, sat with folded hands awaiting the end. While it frightened some into silence it made others loquacious, while others again could not help laughing at the comical figure some of the frightened ones assumed.

No sooner did Silas Jordan see the comet than a great fear seized him, and he sat down in the kitchen, a millstone of desolation holding him in his seat.

Hardly a day passed that I did not run up to the Jordans', and on this evening, instead of hearing Mrs. Jordan singing one of her favourite hymns, I listened to a monologue which contained a note of sadness.

When Kezia came in with a chicken which she had just killed and was about to scald and pluck, a glance at her husband told her of the great and sudden change.

"Dear me, suss! Zack Caverly said ye'd be apt to feel a touch o' fever when ye broke that piece o' land down by the Log-House."

She expected an answer, but none came, and she went on:

"I don't know what we'll do with so much work waitin' to be done."

She took from the highest shelf in the cupboard a large box of quinine pills and offered Silas two, but he refused them with a stubborn shake of the head.

Mrs. Jordan put the box aside and began to pluck the chicken with a will that might have inspired her husband with courage had he noticed what she was doing.

"It ain't no use givin' way and broodin' over yer feelin's," she said quietly.

Alek came in and told his mother a comet was to be seen, and she stepped to the door to look.

She had heard the rumours and prophecies, but they left her indifferent. Her deep religious faith made it impossible for her to worry when worry seemed almost a sin, and it never occurred to her that Silas was not ill of malaria, but of fear and despair.

"Pap's ailin'," said Alek. "If he ain't no better tomorrer I'll go fer that yarb doctor that cured Ebenezer Hicks o' them faintin' spells."

He had a horror of long illnesses, and would call in a "doctor" at the slightest sign of a break-up in health.

The next day I was at the Jordan home again, this time with tempting eatables for the invalid, who, however, refused everything.

The doctor arrived shortly after; then, on his heels, came Socrates, who, when he saw the doctor's horse and saddle-bags, guessed there was something wrong with the Jordan household.

The doctor was looking about the room like a rabbit let loose in a strange place. Lank and bony, clothed in blue jeans, he looked a picture of unsophisticated ignorance.

"My husband's ailin'," said Mrs. Jordan, as she took a chair and placed it before Silas for the doctor.

"How long's he been feelin' this a-way?" he asked in a drawling voice as he sat down and took hold of the patient's limp hand.

"Sence yesterday."

"Chills en fever, I reckon," he said, looking at Silas with a blank stare.

"He ain't had any chills," returned Mrs. Jordan.

"Ain't hed no pin-feather feelins?"

"I don't reckon he hez."

"No chatterin' o' the teeth?"

"Not ez I know of."

"Been wanderin' in his mind?"

"Not ez I know of."

"Ain't felt overly het up?"

"I guess not."

"Then I reckon it's dumb ague," concluded the doctor, at his wits' end.

"I guess it is," said Kezia, "fer he ain't spoke a word sence he was took."

The doctor now asked to see the patient's tongue, and after much persuasion Silas slowly put out the tip, then closed his jaws with a smart snap.

"Mighty peert fer a man thet cain't talk," observed Zack Caverly. But the doctor, more and more bewildered, simply nodded his head, and then moved his chair back several paces as if to be well out of the reach of a patient who might suddenly do him an injury.

He looked fixedly at the little wiry-faced man, not knowing what to say or do.

Suddenly a thought struck him.

"Hez he ever hed quare idees?"

"I don't know thet he hez, 'ceptin' he's been figurin' on jest how long it would take to buy out the folks at the big Log-House."

"En ye say he ain't et no vittles sense yestiddy?"

"Not a morsel."

The doctor considered for a while, pulled at his goatee, and said:

"I 'low his symptomania air summat confoundin', but jest at this perti ckler p'int whar, ez ye might say, the fever hez kinder thawed out the chills, en the chills hez sorter nipped the fever in the bud, both on 'em hev been driv' in. They're a-fightin' it out on the liver, en a man ain't calc'lated te know jest how things air a-workin' up on the inside."

"Will it last long?" demanded Alek.

"Wal, thar ain't no cause to be frustrated. T'other day I see a man over B'ar Creek way thet rolled on the floor fer nigh an hour, en I'm doggoned if the chills en fever didn't stay right whar they war. His wife allowed I hed giv' him too much senna en calomel, but it takes a powerful sight te make 'em go different ways—more pertickler when the chills air dumb."

The doctor, after ordering huge doses of calomel and quinine, shuffled awkwardly out, and Socrates took Silas Jordan's hand and considered for a moment. Then, looking about the room, he observed:

"If chills means bein' cold, he ain't got no chills, en if fever means bein' hot, he ain't got no fever."

"What hez he, then?" inquired Alek, with a startled look.

"He's got the funks!"

"I want to know!" exclaimed Kezia, rising to face the new situation.

Alek, appalled at the sound of a word he had never heard till now, gasped out:

"Is it ketchin'?"

"Ketchin'! I'd like te see ye ketch a weazil in a haystack," observed Zack Caverly.

Mrs. Jordan looked at one and then at the other, but before she had time to say anything further, in came Uriah Busby.

He had come in a great hurry.

Of middle age, somewhat portly, and slightly bald, he now looked ten years older than when I saw him at the meeting-house. To-day his face wore a haggard and woe-begone expression.

Uriah Busby had come to find out what his practical, cool-headed neighbour, Silas Jordan, thought of the comet.

"Glad to see ye," was Kezia's gentle greeting.

She handed him a chair, and Uriah sat down, heaved a deep sigh, and began to wipe his perspiring head and face with his big handkerchief.

"No," resumed Socrates, where he had left off; "he ain't sick, he's only skeered."

Uriah Busby could hardly believe his ears. He had come, thinking that Silas Jordan would have some counsel of hope to offer, and there he sat scared into helplessness!

Nevertheless, Uriah felt called upon to say something:

"These be times of great affliction. It looks like the preacher war plumb right, en the Lord's hand is stretched agin us."

"Mebbe ye're right," interrupted Socrates; "but ez fur ez I kin see the Lord ain't tetched any of ye with more'n a thumb en forefinger."

The eyes of the invalid were now wide open; he sat bolt upright as if shaking off the effects of a horrid nightmare, and blurted out:

"Arter all, like ez not it ain't a-comin' our way!"

Uriah Busby pointed upward, his voice tremulous with emotion:

"Mebbe it's only a sign o' grace fer the elect."

But Socrates simply remarked: "It's a sign ye've been settin' on a chinee egg like a wet hen, en it's 'bout time ye war up en dustin'."

Kezia's dark face was all aglow; she looked as if she had no words to express what she felt.

Uriah Busby's confusion increased with every remark that came from Socrates, who seemed to expose everyone's secret.

"It's jest ez ye say," he stammered at last; "if the Lord's willin' it's our dooty te work en not te set waitin'."

"En he's been settin' there ever sence he took," said Mrs. Jordan.

" 'Pears like ye'll hev te pull him up like ye would a jimpson-weed," added Socrates. "Mebbe thet med'cine man hez got more sense than I 'lowed he had; mebbe ez like ez not Si needs a thunderin' bit shakin', en if we'll jes' set te work we kin bring him te rights. Did ye ever see a b'ar come out arter the fust big thaw, hoppin' roun' on two legs, this a-way, gettin' his sinoos sorter stretched en his blood sorter warmed up?"

He began to imitate a dancing bear, stepping first on one leg, then on the other, swaying, nodding, and bending his head, with comical glances at Silas.

"Do like mister b'ar; shake yerself!"

And with this he pulled the invalid out of his seat with a sudden jerk, forcing him round and round, dancing, bending, and hopping, with growls and grimaces to harmonise with his bruin-like antics.

"Keep it up," shouted Uriah Busby; "it'll do him a heap o' good."

Socrates kept up the hopping and swaying until Silas Jordan was exhausted and Alek's fear had changed into a broad grin that was almost laughter; and hardly had the mad dance ceased when Silas asked for fried chicken, the chicken which Kezia had killed and dressed, and kept for some such occasion.

"The ways o' the Lord air past findin' out," remarked Uriah, wiping his face.

When the chicken was ready Silas walked about picking a wing which he held in both hands.

"He's ez hungry ez a wolf, I do declare," said Kezia in a half-whisper, as she went about her duties, relieved of the long strain of watching and waiting. Then she added:

"I never see his ekil!"

"I 'low ye never did, Sister Jordan," rejoined Socrates; "but ye're mistaken in the varmint—ye mean he's ez hungry ez a catamount!"

CHAPTER 6

The Cabin of Socrates

"SONNY," said my father one afternoon, "you can come with me and you will have a chance of seeing Socrates, for I am to call at his cabin to see a drover on some business."

I accepted the invitation with joy, for I never tired of hearing Zack Caverly talk; even to sit and look at him was to me a great treat.

Socrates was sitting at his cabin door, smoking, dreaming, and listening to what strange sounds might reach him from the woods. As he sat there he felt himself detached from the world, yet near enough to human beings to have all the society he desired. He thought of the new settlers, their troubles and vexations, and he wondered how many of them were as free from care as himself.

Under the cabin the hounds were sleeping, all cuddled up, and now, after a somewhat busy and exciting day, Nature seemed more intimate and satisfying than ever. Age brought with it less and less ambition, less and less desire to do useless things, to speculate about vain theories and impending political events. To the mind of Socrates worry and ambition were unnatural and foolish things, and eternity meant to-day.

As he sat at his door he felt at home in the universe. The wilderness was his kingdom; his subjects, the birds and beasts; his friends, the hounds and his rifle; and he rode out among the settlers like a king on a tour of inspection, with advice here and a greeting of encouragement where it was needed, and when he returned to his cabin, peace and contentment issued forth from every log.

His cabin was his palace. A huge stag's head nailed over the entrance might have been taken for a coat-of-arms in the rough, while inside another set of antlers adorned the chimney-place.

From the rafters hung the pelt of fox and wild cat; a low couch was covered with a buffalo robe, and on the floor were some old skins of the black bear. Several trophies of the wolf were stretched on nails, and strings of Indian corn hanging about here and there made the inside of the cabin a picture of indolence as well as activity.

Zack Caverly was the last of his peculiar mode of life in this part of the country, and towns and railroads would soon put an end to such a mode of living.

The cabin adjoined a deep wood not far from a creek, with the prairie in front, and from his door not a house could be seen.

Socrates had been here some twenty-five years, and knew the history of every family within a radius of many miles: their peculiarities, virtues, and vices. He could sum up the powers and failings of a newcomer at a glance. As for himself, he knew where his food would come from for a year, good weather or bad; he knew the work required at his hands, using his own time and pleasure in doing it. For often when the weather was fine, and the ground dry, he would spend whole days hunting in the bottoms, many miles from home. He ploughed when it suited him, and reaped much in the same way. He read no books, did not belong to any religious sect, never had been to school, and, owing to his wanderings in his younger days, had no prejudices.

He knew the haunts and habits of all the animals and birds of field and forest, and the time to expect certain wild flowers; and he had his own weather signs. He loved everything wild, regarding his solitary mode of life as the most natural thing in the world.

As the days and hours came and went, so he passed from one mood to another without being conscious of any change, without grief or regret, rising in the morning and lying down at night with the same feeling of security and contentment. And principally for this reason he was welcomed everywhere, bringing with him an atmosphere of mental vigour and confidence at a time when these forces were so much needed. His mind was on the present; thus no time was lost in idle sorrow for events of yesterday.

It was nearly dusk when we arrived at the cabin, and my father had not long to wait for the drover. Soon after Socrates set about getting us supper of bacon, eggs, hoe-cakes, and coffee, which we ate with keen appetites.

Shortly after supper was over Elihu Gest, the Load-Bearer, came driving up, and hitched his team to one of the logs near the door. He was on his way home from the post-office.

"I war kinder moved te come aroun' en see ye," he said.

"Right glad ye come; ye're allers welcome ez long ez I'm alive en kickin'," answered Socrates, with his usual good humour.

"The feelin' come jest ez I got te the cross-roads, thar by Ebenezer Hicks's cornfield."

Just then Lem Stephens rode up.

Socrates had come out to greet the Load-Bearer, and the three men sat down on the logs while I sat at one side. My father and the drover were inside discussing some matter of business.

But oh! how shall I depict the company outside? the objects fading in the deepening dusk, the stars growing brighter every moment, the stillness broken now and again by the cries of the whip-poor-will and the conversation of the men!

After a long spell of cloudy weather the sky had cleared; the air was warm and dry, and when darkness closed in the night came with a revelation. Never in that region had such a night been seen by living man, for a comet hung suspended in the shimmering vault, like an immense silver arrow, dominating the world and all the constellations.

An unparalleled radiance illumined the prairie in front of the cabin; the atmosphere vibrated with a strange, mysterious glow; and as the eye looked upward it seemed as if the earth was moving slowly towards the stars.

The sky resembled a phantasmagoria seen from the summit of some far and fabulous Eden. The Milky Way spread across the zenith like a confluence of celestial altars flecked with myriads of gleaming tapers, and countless orbs rose out of the luminous veil like fleecy spires tipped with the blaze of opal and sapphire.

The great stellar clusters appeared like beacons on the shores of infinite worlds, and night was the window from which the soul looked out on eternity.

The august splendour of the heavens, the atmosphere, palpitating with the presence of the All-ruling Spirit, diffused a feeling of an inscrutable power reaching out from the starry depths, enveloping the whole world in mystery.

I sat and gazed in awe and silence.

Socrates was quietly smoking a corn-cob pipe, while Elihu

Gest, rapt in wonder, contemplated the heavens as if seeking an answer to his innermost thoughts.

"I knowed we war clost to it," he exclaimed at last, referring to the comet; "the hand o' the Lord air p'intin' straight!"

He stopped to meditate again, and no one broke the silence for some little time.

Then he proceeded:

"I've seen it afore, but never like this. 'Pears like over around here the hull heavings air clairer, and the stars look like they war nigher the yearth."

"Be you on risin' groun'?" asked Lem Stephens, addressing Socrates.

"Not onless it's riz sence we've been settin' here."

"I allowed ye warn't," said Lem; "but I thought mebbe I war mistaken."

"It's the feelin's a man hez when mericles air a-bein' worked," said the Load-Bearer, with familiar confidence. "A man's thoughts en feelin's ain't noways the same when the Lord begins te manifest His power. He ain't afeared te show His hand; but I ain't never see a kyard-player thet'll let ye look at his kyards."

" 'Kase it air we uns thet do the shufflin'," observed Socrates; "Providence allers leads and allers wins. But some o' these settlers knows what spades air, I reckon."

"En some'll suttinly know what clubs air if they keep on with thar nigger stealin'," spoke up Lem Stephens.

To this the Load-Bearer paid no attention. His thoughts were on the signs of the times and the man who was to lead in the great struggle.

"Thar's a new dispensation a-comin'," he said with calm conviction; "but it warn't made plain what it ud be till I heerd Abe Lincoln en Steve Douglas discussin' some p'ints o' law fer the fust time. When I heerd Lincoln war a-goin' te speak I sez: 'Now's yer time. If ye miss this chance ye won't mebbe hev another.' When I got thar I see Jedge Douglas war 'p'inted te opin the meetin'."

"Thet give ye a chance te see how the leetle giant ud look alongside o' the six-footer," interrupted Socrates. "When I heerd the Jedge he give chapter en verse for every hole he bored in the Republican plank; but when Abe Lincoln riz up he held some thunderin' big Abolition nails te plug 'em with. 'Peared like he ez much ez sez te Steve Douglas: 'You jes' keep on borin' en I'll do the drivin'; it's a heap easier; fer when you fellars git through borin' I'll hev my plank nailed te the constitution o' this hull kintry!' "

"I 'low Steve Douglas hed the law on his side," rejoined Elihu Gest; "but lawyer Lincoln hedn't been speakin' more'n ten minutes afore I see he war a-bein' called on, en 'peared like I could hear the words, 'jedgment jedgment!' a-soundin' in the air; en if all the prairies o' this here State hed been sot on fire, I'd a-sot thar till he'd a-spoke the last word!"

"Shucks!" exclaimed Socrates; "I don't reckon Steve Douglas keers; but I 'spect he see it warn't no use sassin' back."

Lem Stephens struck the log several hard, quick blows with his wooden leg.

"But laws! What kin words en book-larnin' do agin the Ten Commandments?" ejaculated the Load-Bearer.

"I reckon Jedge Douglas war relying' on saft sodder; but it won't hold the spout te the kittle if the fire's anyways over het and the water's mos' b'iled away," said Socrates.

"Ez I war a-goin' te say," continued Elihu Gest, " 'tain't words ez counts ez much ez it air the feelin's. A politician's 'bout the same in this here ez a preacher: he hez te possess the sperit if he wants the power. Accordin' te my thinkin' he hez te throw it out till it kivers the hull meetin'."

"I b'lieve ye're right," assented Socrates nonchalantly. "I've heared the leetle giant more'n oncet, en I 'low he did look spry en plump, en ez boundin' ez a rubber ball. But it ain't the hoss thet jumps the highest thet kin carry the furdest, en I reckon a man's got te be convicted hisself afore he convicts ary other."

"The sperit air more in th' eye than it air in the tongue," said Elihu Gest, rising from his seat; "if Abe Lincoln looked at the wust slave-driver long enough, Satan would give up every time."

" 'Pears like ye're right," observed Socrates again.

The Load-Bearer continued, with increasing emphasis:

"I see right away the difference a-twixt Lincoln en Douglas warn't so much in Lincoln bein' a good ways over six foot en Douglas a good ways under, ez it war in thar eyes. The Jedge looked like he war speakin' agin time, but Abe Lincoln looked plumb through the meetin' into the Everlastin'—the way Moses must hev looked when he see Canaan ahead—en I kin tell ye I never did see a man look thet a-way.

"The Jedge is some pum'kins fer squeezin' hisself in, but I

reckon the six-footer hez got the rulin' hand this time."

"They're at the cross-roads!" ejaculated Lem Stephens; "but them thar Abolitionists air in a howlin' wilderness, en the partin' o' the ways don't lead nowheres; thar ain't no sign-posts, not in this 'ere case. I've been lost more'n oncet by takin' the wrong road jes' when I felt dead sartin' I war on the right track. Gee whizz! I kin take ye te a place over near Edwardsville whar nothin' walkin' on two legs kin tell the difference a-twixt the p'ints in campass on a cloudy day; en even when the sun's a-shinin' ye've got te smell the way jes' like a hound, fer seein' don't do no good.

"I'll tell ye what it is, in this 'ere business whar politics is right on the cross-roads they want sunthin' more'n two eyes te see with. A man's got te know whar he's a-goin'. I see an Injun oncet put his ear te the groun' te tell which road te take. Arter a while he got up, give his breast a thump, en struck out ez if he war a bloodhound arter a nigger. En don't ye go te thinkin' he tuck the wrong road neither. How d'ye allow they air goin' te free the niggers? They ain't got no weepons, en the slave-owners air a sight cuter with shootin'-irons nur the Abolitionists be. Ever sence Daniel Boone settled t'other side the Ohio the white folks o' the South hev been aimin' at movin' targets—all kyinds o' birds en varmints, flyin' en runnin', includin' niggers en Injuns."

"Ez fer settin' on 'em free," said the Load-Bearer, "I ain't allowin' nothin' but God Almighty's hand; en shorely with thet comet up yander we air movin' into conflictin' times. If I hed any doubts my mind war set at rest when I heared Abe Lincoln speak; if he had jes' riz up en looked at the folks they would a-felt his power jes' the same."

"I've seen him," said Zack Caverly, "when he played mournin' tunes on their heart-strings till they mourned with the mourners."

Elihu Gest straightened himself up, and the tone of his voice changed.

"But somehow it 'peared like Abe Lincoln would hev such loads ez no man ever carried sence Christ walked in Israel. When I went over fer te hear him things looked mighty onsartin; 'peared like I hed more'n I could stand up under; but he hadn't spoke more'n ten minutes afore I felt like I never hed no loads. I begin te feel ashamed o' bein' weary en complainin'. When I went te hear him I 'lowed the Lord might let me carry some loads away, but I soon see Abe Lincoln war ekil te carry his'n en mine too, en I sot te wonderin' 'bout the workin's o' Providence."

"But ye war only listenin' to an Abolitionist a-stumpin' this hull tarnation kedentry," remarked Lem Stephens with all the bitterness he could put into the words.

"Arter all, I reckon religion en politics air 'bout the same," broke in Socrates.

"Sin in politics," answered the Load-Bearer, "air ekil te sin in religion—thar ain't no dividin' line," a remark which made Lem Stephens begin a loud and prolonged tattoo on the log with his wooden stump.

"Pete Cartwright," he blurted out, "hez allers been agin Abe Lincoln; how d'ye kyount for it?"

"I 'low Brother Cartwright hez worked a heap o' good ez a preacher," was the cool reply of Elihu Gest, "but things ain't a-goin' te be changed by preachin' alone. There'll be fire en brimstone fer some, er that blazin' star up yander don't mean nothin', en thar ain't no truth in the Scriptur's."

There were sounds as of something rushing through the underbrush and the crackling of dry timber some distance away, and when I looked in that direction I saw what seemed a faint flash of a lantern. One of the hounds under the cabin gave signs of uneasiness.

The Load-Bearer continued, lowering his voice:

"I feel like I did afore the war with Mexico, 'cept we didn't see no comet then."

"They did make a confounded fuss over thet war," observed Socrates, "en I remember Clay en Calhoun having it hot over sunthin' er nuther; both on 'em faced the music fer a reelin' breakdown. Clay sez to Calhoun: 'Ye've been expoundin' a p'int o' law I ain't never diskivered in the book o' statues. Yer argiments air shaky, en yer jedgmints air ez splashy ez the Mississippi in flood-time. The hull nation's cavin' in, en thar ain't a man among ye knows 'nough te plug things up en stop the leakin'.'

"But Calhoun put the question ez peert ez a blue-jay: 'What's a-leakin'?' sez he; ''tain't the ship o' State, it's the whisky barrel.'

" 'Jes' so,' says Henry Clay, ez sassy ez a cat-bird in nestin' time; 'you en yer party hev knocked the plug out, but me en my party air a-goin' te double dam thet leakin'.'

"Old Hickory I see oncet at a Methodist meetin'. Pete Cartwright war a-preachin' when Old Hickory walked in. The presidin' elder sez to the preacher: 'Thet's Andrew Jackson'; but Pete Cartwright didn't noways keer. 'Who's Andrew Jackson?' he sez. 'If he's a sinner God'll damn him the same ez He would a Guinea nigger.' En he went right on preachin'."

"Thar's nothin' I despise so much ez an Abolition Methodist," ejaculated Lem Stephens. "Tar en feathers air a heap too good fer some on 'em."

This remark was evidently intended for the Load-Bearer, but he seemed not to hear.

"When ye're corn-huskin'," said Socrates, "ye put on gloves, but ye take 'em off when ye're gropin' roun' fer sinners' souls. Some preachers en politicioners take holt like they war the hounds en the people a passel o' varmints. But a preacher thet knows what he's about allers takes the p'ints iv a meetin' like he would the p'ints iv a horse. He hez te spy out the kickers en the balky ones, en wust iv all, them thet's half mustang en half mule, en act accordin'.

"I 'low a man kin do a sight with flowin' words en saft soap, but ez fer the mules en cross-breeds, saft soap won't tetch 'em."

"I agree with ye thar, brother Caverly," said the Load-Bearer; "when the meetin's anyways conflictin' it air mighty hard te deal with the Word: some wants singin', some wants preachin', en some wants prayin'."

"I reckon it air ez ye say; but ye might ez well send a retriever arter dead ducks with a tin kittle tied te his tail ez te try te land some sinners with a long string o' prayers. A man's got te roll up en wade in hisself if he wants te find them thet's been winged. When folks sets en blinks like brown owls, 'thout flappin' a wing er losin' a feather, I want te know what a pore preacher kin do! 'Tain't easy te tell who's been tetched."

"Thar's a sight o' difference a-twixt what a preacher hez te do en what a politician hez," answered Elihu Gest. "A preacher hez te wrastle with the sins o' the world every time he stands afore the people."

"Ye see," continued Zack Caverly, filling his pipe, "the 'sponsibility ain't the same. In the meetin'-house the man o' God ain't got but one kyind te wrastle with, en thet air sinners.

He's arter game what cain't fly, seein' ez how they ain't angels yit; en ez they's occupyin' the floor he's 'bleeged te shoot low, allowin' the crows a-settin' on the fence to set right whar they be.

"But a politicioner's in a heap wuss fix; he's 'bleeged to deal with them what's on the fence, kase he knows the crows air jes' waitin' to see which side the fattest worms air a-comin' up on. But them thet's plumb full o' religion ain't got no room fer worms."

He lit his pipe, took a few puffs, and then went on:

"I 'low them lawyers en jedges en stump-speakers over at Springfield ain't fishin' fer snappin' turtles with nothin' but red feathers from a rooster's tail. A politicioner nowadays hez got to be ez cunnin' ez a possum thet's playin' dead, en a heap cuter'n a catamount a-layin' roun' fer the hull hog—fer if he ain't he'll be ketched hisself. Think o' the all-fired predicamints they find tharselves in! Talk about wrastlin' with sin en Satan, Elihu! Why, thar ain't a stump-meetin' but what a Republican hez te spar the Demicrats on a p'int o' law, en trip up the Know-nothin's on a question o' niggers; en while the Whigs air fannin' him with brick-bats he's mighty lucky if he ain't 'spected te hold a candle te the devil while he's a-bein' robbed o' purty nigh all his cowcumbers en water-melons en more'n half his whisky en character."

At this moment the sudden arrival of three men on horseback interrupted the conversation.

"Good evening, gentlemen," said the leader; "have you heard of any runaways about here within the last day or two?"

"I ain't heared o' none; they don't never come this way," Socrates replied.

"We're looking for three runaway slaves that are said to be somewhere in this vicinity."

" 'Bout how long hev they been out?" asked Lem Stephens.

"We lost track of them two days ago; they are somewhere near this creek."

"How many be they?"

"Two women and a boy; there's a reward of five hundred dollars."

"Let me go with ye," said Lem Stephens, hurriedly going towards his horse; "en if we don't see nothin' of 'em to-night I'll help ye find 'em in the mornin'."

After some futile words the three men and Lem Stephens wished us good-night and rode away.

By a sudden turn in the chain of events we had been brought to the verge that divides the high level of freedom from the abyss of bondage, and a feeling of distress seized hold of the company. The two men could find no words for speech. But out of the depths of the night the voices of Nature assailed them: from the woods behind us came the hooting and cries of owl and wild cat, from the prairie came tiny insects that floated past with buzzing whispers in the ears of conscience, crickets sent a thrill of warning from under the logs, tree-toads whistled near the creek, and a whip-poor-will soared and called over the cabin and the ghostly outlines of the woods.

Everything was free except the fugitives hovering somewhere near the cabin: birds and animals could roam about at will, the comet had the universe for a circuit, Socrates, in his humble cabin, was a king in his easy independence, my father, with all his cares, could go and come as he pleased, Elihu Gest, in spite of his "loads," enjoyed the freedom of the earth as far as his eyes could see or his horses carry him; and now, perhaps within a few hundred yards of us, three human beings were still panting in the throes of bondage.

But the time had come to speak, and as my father and the drover joined us the Load-Bearer said:

"It air the mother en her boy en gal. I 'low they ain't a-goin' te be separated in this world."

"Ye talk ez if ye knowed all about it," remarked Socrates; "but they'll be ketched afore to-morrer noon if they air any-whar's roun' here."

"I'm only tellin' ye my idee, en I reckon ye'll find I'm right."

The Load-Bearer walked to the other side of the cabin and stood for some moments without speaking.

"Jes' you keep still en set right whar ye be till I come back," he said, returning towards us.

He walked along the road where it bordered the woods. The three mounted men had come down this road. We all wondered what impulse could have induced him to take that direction.

The Load-Bearer had not been gone more than two or three minutes before Zack Caverly's favourite hound set up a plaintive whining under the cabin.

"Spy! Keep still thar!" said his master.

"Ye see," he went on, "thet ole dog's got wind o' sunthin' quare. I've larned 'em all te keep ez still ez mice when me en other folks air about, but thar's sunthin' unusual a-gettin' ready er Spy wouldn't ez much ez sneeze. He beats all the dogs I ever hed. Thet hound *kin* smell! En ez fer hearin', I b'lieve he kin hear what's a-goin' on most anywhar's.

"But ye wouldn't think he could tell shucks from hoe-cakes, his looks air so innercent en pleadin'! He uster be the best fighter among 'em, but now he knows 'tain't wisdom te be brash.

"It took me nigh on three year te larn him the difference a-twix wolf en b'ar, en skunk en wild cat, en all the other varmints, en thet ain't sayin' nothin' 'bout two-legged creatur's. Ye see, it war this a-way: I war 'bleeged te p'int te the head iv any varmint thet hed been shot er trapped, usin' only one word, en thet word meanin' the varmint; en by callin' the names over en over ag'in he got te know what I meant when I asked: 'Air it wolf?' 'Air it b'ar?' en so on plumb down te 'Air it nigger?' "

Socrates now called on the hound to come out.

Spy came to his master, and, looking into his face, seemed to expect some command. Socrates began:

"Air it wolf?" The dog gave no sign. "Air it b'ar?" Still no response. "Air it nigger?" The old dog gave unmistakable signs of assent.

"Them runaways ain't fur off," said Socrates; "but I ain't a-goin' te let Spy go arter 'em, he might skeer 'em away from Elihu, en he'll bring 'em in if they're alive en kickin'. If thar's anyone in this hull kintry ez know's more'n thet old hound it air Elihu Gest. He's arter loads day en night, en he ain't happy onless he's gettin' hisself into a bushel o' trouble. Ole Spy en him war clost friends from the word Go, en I reckon Elihu hez rescued more runaways than ary other Abolitionist in this deestric'; but they ain't never ketched him at it; they might ez well look fer a sow's ear in a b'ar's den."

I thought I could hear the sound of voices in the direction the Load-Bearer had gone, but I soon began to think I must have been mistaken, for not till nearly half an hour later did we hear him coming towards the cabin.

He was walking as fast as he could, with a boy in one arm and a woman leaning on the other.

"Great Jehosephat!" exclaimed Socrates; "if Elihu ain't got

more'n enough fer a load. But he's mistaken 'bout thar bein' three on 'em. I 'low two's enough, sech ez they be."

Elihu Gest came full into view; even with his firm support the woman hanging on his arm was hardly able to walk. But scarcely had he put down the boy when another figure was seen approaching. It was the woman's daughter—a handsome octoroon of about seventeen—hobbling along with the aid of a crutch made from a dry branch.

"I'll be durned if he warn't right arter all," observed Socrates, hurrying into the cabin to make a fire.

"We got plenty time; them thet's scoutin' roun' these diggin's won't be back ag'in to-night."

The fugitives were placed on the ground, with the logs behind them as props, and the Load-Bearer asked:

" 'Bout how long air it sence ye hed any vittles?"

I could not hear the answer, but Elihu Gest exclaimed:

"Three days without vittles, en all on 'em mos' dead!"

Elihu made haste with the coffee, while Socrates was hurrying with the supper.

Once in a while a groan came from the group of figures. The sound mingled with the mysteries of the surrounding darkness. It put fresh courage into the heart of the Load-Bearer, and strengthened him to assume still greater burdens. Socrates worked in silence, and during this time we were all wondering what ought to be done with the fugitives. To let them be caught was out of the question, but what to do with them after they had partaken of supper was a point that puzzled everyone. My father thought it dangerous to leave them so near the cabin.

To the great relief of all, the drover mounted his horse and rode away, perhaps not wishing to become involved in any responsibility and to steer clear of a situation which might compromise him in the eyes of the law.

"Looky here," remarked Zack Caverly to the Load-Bearer, "ye don't reckon he's goin' over Lem Stephens's way, do ye?"

"I don't reckon he air; 'pears like he allers turns off thar by Ebenezer Hicks's cornfield."

The coffee was ready and the Load-Bearer and Socrates were serving it out in the big blue china cups which we had used at our supper—the bacon and hoe-cakes would soon follow.

Every moment now seemed like an hour.

My father, Elihu, and Socrates went into the cabin to talk over the affair and decide on what to do.

They were coming out of the cabin when the drover returned bringing the news that the slave-catchers had decided to pay Socrates another visit that night.

It did not take long for the Load-Bearer to come to a decision. He called for aid, and one by one the three runaways were lifted into his wagon.

"Whar be ye goin', Elihu? They've seed ye here, en ye'll be called on shore en sartin."

"I don't know no more'n you; but I ain't a-goin' te stop till God Almighty tells me."

He drove off into the night, taking the road to the east. We followed on the same road shortly after, but met no one on the way home. When we arrived at the Log-House we found that it, too, had been visited by the slave-hunters.

CHAPTER 7

At the Post-Office

ONE morning I went with my father to the post-office, which was in a small store by the railway station, about six miles distant.

How bleak and forsaken it was! The place consisted of two houses and some freight cars shunted off the main line. The prairie here had a desolate look, but to the north lay a wooded district, and here my father brought me to stand on a small embankment to watch the train coming up around a curve out of the woods.

The sight made an impression that was lasting, for at this moment it is just as vivid as it was then. It made my nerves tingle and opened the door to a new world of wonders. The train itself, filled with passengers, did not interest me: it was the engine, with its puffing steam, its cow-catcher, and its imposing smoke-stack, that possessed the attraction.

The day soon came, however, when the locomotive took the second place in my imagination and the passengers the first. What, after all, was the steam-engine compared with human beings, animals, and birds? What was its smoke and movement compared with pictures of earth, sky, and water? At rest, the locomotive ceased to interest; but the aspect of the world was always changing. A landscape had its four seasons. Every manifestation of Nature harmonised with some mood or condition of the mind, and I watched the buzzards and bluebirds, the cranes and chick-a-dees, the rabbits and squirrels, with renewed and ever-interesting interest. Nature changed, but never grew stale. The air was full of song and colour, the earth full of forms and movement, and the rapid motion of a garter-snake was, after all, more fascinating than the movement of an engine with its train of cars; and how could the noise of the puffing compare with a chorus of red-winged blackbirds? Nature is the one perennial charm.

But this was not the opinion of poor Monsieur Duval, one of the unfortunate settlers who had mistaken the wilderness for a ready-made paradise. All the loungers at the post-office looked like members of the same family excepting this Frenchman and a German settler whom they called "Dutchy." Duval resembled a shipwrecked mariner among the inhabitants of some remote island, the secret of whose language and customs he could not fathom. But he and the German were full of life, while the others seemed too listless and lazy to do more than whittle sticks and once in a while hit a cetain spot by an expectoration of tobacco-juice.

The scene was set off by rows of tea-canisters, coffee-sacks, bolts of calico, sugar-barrels, bacon, rice, and plug-tobacco, with sundry farming implements stored at the back, and a few pigeon-holes for letters.

The shuffling figure of the goateed proprietor stood in the midst of all, a little taller and perhaps a little more languid than any of the others, too indifferent to talk, yet putting in a word now and again mechanically without stopping to calculate the effect of what he said and without being interested in any person or thing. He aroused my interest as soon as he said to my father:

"Wal, I'm going to wind her up—goin' to vamose."

"Going to leave us?"

"Ya-as," he drawled; "goin' to wind up and move on."

A man sitting on the edge of a large box, half-filled with empty sacks, called out:

"Which a-way?"

"Over to Pike kyounty," was the answer.

The Frenchman, who was standing against the counter, straightened up.

"Me, too," he exclaimed, tapping his bosom once for each word, "me, too, I wind her up, I go vamose."

"Goin' to sell out, too?"

"If I no sell heem I geef heem way," he answered with a gesture of supreme disgust.

"How long have you been here?" asked the storekeeper.

"Two, tree year."

"Hardly long enough to give the country a fair trial," said my father.

"Try heem! I geef him plenty tam. Ze farm he try me lak Job was try wiz hees sheep an' hees camelle!"

"Have you had much illness?"

"Do I look seek? My wife, my son, meself, we work lak niggair. We haf no tam for eat, no tam for sleep, no tam for wash ourself."

"You must have taken up too much land. Most of the trouble comes from that."

"No, monsieur, we no haf too much, but we been too much for ze land."

"I suppose you are from some part of the South?"

"Me, I come from New Orleans. I haf one big family; I lose heem wiz ze yellow fevair. My friends say, 'You go up ze Mississippi, you 'scape ze fevair.' I tak my wife an' son to Saint-Lewis. Someone say, 'You tak one farm in Illinois, ze soil she been so rich you scratch heem two, tree tam wiz hoe, everyzing come up while you look!' Wen I come on ze farm ze soil she been too hard for scratch; I get one plough, so long, for cut ze bit root, an four pair ox for pool her. But ze wild cat come in ze night; she clam up ze tree an' tak ze turkey; ze fox brak in ze hen-house an' tak ze chicken. In ze morning I find ze haid an' some feddair."

He stopped to consider a moment, then continued: "I keep some bee for make bees' wax. I go look—I find ze hive sprawl on ze groun', zey haf left me nozzing!"

"What animal do you suppose it was?"

"Tell me, monsieur, do ze fox lak for eat ze bee? Do ze wild cat lak for chew ze bees' wax? Do ze mink lak for haf her nose sting? Ah, monsieur, I lak for someone tell me zat!"

Duval gave a fierce look at the man sitting on the box, for he had just fallen over on the sacks in a spasm of laughter, his feet in the air, and we concluded he could tell what had become of the Frenchman's bees if he chose.

"But zat is not ze worst," he went on. "One tam I haf ver' good crop. Ze corn, ze legume, ze poomkin, she been all plant an' come up. But ze army-worm she come! Next day I go look—she leave me nozzing but ze cobble-stone."

Then as if he had forgotten something, he added:

"Ze cow come home an' I go for milk her—she been dry lak

my old boot; ze worm haf eat her foddair!"

He let his arms fall in a limp gesture of resignation, and taking from his pocket a cheap cigar, and leaning with one arm on the counter, he began smoking, letting out great puffs through his nose as if in this way he were getting rid of all the evil things connected with pioneer life.

The hang-dog faces of the men sitting and lolling about were enlivened by grins, and ironical remarks were freely indulged in.

"Say, Frenchy," said the man sitting on the box, "what'll ye take te hire out jes' te keep away b'ars en' skunks?"

Duval gave the man one contemptuous look. Evidently he was not going to answer. He smoked while he walked carelessly towards the box, and when within a few feet of it made a sudden, cat-like bound at the man, clutching his throat with the grip of a frenzied gorilla while he forced him down into the box head foremost.

The onlookers, stunned by the suddenness of the attack, seemed dazed and helpless, staring at the scene as if held by some horrible fascination. Then a gurgling sound came from the victim, causing someone to cry out:

"I'll be hanged if he ain't chokin' him to death!"

"I'm durned if he ain't!" exclaimed someone else.

"Haul him off!" shouted the store-keeper, roused out of his lethargy; "we don't want no dead men round here!"

The store-keeper, assisted by one of the man's friends, began to tug at the Frenchman. Hardly had they done so when a man with a knife made a rush for Duval; but the "Dutchman" was waiting his chance; he felled him to the floor by one quick blow from his great, open hand, the hard, thick palm and huge, long fingers making a splitting noise like a blade of steel on a sheet of ice.

"No! By sheemany!" he growled, as he picked up the knife and shook it in their faces. "You don't come dem games here! Ven you gif me dat shifferee I hef some buckshot ready, but mine vife she don't let me shoot nodding. Now I gif you someding mit interest," and with that he brought the same open hand down on the man who had helped to pull Duval off his victim. He fell to the floor as if struck with a mallet, and I shuddered, for he seemed to be stone dead. This was the third surprise within a few seconds. The man in the box was not yet able to rise to his feet, but Duval was looking about him ready for more work and well inclined to keep it going. His eyes were bloodshot and his face was all afire. He stood like some ferocious animal in the arena ready for any opponent, with a firm faith in his two hands, his two legs, his nimble body and his quick wit, while the "Dutchman" had good reason to pin his faith to a pair of broad palms, which resembled the paws of a bear in thickness, and a body unimpaired by fiery whisky and malarial fever.

Two of the gang were now placed *hors de combat*, and this without the use of knives or firearms. It was now four against two, and the Frenchman had evidently summed up the situation at a glance; with a quick, twisting movement he turned his body like a practised wrestler, and the man standing beside him found himself sprawling on the floor, his feet knocked from under him by the deft manoeuvres of Duval's foot.

All was now over. After this the gang resembled nothing so much as a pack of whipped dogs, and the stillness that reigned in the store had something of the stillness of the battlefield after the fury of the battle.

Duval and the "Dutchman" left the store together and became close friends from that day.

CHAPTER *8*

My Visit to the Load-Bearer's Home

MY MOTHER was busy getting ready for another baking. She had baked the day before, and I could not help wondering what all the extra bread was for.

I had not long to wait for an answer to my thoughts: she stopped in the middle of her work, cleaned the rolling-pin of dough, and went to the pantry, where she stood and looked for some moments at the things inside.

"Oh, dear!" she said, with one of her gentle sighs which I always understood so well; "there is not much, but what there is must go to-day, and in a day or two I shall send more."

Out came all the bread and the meat and a pound of coffee, with sugar. These were stored away in the saddle-bags, for she said it was too far to walk and I would have to saddle my pony.

"But where to?" I asked with surprise.

"To Mrs. Gest's; these things are for her."

"The Load-Bearer married!" I exclaimed.

"Why, of course he's married, like all good Christians," she observed, smiling; "and you'll be married too, some day, when the proper time comes."

I had pictured him as a kind of hermit, living somewhere all alone, perhaps being fed by ravens, like Elijah the prophet; and even now I could hardly believe that he had a regular, fixed abode.

I was to tell Mrs. Gest she could count on my mother's aid when she had "visitors from the South," which meant fugitive slaves trying to reach Canada.

The affair at the cabin of Socrates had been discussed between my parents, and this was the result.

No member of the family had ever been to the home of Elihu Gest. We knew he lived near a large creek, some four or five

89

miles south-west of the meeting-house; so off I went in the full belief that I would find the place by asking here and there on the way.

The country beyond the meeting-house was like another world to me. The prairie, the dim outline of the woods beyond, the atmosphere, all combined to produce a sense of freshness and novelty, and the effect on my mind could not have been greater had I gone a hundred miles from home.

After riding what seemed to me a long distance a man in a wagon directed me to a road bordering a strip of wood which led into a region of trees and underbrush, with patches of prairie here and there, and vistas of the creek and the undulating ground beyond. The land had a gentle slope towards the water. The beech trees rose to a great height, and now and then, through an opening in the woods, I could see a distance of two miles; but in most places the world all around was hidden by rocky knobs, thick underbrush, and immense trees.

"What a place to hide in!" I thought; and I was beginning to fear my search for the house would not end in success, when I heard the barking of a dog some considerable distance to the left. Stopping to consider what to do, I detected faint tracks of wagon wheels leading in that direction. I followed as best I could over a parterre of leaves, moss and the *débris* of decayed timber.

Penetrating still farther, I came upon a clearing, and then I caught a glimpse of a small frame house almost hidden by trees and shrubs. As I approached, three savage dogs, which I at first took to be wolves, chained up, began a fierce barking and howling. As I was about to get off my pony and ask if Elihu Gest lived here, a thin, pale-faced woman, her hair streaked with grey, opened the door. Then, wiping her mouth with her apron, she exclaimed:

"Bless ye, sonny, ye ain't come with bad news, hev ye? My ole man's been gone two full days en nights!"

It was Cornelia Gest, the Load-Bearer's wife.

I told her who had sent me and what I had brought; but it did not allay her anxiety when I recounted the incidents at the cabin of Socrates.

"Git right down en come in, en tell me all about it," she said; "I 'spect ye need a rest. It allers makes my head ache ridin' over the prairie in the hot sun."

I got off the pony, and after tying up took the things into the kitchen.

"Land! How good yer ma is," she exclaimed, "sendin' me all these things, in case o' needcessity. Elihu told me 'bout her. Some folks don't need te hev wings te be angels. How did yer ma know I hedn't but one loaf o' bread left? It do beat all how things work out! I 'lowed te do some bakin' to-day, but somehow I couldn't git te work. 'Pears like when Elihu's away en I don't know his whereabouts I cain't git nothin' done! Law me! if here ain't coffee! Elihu ain't never ceased talkin' 'bout yer ma's coffee. What does she cl'ar it with?"

All this time I was wondering what she would do if her husband should fail to return before evening.

"I'm right glad ye've come te cher a body; the hours air longer when ye're mos' dead worryin'. When he stayed away afore he 'lowed he wouldn't hev time te git back, en I warn't noways a-feared he'd got hisself into trouble."

There was something in her voice and look that aroused my sympathy.

"I set up all las' night prayin' en readin' in the Good Book," she went on; " 'twarn't in mortal natur' te sleep."

She seemed far away in thought. Her eyes were fixed on the floor, and I began to ask myself why everyone had so much trouble. As I only sat and listened she had become unconscious of my presence in the house; but after a while she straightened up and resumed:

"I recken he tuck the runaways over te Uriah Busby's, en from there he'll take 'em on te the nex' station."

She mused for a time again, and then continued:

"But it ain't easy; the resks air turrible, but then, ez Elihu sez, when the Lord en His hosts air with ye thar ain't no call te feel skeered. Elihu en Ike Snedeker en Ebenezer Carter en Tom Melendy, they don't none o' them know what it air te fail."

After sitting for some time without speaking, all of a sudden she clasped her hands and rose from her seat, and stretching out her thin, bare arms, with trembling body and quivering lips, her voice went up in a long, loud wail:

"Lord help a pore fersaken woman! Help me this day, fer my troubles air more'n I kin bear without Ye. Make it so I kin set here alone without repinin'; send Elihu home, oh my Lord en my God, fer I cain't live without him."

Her look appalled me. I saw grief manifest in words and gesture. . . . I pictured to myself my mother pleading with the Eternal. I imagined what the Log-House would be with my father absent and his whereabouts unknown.

How I wished to say something comforting to the lonely woman standing there, but I, who could never express to my mother what I thought and felt when she was in trouble, could not find words to comfort a stranger. I was overcome with a pity and sympathy which I was powerless to express, and I wondered what would become of the little home in the woods if the Load-Bearer never returned. It seemed as if I had known this house and its occupants all my life. that we were in some way closely related.

I proposed to ride over to the Busbys for any news I could gather there. It would take about an hour and a half. But we could arrive at no decision, and I was thinking of returning when we saw Elihu Gest slowly wending his way home through the most unfrequented part of the woods. He had followed the creek a good part of the way, and his wagon seemed full of farming implements and sacks of grain.

Cornelia Gest stood at the door awaiting his arrival.

"Fer the Land's sake!" she ejaculated when he got within talking distance, "whar hev ye been?"

She paused a moment and then continued:

"I don't know whether I'm lookin right at ye er whether it's yer ghost a-drivin' them hosses. How d'ye 'low I've been settin' here two endurin' nights through without ye?"

"Now, Cornely," he pleaded, "don't ye take on so. When I tell ye all about it ye'll be sprised en mighty glad I didn't come right home from the post-office. But I want ye te help me unload right here, fer it don't matter whar we set these things."

We all went to work. The implements, or what I took to be such, were soon placed on the ground, but the sacks, instead of containing grain or potatoes were filled with straw. We lifted off those nearest the dash-board, the Load-Bearer flung back a horse-blanket, and three faces, frightened, haggard, and woebegone, looked out from the hay underneath. It was the quadroon mother and her two octoroon children.

"White folks!" gasped Cornelia, stunned by the unexpected.

"I 'low the two air white enough, more's the pity," assented Elihu.

"Goodness me! Elihu Gest!" protested Cornelia when the two stepped into the kitchen; "we ain't got no place fer white folks. Thar's plenty vittles, but we ain't got no room, ye know we ain't; en two on 'em look like they hedn't but one more breath te let out en they war holdin' on to it till they got here."

"Wal, now," he said, "jes' give me a leetle time to let out *my* breath, fer me, too, I've been holdin' it in ever sence night afore last."

But she persisted:

"Whar on the face o' this yearth hev ye fished out sech a load? Ye ain't never carried home nothin' te ekil it! Whar *hev* ye been? Do tell!"

"Why, ain't Bub here told ye?"

"He told me 'bout three runaways ye found over at Zack Caverly's, two on 'em mos' dead."

"Jes' so, en I driv 'em te brother Busby's, whar I war obleeged te wait fer a good chance te git away, en now they air in the wagon thar."

Cornelia sank into a seat. Amazement and indignation were depicted on every feature. Her jaws were firmly set and I could hear her teeth grate.

"White slaves!" she groaned. "I know ye ain't given te jokes, Elihu, but I cain't git it into my head how thar kin be slaves thet air ez white ez we be; somehow I couldn't never believe it; but accordin' te your tellin' I've got te believe it, and now I've seen it with my own eyes."

She did not seem like the woman who, a short time before, was complaining of her sorrows and tribulations. Indignation had given way to a desire to act, to help, to save the lives of the fugitives and send them on their way towards Canada.

"I war calc'latin' te bring 'em in the house," remarked the Load-Bearer, as the two left the kitchen and walked over to the wagon, "but I reckon it air safer to take 'em te the barn. Thar'll be a mite iv a chance thet if anyone comes arter 'em they won't go te the barn te look."

"Wal," agreed Cornelia, "thar ain't no objections te clean, new hay fer beds, en we kin take some things over from the house."

"To-morrer I'll hev te step about en find a new hidin'-place, fer I heared another band o' runaways air summairs south o' here, en they may be along afore we know it."

"Don't ye go te doin' too much all te oncet," interposed his wife, "er ye'll be ailin' en things 'll be a sight wuss."

"To-morrer I'll take 'em te the cave by the creek. I 'lowed te hev it all fixed afore now, but things hev come about mighty sudden. Thet cave needs a heap o' fixin'. I ain't hed no sleep fer two nights en I skasely know what I'm a-doin'."

For the first time I took notice of the Load-Bearer's tired face. His eyes expressed the hope and faith which inspired him, but a great weariness made his walk heavy and his movements slow.

It was all Elihu and Cornelia Gest could do to get the eldest of the two women out of the wagon and into the barn. There was enough to keep all hands busy. I ran to and fro with blankets and pillows, while Mrs. Gest attended to the immediate wants of the fugitives.

When I had done all I could at the barn and returned to the house, I found Socrates standing close to the dogs. He was evidently in one of his keenest talking moods.:

"Ye kin kyount on what I'm tellin' ye," he was saying. "I hev fit varmints my hull life, en hev teached dogs, en I hev fed 'em so ez te make 'em win. Mebbe ye'll be in fer a fight afore long, en ye cain't keep 'em chained 'thout hevin' 'em fall off some en git sorter limp in the fore-legs—reecollect a dog fights ez much with his legs ez he does with his teeth. If Lem Stephen's bloodhounds come nosin' up this way ye'll be in fer a lively kick-up."

"I've been wonderin' how ye keep yer dogs so sleek and spry," remarked the Load-Bearer. "What d'ye feed 'em on? Any pertickler kyind o' meat?"

"Give 'em mos' anythin' but liver, en let 'em run roun' consider'ble. But tie 'em up en starve 'em fer a day er so afore ye calc'late te use 'em fer any fightin'."

Zack Caverly was eyeing with extraordinary interest the three huge wolf-hounds, whose cold, agate eyes conjured up in my imagination images of the haunts of wolf and bear and the cruel romance of wold and wilderness. Compared with the Load-Bearer's dogs the hounds at the cabin of Socrates were the incarnation of docility and affection.

The wolf-hounds gave us a look now and then of glacial indifference. There was no caressing to be indulged in here, no patting on the back, no words of encouragement expected or needed. I could not distinguish any difference between them—

they all looked the same height, colour, and size—but the Load-Bearer knew the characteristics of each.

As I looked at the wolf-hounds, and then at the meek, compassionate face of Elihu Gest, I was struck with the incongruity of the scene: the dogs all ferocity, the man all meekness. But from that moment I saw the Load-Bearer in a new light. Under the humane countenance there dwelt the inflexible will, the inexorable determination to dare and to do. How different he was now, standing beside his wolf-hounds, from what he looked on his first visit to the Log-House! The benevolent look was still there, but the vague, dreamy expression was gone, and in its place appeared a realisation of present responsibilities. Plotting and planning had taken the place of dreams.

"They don't need no coddlin'," observed Socrates, as he eyed them one after the other, slowly and critically. "I ain't seed no dog-flesh ekil to 'em sence I war down in Tennessee, en if ye treat 'em ez I say ye'll hev good reason to be thankful, Elihu."

"The Lord made 'em, brother Caverly, en they air here accordin' te His will, en I'm right glad ye see thar p'ints air p'ints te reckon on."

"I ain't seed thar ekil," he declared, giving the Load-Bearer a knowing look; "they're ez full o' p'ints ez a porcupine air o' quills, en I reckon it ain't no ways discommodin' fer a man in your cirkinstances te hev sech pets layin' roun', jes' pinin' away kase thar ain't no live meat fer te clean thar teeth on."

" 'Pears like they ain't got no feelin's, 'ceptin' fer huntin' en fightin'," remarked Elihu, contemplating the animals much as he would so many savage Indians.

"They don't show no pertikler likin' fer anybody," returned Socrates; "but ye'll allow a good wagger makes a pore watcher, en some on 'em gits more'n enough te eat by not knowin' they hev tails."

"If thar ain't Sister Busby!" exclaimed the Load-Bearer, as Serena emerged from the woods on a big, slow, floundering sorrel.

Elihu Gest seemed ill at ease when he saw her coming. She came like a rain-cloud, and her presence threw a cold douche over all. Serena Busby's tongue was all the more dangerous because her intentions were good and everybody liked her, but she was apt to tell the gravest secrets without being conscious of what she was saying.

"Where's Cornely?" she shouted, before the sorrel came to a stop at the kitchen door.

"I've brought ye over some b'ar grease en camphire," she went on as she caught sight of Mrs. Gest coming from the barn. "I forgot all about it this mornin' when Elihu left, everyone bein' so flustered."

"How good ye be!" said Cornelia. "I war sayin' to Elihu jes' now thet we hedn't nothin' in the house to rub with, en the gal's ankle do need 'tendin' to. Ez fer gittin' a doctor, 'tain't no use thinkin' o' sech a thing. Thar ain't no one 'cept Doc. Reed in Jacksonville we could trust to keep the secret, en he's too fur away."

"This is what we all use fer sprains en bruises," replied Serena. "Ye know she ain't hed no bones broke. It all come about by havin' te jump over logs like rabbits with hounds after 'em that night when the slave-hunters were on thar tracks. It's horrible te see the poor thing suffer so! But her mother is plumb used up; she wouldn't taste a mite o' vittles over to my house, en I tried her with everything. Sakes alive!" she exclaimed, putting her hand into a deep pocket and taking out a small parcel, "I mos' forgot the tea; it's *green* tea, Cornely—some that Uriah got the last time he was down to Alton, en if *that* don't make her set up nothin' will. It'll give her backbone. But law! ain't the children white! It was the boy's curly hair made me think o' runaways, but I declare I'd take 'em fer white folks if they was dressed up real nice."

"I didn't take no pertickler notice the night Elihu diskivered 'em," observed Socrates, "en I ain't seed 'em since—not te look squar' at 'em."

Cornelia Gest had no more to say. She pretended a deep interest in the things Mrs. Busby had brought, but her mind was elsewhere. Her face looked what she felt.

"Ain't ye goin' te git off en stop a spell, Sister Busby?" inquired the Load-Bearer, with bland apathy.

"Yes, do," said his wife; "shorely ye ain't goin' back 'thout seein' whar we've put 'em. We've done the best we could; it's a sight cleaner'n some beds I've slept in afore now."

"I promised Uriah te be right back without tyin' up, but I'll git off en make 'em a real nice cup o' this here tea, en we'll take it over to 'em."

"They've hed coffee," observed Cornelia, with an effort to be polite and as a mild protest against green tea.

The two women went into the kitchen, and I heard the Load-Bearer remark:

"Sister Busby's got a sight o' hoss sense, but she do need the bridle now and ag'in."

"Sereny's jes' like a skittish yearling," commented Socrates; "but don't ye go te bridlin' her tongue er she'll take the bit 'twixt her teeth en a prairie fire won't head her off. Give her plenty tetherin'-groun' en plenty fac's te nibble on, but don't let her chaw too close te the stumps."

"Ye kin lead a filly te the trough, brother Caverly, but ye cain't make her drink more'n jes' so much. Some folks air allers thirstin' fer water from other folks's wells, but nothin' but a runnin' stream o' gossip will slake Sister Busby's thirst fer more knowledge."

"Thet's a fac', thet's a fac'; but the wust is the stream runs squar' through your diggin's."

"Ez things are goin' now, Sereny knows 'nough te want te know a heap more. I'm plumb with ye when ye tell me not to let her nibble till she comes to the cobble-stones."

The tea was soon made, for Mrs. Gest had kept the fire going and the water hot.

No sooner had she and Mrs. Busby disappeared into the barn than Alek Jordan came galloping up by the shortest cut from the main road.

"Marm told me te give ye this," he said to the Load-Bearer, handing him a letter; "it's from Isaac Snedeker; he give it te marm te send."

Elihu opened and read, while Zack Caverly stood and waited for the news.

The Load-Bearer heaved a sigh:

"Brother Snedeker sez he's a-comin' here to-morrer night with eight runaways."

"Whoop-ee!" exclaimed Socrates.

Then a thought struck him.

"Looky here Alek," he said, "you jes' light out ez quick ez ever ye kin; thar's some un at the barn thet mustn't know ye've been here. Don't ye wait a minnit; take the trail through the woods by the creek ez fur ez ye kin er mebbe the runaways 'll git ketched."

The Load-Bearer had his eyes fixed on the barn, expecting

every moment to see Mrs. Busby emerge and then ride part of the way home with Alek Jordan, when more than one secret would be revealed concerning the intentions of Isaac Snedeker.

Alek, whose horse was young and in fine condition, was off at a bound, the animal clearing like a buck every obstacle in his path.

Hardly had he got out of sight when Serena Busby made her appearance, followed by Cornelia Gest, who, weary and distracted, let the visitor do all the talking.

CHAPTER 9

A Night of Mystery

ON CERTAIN evenings my father would sit before the big, open fireplace and watch with unalloyed satisfaction the burning logs. He would see pictures in the blazing wood, and he had a science of his own in the mingling of different logs.

"How well that dried hickory burns with the damp walnut!" he would say, taking the tongs and shifting the pieces, now a little more to the front, now a little farther back.

He taught me to see castles, people, and faces in the flames and embers, and I knew what colours to expect from the different woods. He kept some that were full of sap, that would burn slowly; others were split up to dry. While sitting before the fire on a clear, bracing night my father was wont to forget every care and abandon himself to the pure pleasures of the hearth. He would dream of the past, of friends in the old country, and more than once he would remark to me, taking the tongs and pointing: "There's a face that reminds me of poor So-and-so." He loved to revisit the old familiar scenes while the fire gave them momentary life and set them before him in frames of gold and flaming opal. Then he would tell me stories of the wild animals of the old homestead, of the tracks of the marten in the snow, and how he discovered its hiding-place; of a memorable fox hunt when one of his friends held the fox up by the tail and another friend cried out from a distance: "Don't hurt the fox! don't hurt the fox!" and of his sojourn in Paris during the reign of Louis Philippe.

At such times my mother added a spirit of cheerfulness by some joyful exclamation, such as: "There's a letter in the candle!" as if the simple expression in itself would assist the arrival of good news from afar; and when I looked I saw a large flaming blot, on the side of the wick, pointing toward us.

I cannot remember whether the letters arrived, as the candle so often announced; but how vividly I recollect the nights when I lay awake in the next room and heard my parents discuss the uncertainty of the future, the imminent need of funds to carry on the work of the farm, and the possibility of failure and ruin! Such conversations occurred after the other members of the family had gone to bed, but I heard everything, and night after night I listened to these talks, and racked my brain, wondering how it would all end. My distress was even greater than that of my mother, for she knew what I did not, and she could still hope.

After such talks the quivering song of the cricket dotted the stillness with an accent of deeper melancholy, while the heavy pendulum slowly measured out the minutes between midnight and the dismal twilight of dawn.

We were all sitting quietly together the evening after my visit to the Load-Bearer's home, my mother with the Bible in her lap—the only book she ever read while in the Log-House—my father reading a newspaper containing an account of a recent speech by Abraham Lincoln. My mother's face looked paler and more pensive than usual, for, some days previous to this, my father had had a misunderstanding with one of the settlers. The only weapon in the house was a double-barrelled gun, and even this stood unloaded against the wall in a corner of the sitting-room. No dog was kept on the place, for the reason that a dog was regarded as one of the things most likely to cause trouble with the neighbours.

The wind was blowing across the prairie from the east. My mother seemed apprehensive, and I must have caught some of the thoughts which filled her mind with gloomy presentiments. During a lull of the wind a sound reached us from the prairie. It might have been a shout or a call. How vividly it all comes before me now! She looked inquiringly at my father, who was absorbed in his newspaper and heard nothing. I needed no words to tell me what she wwas thinking; her face assumed a grave and anxious look. I was hoping the sound might be nothing more than the noise of belated travellers passing on horseback, when we heard it again, like a confused, mumbling menace—this time a little nearer, still disguised in the muffled wind. She walked into the next room, greatly agitated, but instantly returned and began to read in the Prayer-book.

My father had just put aside his newspaper when a low, hollow murmur came from the prairie.

"What can it be?" asked my mother in a voice scarcely audible. Without answering, he went into the next room for the ammunition, took the gun from the corner and began to load with buckshot. It seemed to me he had never looked so tall, so grim, so determined as when he rammed the wadding down with the ramrod. Then he went to the front door and listened. My mother sat with closed eyes like one in a trance, until it seemed to me as if by some unaccountable hocus-pocus we had been thrust into a world where pantomime and mystery had taken the place of speech, and we were waiting for some sudden and terrible stroke of destiny. What was going to happen? Was it the end of all things at the Log-House?

My father decided not to go out by the front way, and after the light was removed he opened the kitchen door and stood outside in the dark.

"The moon is just rising," said my mother in a half-whisper, looking through the window of the front room. Then I looked, and as the clouds drifted by I saw the moon in the shape of a gleaming scythe. A sudden chill of autumn had come to the house. She hurried out to beg my father to come in, but he was creeping from corner to corner and from tree to tree, with the gun held before him, cocked and ready for that deadly aim for which he was so well known.

After going as far as the smoke-house and waiting there some time, he returned; he thought the sounds must have been due to some prowling animal. He was about to give up further search when the moaning was again heard, out a little beyond the trees, and then, as my mother stood trembling at the door, a voice shouted:

"Don' shoot, massa; don' shoot! fer de Lawd's sake don' ye shoot!"

My father went straight towards the voice.

"We done lost, massa," someone shouted as soon as he reached the open; "we is lookin' fer massa Gest's place."

"Come in, come in."

My father came back into the kitchen with two negro fugitives.

"Where have you been?"

"Mass' Snedeker done drap us ober dere," said one of the negroes, pointing west.

"He was running you off?"

"Yes, massa."

"And finding he was chased, let you down, and so you got lost?"

"Yes, massa."

Just then a loud knocking at the front door came with terrible suddenness, for during the talk and confusion no one had heard any noise in the road.

My father took his gun, and standing at one side of the door asked who was there.

"Isaac Snedeker," answered a familiar voice.

Open went the door and in rushed Ike Snedeker, one of the most intrepid souls that ever risked death for the sake of conscience.

A man stood before us who had never known fear. One glance at this face would be enough to make an enemy stop and think twice before coming to close quarters with such a being. He was courage incarnate, with the shaggy head of a lion, the sharp, invincible eye of an eagle, the frame of an athlete, the earnestness of a convinced reformer. His hair stood out thick and bushy, and his bearded face, with the upper lip clean-shaven, gave to the whole countenance a massive, formidable look that inspired every fugitive with confidence and struck fear into the hearts of his secret foes.

"I've lost two runaways," he said, as he walked through to the kitchen; "had to let them out of the wagon over there near the maple grove—we were followed."

"I think they are here," said my father, "and I came near shooting one of them by mistake."

"I directed them to come this way as near as I could, hoping they would strike through the prairie at this place."

My mother was now bringing the fugitives something to eat when Isaac Snedeker said peremptorily:

"Come along, it's now or never. We've got to get to Brother Gest's with that load before midnight. You see, I've had to gather 'em up here and there in different places, and I have in the wagon out there two lots—one sent over by Ebenezer Carter and the other by Brother Wolcott. If we get caught it'll be the first time; but they'd get a haul that would amount to something—I've got fourteen altogether."

The two fugitives left without having time to drink a cup of coffee, and we all went to the road to see them off. The wagon was full of frightened, trembling runaways: negroes, mulattoes, octoroons. Not a moment was lost. Isaac Snedeker had only to speak to his horses—a fine, powerful team—to send them going at a great speed down the road towards the appointed meeting-place at Elihu Gest's.

We went back into the house, where my mother sank exhausted into a rocking-chair.

But she had still another ordeal to go through. Prayers had been said, and we were all about to retire for the night, when the noise of galloping horses and men talking could be heard in the road. One moment of suspense followed another. Footsteps were heard near the kitchen door, then there came a light and somewhat timid rapping as if the persons outside were not certain about this being the right place. My father opened, this time without asking who was there. Two disreputable-looking men stood before him, one of them scowling at us through the door like some ferocious animal. They carried pistols and dirks. Their eyes were shaded by slouched hats that partly concealed the upper part of their faces, so that, for all we knew, they might have been neighbours living at no great distance from the Log-House.

"Hev ye seen any runaways hangin' round hyar?" asked the elder man, looking up from under his hat, and with an expression that told of a fearful admixture of malicious cunning and moral cowardice.

"I have," answered my father. "Who delegated you to look for them?"

The fellow hesitated. Then he stammered:

"Be you a fire-eatin' Abolitionist?"

"I have voted for Abraham Lincoln once, if that is what you mean by being an Abolitionist."

"Ye ain't been long in this country," observed the younger man.

"Long enough to become an American citizen, and vote."

This surprised them. They looked confused, but they braced themselves for a final effort.

"We're arter them runaways, en we don't calc'late te leave hyar without takin' 'em along."

"They went from here some time ago, so you'll have to look elsewhere if you want to find them."

"Let's go over to the barn," said the elder of the two.

They started for the barn, but stopped just beyond the big locust tree, and I heard the words:

"Say, Jake, I don't like the look o' that old Britisher."

"No more do I."

"He'll shoot the fust thing we know. He's got sunthin' mighty juberous in thet eye o' his'n."

Not another word was said. They wheeled about, made for the road, mounted their horses, and were off.

They had been cowed and disarmed by my father's coolness, his independence, by his towering height, and a scorn that was withering to the two slave-hunting villains.

CHAPTER 10

Sowing and Reaping

THE wide strip of prairie to the west of the Log-House was now ready for planting, but not without immense labour. A huge plough which descended into the primitive soil was drawn by four or five pairs of stout oxen, driven and directed by a man with a whip as long as the team itself. My father held the plough, and frequently stood on it in order to drive it deep enough to cut through the roots that were often formidable in their thickness.

Oh, the delightful souvenirs of that ploughing and planting! The odour of the fresh, rich soil, never broken till now, the turning up of snakes, insects, and queer stones, with here and there the rough flint-head of an Indian arrow, the flocks of red-winged blackbirds settling down to feast in the wavy sods, the excitement which had in it no reaction—how is it possible that such things pass as in dreams?

The whole day I followed the oxen, never growing weary of the wonders of Nature, and when this rough piece of land has been ploughed, harrowed, and duly prepared for the first crop of Indian corn (maize), then came what was to me, the climax of the whole proceedings, the actual sowing of the seed. It was like some rare holiday, a festival, a celebration. All Nature seemed to partake of the joy; a new world of marvels seemed to be on the eve of consummation. The weather was perfect and as we three—my father, one of my sisters, and myself—went forth with a sack of seed, we dropped the large golden grains into the proper places all along through the soft, dark loam, closing up each hole, keeping up a ceaseless chatter, mainly, I think, about the pure delights of the work we were doing.

Perhaps never since have I felt the same kind of thrill. There are days that shine out like great white jewels in the crown of years.

After the planting there was little to be done except watching and waiting. We watched the sprouting of the corn till it grew through the first period. Its second period was one of flowing, silky tassels, clear and pure, with a silvery sheen, the whole field decked in opulent hangings that waved in the wind and sparkled in the sun, the stalks rising in places to a height of ten feet or more. The third period came about August, when the ripening began. It was slow, the stalks turning to a light, faded gold, the big ears hanging in heavy clusters and in countless numbers, one rivalling another in length and size. And the field now afforded another pleasure—that of getting lost in its mysterious depths. It was a happy feeding-ground for birds and by night a hiding-place for wild animals.

Then came two later stages—the cutting and stacking. The cutting was rough work. It was done by hired hands; and when the corn was stacked the field assumed another air, and the face of Nature thereabouts was changed beyond recognition. The stacks resembled innumerable huts or wigwams, and this was not without a charm of its own, for it made the surroundings less lonely-looking; but when the ears of corn were taken from the stalks and the field stripped bare the view was one of vacant desolation, without a symbol of saving grace—naked, barren of romance or joy, a thing plucked and polluted by the ruthless hand of necessity.

Then came one of the last stages in the progress of the corn towards the bread-pan of the household. The big, stout ears had to be stripped of the thick outer envelope, and this was called a "corn-husking." It was done by all hands, great and small; the neighbours were invited, the company assembling in the evening, mostly young people; a husking-glove was worn on one hand, and, with a small, knife-shaped implement, the shuck was stripped off and the beautiful gold-red grain was laid bare. This was a time of merry-making, love-making, and gaiety. In the earlier days it was a time of dancing and heavy drinking, but here at the Log-House the evening passed in sober enjoyment, as became the rigid tenets of the master and mistress, almost Calvinistic in their religious views; and so nothing stronger than coffee was drunk at the merry supper which followed.

Six months had passed since the prairie soil was broken for the corn, and now we should see it no more till it came into the house in the form of golden meal, all ready to be prepared for the bread-pan, baked in the oven, and set steaming hot on the table for breakfast or supper, about an inch and a half thick, as yellow as rich gold, the top baked to a brown crust, the whole cut into good-sized squares in the pan. We cut the pieces through the middle and spread them with fresh home-made butter; and this, with home-cured bacon, and eggs laid in the sweet-smelling hay of the old barn, by hens fattened on corn, surpassed any dish I have ever eaten, in the palaces of kings, in the mansions of millionaires, or any of the great restaurants of Paris or London. How many times, when dining with the great ones of the world, undeceived by the illusions of sight, taste, and smell, my mind has wandered back to the delicious breakfasts and suppers at the Log-House, certain that nothing could rival hot corn-bread properly made.

In many of the principal States corn is the staff of life. It is given to pigs, cattle, turkeys, and chickens. It fed the negroes as slaves, the whites when flour was a thing unattainable, gave Abraham Lincoln his robust frame, developed the physical frame of most of the famous men of the South and West of early days, and made victory over malaria and adverse conditions possible. Neurasthenia was unheard of till the people began to eat bread made from wheat. The eating of hot white biscuits (muffins) for breakfast and supper developed America's national disease—dyspepsia.

Up to the time of the great Civil War, the general type of the South and West was characterised by height, muscular litheness, immense powers of resistance, sound digestion. The fashions in eating kept pace with fashions in dress. Previous to 1820 the dress was mainly of buckskin, cap of fur, such as the raccoon, and moccasins on the feet. Then came the period of jean and linsey-woolsey, dyed blue or copperas-coloured; then what I may call the calico period, when young women were considered to be beautifully dressed in plain dotted or striped coloured calico patterns with sun-bonnets to match. This was followed by a step nearer the city fashions, and ginghams and delaines were introduced here and there; but the silk and lace period did not dawn on the smaller towns of the West till the war suddenly scattered bank-notes broadcast through the land and brought in its train tumult, movement, money, and the latest fashions.

In the autumn there were other gatherings, such as "apple parings," and "quiltings," and the inevitable country fair which everyone attended. The autumn was the most sociable time of the whole year, and for several weeks there would be plenty to do and plenty to talk about. The quilting brought together the most instructive and entertaining visitors. It was a woman's affair, but the husbands usually came for supper at six, or later in the evening, and so there was talk on every subject of any local interest, from politics to mince pies.

After one or two cups of tea Mrs. Busby would talk by the hour, and a word, a hint, would call forth the description of an event or a new version of some disputed story.

"Law me! How this section hez settled up sence we've been here! When we fust come there warn't no stores within a ten-mile ride. It *wuz* rough, and in some places a mite dangerous, especially over in what they called the 'chivaree' district. There wuz a band that chivareed every couple that got married fer miles around; en speakin' o' chivarees reminds me o' the time when ole man Snyder married a yaller-haired gal from down Jerseyville way. They hedn't more'n got home when 'long come the wust crowd ye could pick up in the hull country, headed by Bub Hawkins en Jack Haywood. They brought ole tin pans, kittles, whistles, cow-bells, horns en everything they could make a howlin' noise with, en set up a kinder war-dance round the cabin. Ole man Snyder was fer shootin', bein' tetchy en not given to lettin' words melt in his mouth, but his bride got riled en took a raw hide en made fer the door, en out she went into the crowd.

" 'Who's the ringleader here' she says. 'Who's the ringleader? I want te know; en if ye don't tell me I'll cow-hide ye all, en won't be long about it.'

"With that Bub Hawkins started snickerin' en steppin' roun' like a turkey on a hot gridiron, half ashamed like en not know-in' jes' what to do or te say, en Sal Snyder standin' there with her yaller hair all hangin' loose en her eyes a-snappin' like a wild cat.

" 'Ain't ye goin' to tell me?' she shouted; but there warn't a man there that could stand en look right in them eyes.

" 'Looky here, Bub Hawkins,' she says, 'you've come te chiva-ree me en my ole man, but I'm a-goin' te give ye somethin' te make ye shiver en keep it up all night,' en with that she lit in en let him have it, head en face, neck en body, en when he broke en ran she wus after him, lettin' him have it from behind; en ye better b'lieve she hed sinews in her arms like the strong man in th' Good Book; en every time Bub Hawkins jumped a log she brought down her cow-hide from behind with a reg'lar war-whoop that made the woods ring. When she had chased the ringleader she come back te tackle the others, but they had all vamosed. They do claim that Sal Snyder plumb broke up that gang.

"They did need religion," she went on, "en it was time Pete Cartwright come along en got Jack Haywood side-tracked from his good-fer-nothin' ways. Ye see, it wus like this: Jack Haywood's wife died en left him with six young uns, en he 'lowed his home wus like a hive without a queen bee. Anyhow, that's what he tole widder Brown when he merried her. Things went 'long purty smooth fer some time, en it looked like he wuz well fixed en settled; but one day she up en said:

" 'Looky here, Jack Haywood, I 'low yer hive's all right, en it sets close te a clover patch; but whar's the honey? I ain't never see ye bring home nothin' but what sticks te yer feet, en thar ain't no mistake 'bout it, thar's plenty comb—fer it's comb, comb, all day long tryin' te get the hay-seeds out o' yer six sassy tow-heads. Now I tell ye what it is,' she says, turnin' from her dough en p'intin' the rollin'-pin straight at him, 'you've got the hive en you've got a bee te boss it, but what hez *she* got? Why, she's got six young drones, not includin' two yaller dogs en yerself, en if I had wings, ez I hed orter hev, I'd take a bee-line fer a hive that's got some vittles in it.'

"When Uriah asked him how he wus gettin' on with his queen bee, he said:

" 'She's workin' the comb all right, but she stings with her tongue wus'n any hornet I ever bumped agin.'

"His fust wife druv him te drinkin' en this one druv him te religion. He got converted, but fust off she wuz dead set agin preachers, en scuffled up agin preachin' en prayin' in dead earnest till Haywood was most druv crazy. When Pete Cartwright come 'long one day he says she stormed en raved en used cuss words, en when he said he wuz goin' te pray right in the cabin she shook her fist in his face en 'lowed she wuz one half alligator en t'other half snappin' turtle, en dared him te put her out, ez he said he would if she didn't behave; she said it 'ud take a better man than he wuz te do it.

"While he wuz prayin' she got awful mad. She called him all

the names she could think of, en threw the cat at his head, en then Pete Cartwright up en took hold of her arm en swung her clean te the door, en out she went. He slammed the door in her face, en of all the rippin' en roarin' ye ever heared that wuz the wust.

"He barred the door agin her and went right on with his prayin'; but land! with a she-devil scratchin' te get in a man ud hev te be a reg'lar angel with wings not te be riled en flustered in his pleadin's; so he jes' turned the table on her: stopped prayin' en begin to sing ez loud ez ever he could beller—en ye better b'lieve he *could* shout when he got fixed fer it; en the louder she screamed en roared outside, the louder he sung inside, en they kept it up till she begin te pant fer breath. He kept right on till she knocked on the door an hollered out:

" 'Mr. Cartwright, do please let me in!'

" 'Well,' he said, 'I'll let ye come in if ye'll promise te behave yerself.'

"She said she would; so he opened the door en let her te a seat near the fire-place, en he says he never see a woman so pale en tremblin'.

" 'I've been a big fool,' she says.

" 'I 'low ye hev,' says Pete Cartwright, 'en ye'll hev te repent fer all yer sins or ye'll go te perdition.'

"She hung her head en plumb give up fer shame. The poor little children were all huddled under the bed, en he called 'em out en told 'em their mother wouldn't hurt 'em now, en with that he started prayin' agin with Haywood, en in six months she was converted en the folks in that cabin made real happy."

In the evening the riding of the young ladies for prizes at the county fair was discussed. All had something to say concerning this momentous incident.

"I've been attendin' kyounty fairs 'most all my life," said one, "en it did take the rag off the bush te see the way the cuttin's up o' thet ole chestnut sp'iled the ridin' o' them po' gals."

"What I want te know is who put Almedy Sinclair te ride on sech a critter," said another.

"Well," said Mrs. Busby, "ye don't reckon Almedy Sinclair's green enough te pick out sech a rib-breaker te ride on all by herself, do ye?—en she one of the best jedges o' hoss-flesh in this hull district. Why, that gal thinks nothin' o' ridin' bare-back en breakin' the wust mustang ye kin bring her. I've see her do it. She sets a-hossback ez easy ez ye're settin' in that rockin'-cheer. No, sir-ree, ye better look fer someone with more green in their eye before ye ask me te b'lieve she went roamin' roun' the country jes' te choose sech a rip-tearin' bucker fer a saddle-hoss, en she settin' her cap fer fust prize! Almedy Sinclair ain't that kind. Ye see," she continued, warming to the subject, "the man that owned thet chestnut fust off went te the Mexican War en rid him in the battle o' Bueny Visty, en there's where a bullet nipped the top off one o' his marrer-bones, a leetle behind the saddle, en that wuz the beginnin' o' the kickin' en the buckin'; but some say after the wowned got healed he kept the buckin' up jest fer old times' sake. When his owner come back from the war he sold him fer a good draw-hoss, b'lievin' him te be right safe te pull a wagon, en when the man that bought him was fordin' a creek in flood-time the hoss kicked everything te pieces right in the middle o' the creek. His next owner was a Baptist preacher who took te dram drinkin' te drown his sorrer at bein' so tuk in by a sleek, fat hoss en a professin' christian. The fac' is, the wowned in his back got healed quick enough, en it never showed no signs on th' outside, but the bone wuz allers tender, en when the saddle wuz put a lettle too fur back, er when it happened te be a leetle too long, there was sure to be trouble; en that double-dealin' rascal that owns him now knows it, en he fixed te hev Almedy lose en his own gal win, fer he knew if Almedy hed a good hoss she'd surely carry off the prize. Ye see, when a body's used te ridin' hosses that chaw the bit en prance te one side en rear on their hind legs, it looks like hoss en gal's both cunnin' 'nough te show off their good p'ints all te oncet, en Almedy Sinclair kinder looked fer sum'thin' like that in the critter she was ridin'. She expected te be h'isted a couple o' times, fer a man hollered out to her, 'Sit ez tight ez ye kin!' en she knowed what that meant; but it didn't mean what she thought. Th' old chestnut warn't no ways stiff in the hind legs when he started; but that ain't allers a good sign nuther. It allers takes time te git right down te the weak spot of any beast, but in this here case it looked like the time wus fore-ordained, ez the preachers say, right down te the minnit, fer just ez th' ole hoss come along in front o' the jedges stand the saddle worked back till it come agin the tender marrer-bone, en he stopped like he'd been struck with a bullet. Right then I hear a man say, 'Watch out!' en skasely hed he spoke when the critter up en give his tail en hind legs sech a twist that it looked like Almedy'd surely land on the critter's neck. It warn't expected; the hoss riz at the wrong end. There he stood, stock still, leavin' Almedy Sinclair settin' like a sack o' seed pertaters while t'other gal rid by on her prancin' roan ez big ez life en twicet ez sassy. Pore Almedy sot till her hoss riz en shuk his heels ag'in, en ye kin b'lieve she made a break from that saddle ez mad ez ever ye see a gal in all yer born days."

CHAPTER 11

The Flight

THE Indian summer had come, the season of seasons, with its golden memories, its diaphanous skies, its dream-like afternoons, its gossamer veils spread over the shimmering horizon, transforming by its own transcendent magic the whole earth and atmosphere.

Smoke rose from wooded places in long, thin columns of hazy blue, and once in a while a whiff of burning grass and leaves filled the magnetic air with fragrant odour. The settlers ceased to fret and worry; there was neither reaping nor repining.

The sun was setting when I arrived at the Load-Bearer's home, two days after Isaac Snedeker's visit to the Log-House. I had brought more provisions for the fugitives.

"Dear me! but yer ma *is* good te send all these vittles fer the runaways." exclaimed Mrs. Gest as I emptied my saddle-bags on the kitchen table.

As I was going to stay there till morning we sat about here and there waiting for the hours to pass and the coming of Isaac Snedeker, who was to take the fugitives to the next station that night. We expected his arrival some time between ten and eleven o'clock.

How calm and peaceful was the evening!

Now and then a gentle current of wind stirred the branches, and the leaves fell in flaky showers like snow on ground already strewn with the dead foliage of autumn.

Far away, the tinkling of bells told of cattle peacefully grazing, and the prairie, immense and tranquil as a golden sea, inspired a feeling as of ages and ages of repose.

In the west a bank of filmy clouds edged with silver floated against a sky of glassy green which gradually melted into serried ranks of flaming amber, and the sere, crisp leaves of the beech were interlaced with the red and purple of oak and maple, while the trees by the creek glistened and sparkled in the genial rays of the setting sun.

And there was something in the early hours of the evening that throbbed in ceaseless unison with the constellations over-head. After darkness closed in all the witchery of Nature seemed at work in earth and sky. Above the tree-tops a host of twin-kling stars looked down on the anxious watchers and refugees. Presently a thin mist descended about us through which the starry vault and dark masses of trees could be discerned, with tracings of dim, fantastic forms in the scattered underbush.

The slanting rays of the rising moon came reaching in long gleams across the roof of the little frame house, while its weird shafts shot through the narrow interspaces of wood and thicket, and gleamed in small round patches on the green moss under-neath. The scarlet vines all around on the boughs were tipped with a soft, glistening pallor that fell as from some ghostly lan-tern from a distant world, while just above the horizon, poised like an aerial plume in the deep indigo blue, the vanishing comet waned amidst a wilderness of glittering lights under a shimmer-ing crown of stars.

During a moment of profound quiet, when it seemed as if all Nature had sunk to rest, a wolf beyond the creek began a series of long-drawn-out howls. The woods began to vibrate with low, clamorous calls. The howling drew nearer; one of the wolf-hounds answered back in pitiful cries, then another and another. Everywhere call answered call. A rushing sound filled the space above us where vast flocks of wildfowl cut the air with the swish and rustle of a thousand wings. The honking came and went as flock after flock passed over us in whizzing waves. The whole world was stirring. Earth sent up a chorus of lamentations that mingled with the voices above. The fugitives huddled to-gether in the cave in expectation of some unimagined calamity, and at last, unable to withstand the feeling of terror, they began to creep up towards the house.

The Load-Bearer, who had gone into the kitchen, fell on his knees, with the Bible open before him on the chair, while his wife sat just inside, with her hands tightly clasped, peering in-tently through the open door across the clear patches of moon-light.

Soon he rose and hurriedly walked out.

"Whar be ye goin'?" stammered his wife, noticing his dazed look.

He walked as one in a dream, while Cornelia followed.

"Elihu, whar be ye goin'?"

There was a clinking of the chains at the kennels, and a cry from the wolf-hounds told us they were free. They sped round and round the house in a whirl of excitement, then into the woods and back again to the house, giving the last shudder to the climax of confusion before they made off towards the main road leading south-west.

Then, as by a wave of some invisible wand, the tumult ceased. The woods and the house lay plunged in an all-pervading stillness. The country round about seemed suddenly dipped in a gulf of silence.

The Load-Bearer came back to the kitchen and again fell on his knees. After some moments he began to read aloud:

" 'Alas, for that day is great, so that none is like it; it is even the time of Jacob's trouble; but he shall be saved out of it.' "

"Whar be they?" mused Cornelia, not listening to her husband, "It's gettin' late . . . Brother Snedeker said he'd be here at ten o'clock."

Her hair had fallen down on one side of her face; she looked sad and very troubled. She was overburdened with the loads of others, with loads which she had not sought, which life and death had heaped together in one short, swift period of time, and she felt crushed under their weight. But Elihu Gest, absorbed in prayer, heard nothing, saw nothing, thought of nothing but the Eternal.

Now he read aloud from Isaiah:

" 'Awake, awake, O Jerusalem, which has drunk of the hand of the Lord the cup of His fury; thou hast drunken the dregs of the cup of trembling and wrung them out.' "

He remained silent for a moment, and when he continued it was with a voice full of prophetic faith:

" 'Thus saith the Lord thy God that pleadeth the cause of His people, behold I have taken out of thine hand the cup of trembling, even the dregs of the cup of My fury; thou shalt no more drink it again.' "

The last words had sunk deep into Cornelia's soul. She seemed to have caught all the mystical power of those seven magical words: "Thou shalt no more drink it again." Her eyes grew brighter, her face was lit by a placid smile, all the old religious faith came rushing back.

A faint breeze brought with it an aroma of dried leaves and withering grasses. As the moon rose higher in the heavens the night grew brighter. Not far from the door a group of fugitives stood gazing intently at Cornelia Gest, the pallid faces of the octoroons forming a sort of spectral frame for the black faces in the centre. Here and there, around the house, murmurs and half-suppressed groans and supplications arose, for the runaways had brought to the Load-Bearer's home a new world, with new and unheard-of influences. There were fugitives from nearly every slave State bordering the Mississippi; they brought with them their own peculiar beliefs, their own interpretations of certain signs and sounds of the night. All had been awed by the appearance of the comet, but now a terrible fear possessed them. For each one every sound came as a special menace, every object had a special symbol.

The Load-Bearer rose from his knees, and as he stepped to the door one of the wolf-hounds, covered with blood-stains, was there to greet him. The others were not far off, and all had evidently done their work.

"Somethin' hez happened down on the road," said Cornelia.

"They hev nipped some evil in the bud," returned Elihu.

But Cornelia peered without ceasing in one direction, anxiously awaiting the arrival of Isaac Snedeker.

"Thar's someone a-comin' now," remarked the Load-Bearer.

But we still waited, gazing into the distance. The last hour had seemed endless. We walked down towards the creek to pass away the time, then returned and stood in the moonlight. Elihu Gest was trying to make out what the object was that we now saw approaching from the east. It came looming up on the thin mist that hung over the road, growing bigger as it drew nearer; and the fugitives, seeing it approach, sought refuge in the darkness behind the house, some running as far as the creek.

Not one was visible; not a murmur was to be heard. A ghostly silence greeted Azariah James, the preacher, as he came ambling up on a horse that seemed to glide over the surface of the ground. There he sat for some moments, speechless, and at first I did not recognise him, clad as he was in hunting costume, with a fringe about the cape, a coon-skin cap on his head, a rifle slung over his shoulders, and a pistol and dirk before him.

But the man himself had not changed. It was the same face, naïvely absent-minded and wonderingly mute, that I had seen at the meeting-house—the man who began his sermon by a series of blunders and then glided along by some miraculous means to an unexpected and memorable triumph. Now, as then, he looked as if he were floating along with the tide and the hour, ready for the unforeseen without expecting it, armed for trouble without fearing it.

We stood looking at the preacher and he at us, but no one spoke.

What an enigmatical group we must have been to the peeping fugitives a little distance away! There sat Azariah James, the preacher, twin brother in spirit to Elihu Gest, the Load-Bearer; yet what a contrast they presented! The preacher appeared double his natural size, clothed in a hunter's garb, awaiting some mysterious command; and the Load-Bearer, thinner, smaller, almost wizened, seemed to be awaiting some word or sign on the part of the preacher.

And a sign did come; but not from Azariah James. Down to the south, through the thick groves of beech, a yellow light rose and fell and rose again in slow waving flashes over the horizon, its glow reaching above the wooded cover, and even beyond the belted line of timber to the east.

"What kin thet be?"

It was Cornelia who spoke, for the two men were still rapt in a kind of mystical quandary.

"Thar's sunthin' goin' on down thar er my name ain't Elihu Gest, en the Lord ain't sent ye, Azariah," remarked the Load-Bearer.

"I 'low ye're right," replied the preacher; "the prairie's a-burnin' cl'ar from a mile beyon' Lem Stephens's, plumb te the bend in the creek."

"The prairie on fire, en at this time o' night!" exclaimed Cornelia; "what kin it mean?"

"Why, it means that the Almighty air with we uns, en agin Lem Stephens en the slave-catchers."

"Air it runnin' him clost?"

"Ez fur ez I kin jedge it must be closin' in on him about now," responded the preacher, with surprising nonchalance. "A passel o' good-fer-nothin's banded tharselves together te come over en take off the runaways en git the rewards. They 'lowed te be hyar by this time so ez te head off Brother Snedeker. I come right by Lem Stephens's en see 'em let the bloodhounds loose, en jest ez the hounds lit out over this way the prairie began te blaze, so all hands stayed right thar te watch the place."

The Load-Bearer began to shake off his seeming lethargy.

"Whar be the bloodhounds now?" he asked.

"Whar be they? I reckon they air right whar yer dogs en my pistol left 'em down the road thar."

"They air dead!" cried Cornelia.

"They air dead!" echoed a mournful voice behind the house.

The cry was taken up by other fugitives, who imagined Isaac Snedeker and his friends had been assassinated.

"Dey's all dead! Dey done killed 'em off!" arose on all sides from the dark forms now emerging from their hiding-places.

An ever-increasing glamour shone through the woods to the south, and the runaways now saw it for the first time. It hushed their cries and murmurs as if a damper had suddenly been placed over their mouths.

Azariah James got off his horse, tied up, and followed Cornelia Gest into the kitchen.

" 'Pears like they won't never git here to-night," she sighed.

" 'Bout how many d'ye expect?"

"Brother Snedeker en two er three more; but he's a-comin' te carry the runaways te the nex' station. I don't calc'late he'll stay more'n long 'nough te load up en git away ez quick ez iver he kin."

There were sounds of horses' hoofs and wagon wheels outside.

Cornelia Gest went to the door.

"Thank the Lord ye've got here at last!" she exclaimed, greeting a slender man with a long, greyish beard, who was helping out an elderly woman clad in deep black.

"It's Squar Higgins," said Cornelia; "en Sister Higgins hez come along te cher a body by thet beautiful smile o' her'n; Elihu allers says it's like the grace o' God a-smilin' on the hull world when *she's* aroun'."

And so it was; for Martha Higgins was another of those wonderful women whose very presence diffused an influence of peace and harmony. Her faith and confidence in the Divine goodness were incorruptible and never-ending. She brought with her a radiant power that aroused the preacher to thoughts of praise and thanksgiving for all the mercies of the past and present. With her presence, the terrors of the night receded, and the preacher, with his eyes half closed, began to hum a few bars of a favourite hymn.

Meanwhile the Load-Bearer had quietly slipped away to have a look over the prairie. He had climbed a large withered tree which stood on a knoll, and was watching a thin tongue of fire licking up the grass away towards the bend in the creek not far from Lem Stephens's frame house. From this tree he had often looked out before, but never on such a sight as this. He watched the flames dart up here and there in sudden flashes as they caught the strips of taller grass in the low soil near the water, dying down where the ground was higher and the grass thinner. He could not at first make out in what direction the flames were moving, nor could he yet tell whether they had reached the frame house. The whole region before him lay circled in a rim of fire. Never had he been in such intimate communion with the mighty forces of the Eternal; never had he felt the breath of the night come with so much inspiration and judgment. It seemed to Elihu Gest that fire had descended from the skies, that a ban had been placed on the movements of evil-doers in that section and for miles around; and while he pondered and marvelled over the wonders of the night he felt the "Living Presence" throb through his being with a quickening power that lifted him clear above and away from mortal things. He shouted aloud one of his favourite passages from the Old Testament. He was about to descend when a long sheet of flame leaped into the sky. Lem Stephens's house was ablaze: it was burning like a box of tinder. Now the barn caught; now the brushwood behind the house was blazing. The border of the creek was a mass of flame. It looked as if a fiery serpent were moving in a zigzag along its border, rising and falling on great wings of fire, then disappearing, to rise again in another place.

A current of wind was created by the heat, and flames darted from the other side of the water.

When he returned, Elihu Gest found Isaac Snedeker—who had brought several more refugees with him—the two Higginses, Azariah James, and Cornelia, all sitting in a semi-circle in the kitchen, and after greeting Mr. Snedeker he took a seat at one end.

There followed a period of deep, devotional quietude in

which each one sat as if alone. There was the grey-bearded Squire Higgins, with his big brows and kindly face; there was Cornelia Gest, slender, frail, and shrunken, in her seat; there was Azariah James, whose broodings defied all divination; there was Isaac Snedeker, stern and restless as an eagle about to take wing; and Martha Higgins, whose high, massive forehead and arching nose contrasted strangely with the bountiful kindness of her dreamy eyes, while her smile expressed a faith that was infinite and undying.

At one end sat Elihu Gest, obscure carrier of other people's loads, impulsive and enigmatical seer, last in the long procession of the *ante-bellum* prophets of old Illinois.

A shout was heard, and Elihu looked at Martha Higgins as he said:

"They ain't calc'lated te understand what it air thet's workin' out te save them."

"Martha had a presentiment before we came," observed Squire Higgins. "I have never known her to be wrong."

"Who lit thet fire?" queried Cornelia Gest. " 'Twarn't you, Brother Snedeker?"

"That's what I've been wanting to know. I came near being caught in it, and now I'll have to wait here till I see how far it's going to spread."

"It hez plumb licked up Lem Stephens's house," said the Load-Bearer. "I see it from the big tree."

"I want te know!" exclaimed Cornelia.

"Thar ain't nothin' left by this time. If Lem Stephens en the slave-hunters ain't hidin' in the water they air burnt up. Thar's a mighty power movin' over the yearth; I ain't see a night sech ez this sence the comet fust appeared."

Isaac Snedeker went out with Squire Higgins to survey the land. A wall of fire rose above the creek, to the south; an immense, palpitating glow lit the sky—a glow that flashed like sheet-lightning along the course of the creek, for a wind had risen which forced the flames straight towards the Load-Bearer's home. There was a rushing sound where it began to skim the upper branches; then a current of warm air struck through the open space leading from the creek to the house. The woods rang with the screaming of birds; the howling of a wolf again haunted the lonely plains to the north, and a little later an awful roar told that the fire had reached the tall, thick grass and brushwood that lined the water's edge not more than a quarter of a mile from the house.

"De comet done struck de yearth! De world's burnin' up!"

The runaways no longer thought of slave-hunters and a return to bondage. For them, all was at an end; and from a sort of dumb despair there issued forth groans and exclamations of, "Mercy, Lord, mercy, mercy!"

Yet two or three were on the point of escaping to the woods. Isaac Snedeker, seeing the danger, called out:

"All who run away will be caught!"

Squire Higgins hardly knew what to do. The night seemed like day. The roar of the fire could be heard, ever a little nearer, ever more ominous and awful.

"If we have to quit," he said at last, "there's not a minute to lose!"

He was thinking of the safety of the women.

Even the invincible Isaac Snedeker was shaken by forebodings of evil. But when they returned to the kitchen and beheld the Load-Bearer in the same place, self-poised, self-contained, all doubts departed.

" 'Twixt here and thar, thar's a swamp and a patchin' o' oak thet won't ketch, en the grass air sparse and spindlin', en then comes the big trees. But thar's sunthin' else besides the wind thet's blowin' them flames, Squar Higgins."

Even as he spoke the light from the fire was gradually descending out of the zenith. Lower and lower it fell. In about ten minutes nothing but a dim outline of glimmering yellow could be discerned far beyond the belt of woods, and once more the moonlight reigned; the patches of light were brighter, the shadows deeper; the wings of unrest were folded, and silence returned with a twofold presage.

"It air about time," said the Load-Bearer, rising and placing his hand on the preacher's shoulder. "It air time te begin," he intimated to Squire Higgins and Isaac Snedeker.

They all left the kitchen except Cornelia Gest, Martha Higgins, and myself. Cornelia's face assumed a pensive look; she wiped away a tear, and said in a quavering voice:

"God be praised! He allowed her te pass out o' this world in peace. I'm right happy te have ye here, Sister Higgins, en I jes' knowed ye'd come over when Elihu sent ye word."

"I don't know of anything that could have kept me from

coming, Sister Gest," replied Mrs. Higgins. "I had a presentiment that she would die right here."

"We couldn't git her te talk about herself, nur give her name, nur nothin'; they're all so afeared they'll be sent back te bondage. Thar ain't on'y Mr. Snedeker en Brother James en yerselves ez knows 'bout her havin' died here. If thar warn't so many good people aroun' I'd give right up, seein' so many wicked. But Elihu said he war boun' te have prayers en his favourite hymn sung at the funeral."

Now for the first time I knew that the quadroon had passed away and that this night was appointed for her burial.

We had not long to wait, for presently Squire Higgins came and announced that all was ready. When we got to the graveside, near the creek, all the fugitives stood around, some of them holding lanterns, the black faces appearing strangely unnatural in the flickering light, the faces of the quadroons and octoroons more ghostly. Under the trees, half in the moonlight, half in shadow, it seemed as if a great multitude were crowding up from behind, eager to catch every sound that might pass from anyone's lips.

A soft breeze moved among the last sere leaves of autumn. Now and then a gentle gust swayed the lower branches to and fro, and an infinitely tender sighing came and went and melted away in the eerie moonlight.

The preacher took off his tightly-fitting cap and without it his hair stood out in wild, rumpled locks. He seemed to loom taller and taller. He looked as if he had forgotten all he had intended to say, and was standing there helpless and forsaken at the brink of a grave, over the dead he had come to bury.

"Praise God!" murmured the Load-Bearer, who alone of all the persons there seemed to understand.

Azariah James closed his eyes for one or two seconds; a slight shiver passed through his frame; then he opened them wide and searching, and a wondrous light flashed out over the awed and speechless company. He was no longer an awkward, hesitating dreamer, but a lion aroused, a prophet in his own country. His listeners began to move and sway in unison with his immeasurable compassion, and after he had spoken for ten minutes the Load-Bearer offered up a short, fervent prayer. Then, when the last scene was about to begin, the voice of Martha Higgins rang out above the open grave:

"On Jordan's stormy banks I stand
 And cast a wistful eye"—

A loud, rolling wave of song passed in long, reaching echoes through the woods as the twenty-nine persons present sent their voices calling—

"To Canaan's fair and happy land
 Where my possessions lie"—

for now every voice was attuned to the old matchless melody of the meeting-house and the camp-ground.

As the hymn proceeded the sense of time was obliterated. A far-sweeping chorus, tinged here and there with a nameless melancholy, floated upward into the white silence of the night. On and on they sang, and the old hymn rolled out in a miracle of sound, on a river of golden melody, vibrating far into regions of infinite light and love.

Isaac Snedeker gathered up the runaways and prepared for flight. He separated them into two groups—one he would carry in his own wagon, the other was for Squire Higgins. It did not take long, and the two wagon loads set out in the clear moonlight. A little way towards the north they would separate, each going according to a pre-arranged plan; and every fugitive arrived at last safely in Canada, which was, after all, the land of Canaan for them.

CHAPTER 12

The Camp-Meeting

ON THE morning of the great camp-meeting I stood at the gate for nearly an hour waiting for a sight of the Busby wagon, which was to take us; and when it arrived Uriah Busby was so eager to be off that his wife had barely time to call out to those standing at the door to see us depart:

"You see it's jest as I said, Uriah says he'll git there if it was twice as fur agin."

When we got to the main road we began to see signs of gathering campers, but when we reached a place called the "mud-holes" people could be seen in every direction making for this spot where several roads converged into one.

"Now, Uriah, you ain't a-goin' to land us in the mud, air ye?" said Mrs. Busby, as we neared the deceitful holes. "If there ain't them Wagner boys, plague take 'em! I do hope we kin git through afore they do."

"I reckon they ain't been drinkin yet," said her husband; "it's too early in the day."

"I don't know 'bout that," returned Serena Busby. "They don't look accommodatin', en ye see they're doin' their level best to git ahead of us."

The Wagner boys were urging on their horses almost to a gallop.

"Now, Uriah, don't be a fool; jest rein up en let 'em go it all they want to; the folks at the camp ain't a-goin' to shout much afore we git there; en besides, if ye dump me in the mud it'll be the fust en the last time."

Uriah Busby did as he was told. The Wagner boys made a dash for the crossing, but in the rush to be first they went too far to the right. When they got to the middle, at a place where the mud looked shallow but was in reality deep, over went the wagon and out toppled the brothers.

"Providence air on our side," said Uriah, as he took extra pains to keep to the left.

"It'll take some o' the dare-devil out of 'em, en if it had been a Baptist camp-meetin' it 'ud took some sousin' in the creek to wash the mud from their bodies as well as the sins from their souls," remarked Mrs. Busby.

Other travellers followed, all giving that particular side of the crossing a wide berth. In about three hours we arrived at another point where we could see scores of people in wagons, buggies, and on horseback, making for the camp, now distant about an hour. Many of the horses "carried double," while in some of the big covered wagons sat whole families. A blinding dust filled the air and covered our clothes, as we drove along in the wake of others, receiving their dust and kicking more of it up for those at our heels. As the day began to grow hot we saw many indulging in "drams" from the demijohn, and Serena Busby remarked that there was sure to be some "kickin'-up" at the camp towards evening.

As we got within two miles of the grounds the whole populace, for a radius of many miles, seemed to be on the move, converging towards one point. From a slight eminence which we had just attained, commanding a view on all sides, a scraggy line of white-topped wagons could be seen descending a slope to the right, while to the left, a little below us, another line of twisting vehicles ascended in a slow, weary train, enveloped in clouds of dust, now partly hidden behind clumps of trees, now emerging like the remnant of some scattered army crawling towards the precincts of a friendly country. Once in a while we were passed by young men on horseback who galloped their horses; others, in light buggies, shot past the heavy wagons and were soon out of sight; hundreds were on foot, looking neither to the right nor to the left, and these, as Uriah Busby observed, were the ones in dead earnest, bound to get there no matter how.

We drove into the camp grounds about one o'clock, and found two or three thousand persons already there, with others pouring in by the hundred.

A shed had been erected large enough to shelter several thousand persons, and out in the woods, beyond the confines of the meeting-grounds, groups of old reprobates and young rowdies had taken their stand with whisky barrels and demijohns ready to supply all who cared for strong drink, some of them armed with pistols and murderous-looking knives. Everyone was eating or getting ready to eat, for the women had brought a goodly supply of edibles. Tents were put up by some, while others would sleep in the covered wagons, the men mostly under the wagons or under the shed. It looked like an immense gathering for a picnic; and it was impossible to say from the expression of people's faces what sort of a meeting it was, for no one seemed over-anxious; all seemed contented to be there let come what may. Indeed, Mrs. Busby was right when she said:

"Te jedge by thar looks they hev all saved their souls en air now attendin' to their bodies, not te git te the other world afore their time."

Uriah Busby unhitched the horses at a spot near the creek, and after dinner Serena began to look about her.

Presently she discovered someone she knew.

"Why, if thar ain't Zack Caverly, of all people in the world!"

"Wal, I'll be blamed!" exclaimed Mr. Busby. "Ye don't reckon he's come te sell whisky, do ye?"

"I reckon not. Zack's ez sober ez an owl, en ye know it. Wal! If there ain't Minerva Wagner! I want to know how she got here! Must hev come a-hossback, if she didn't come in a neighbour's wagon, fearin' to risk her neck with them two good-fer-nothin's."

And, sure enough, there was Mrs. Wagner, seated on a big stump, talking to Ebenezer Hicks.

"My word!" said Uriah Busby; "it do give me a disagreeable feelin' te see them fire-eatin' Baptists settin' there waitin' fer te stir up mischief agin the Abolitionists en the Methodists. They ain't out here fer any good, I kin tell ye."

"You better b'lieve they ain't here fer any religion they kin pick up; I believe I ain't never seen her look so sour and spiteful."

Zack Caverly led his horse over and settled himself near our wagon.

"I heared ye war comin'," he said, "en the weather bein' fine I fixed te ride over en take things sort o' easy durin' meetin'-time."

"Hev ye see many folks ye know?" asked Uriah Busby.

"The whole kintry's turnin' out; thar's goin' te be the biggest meetin' ever holdin' in this section. Ye see, it's the fire-eatin' question thet's got hold on 'em, en they all want te see which a-way the black cat's a-goin' te jump. Summow, right er wrong, the people hev an idee that this here meetin' ain't so much fer religion ez it air fer politics, en thet's why ye see so many Baptists en Campbellites en Presbyterians en members o' the Methodist Church South sprinkled all over the grounds. I heerd a man say they've got Abe Lincoln on the brain."

" 'Pears to me," said Mrs. Busby, "it's niggers more likely."

The afternoon and evening of Thursday were given up to preliminary services and to getting the huge meeting into working order, and on Friday afternoon the number of people on the ground was computed at twenty thousand.

Religious services were held three times a day, and in case of a revival the evening service would be protracted far into the night, perhaps all night, as it often happened at such gatherings. But somehow the meetings on Friday seemed without any signs of enthusiasm; the people listened with respect to all that was said, and they sang with a hearty will, but there was something lacking. Uriah Busby remarked to Zack Caverly that it was a spark from Heaven that was wanting, to which the old pioneer replied that he thought so too, as there was plenty of tinder in the congregation.

Before the evening service on this day, Friday, Elihu Gest, Squire Higgins, Azariah James, and several others decided on going out into the woods to a lonely spot and praying for a revival at the next service.

The people were all expectation at meeting-time, the preachers did their best, exhorters exhorted, but there were no happy shouts, no groans of mental misery, no conviction of sins. Squire Higgins said he had often seen the like before, and counselled hope and courage, but the Load-Bearer was certain they had not prayed with sufficient faith and fervour. "The people," he declared, "air all right, but they must be tetched."

Saturday came, and at the morning service it was decided to have a short but positive sermon on the sins of the times, with some pointed remarks against slavery; for a good many were of the opinion that this would fire up the people and prepare a way for a revival in the afternoon. The sermon was preached by a stranger from Missouri, but it failed to do more than create a lively interest in the political questions of the hour, and, curious to relate, just as this meeting was brought to a close the negroes on the ground, who numbered between two and three hundred, began a meeting of their own off at one side of the white camp, where certain freed negroes were found who actually believed in slavery.

Their meeting was conducted in the orthodox Methodist manner; but those of the coloured people who belonged to the Methodist Church South were believers in slavery, while the Methodist Church North was against it, many of its members being extreme Abolitionists. The coloured meeting was conducted by two negro exhorters, presided over by a white preacher, and when the exercises began by the singing of a popular hymn:

> "De golden chariot's hangin' low,
> My breddern you'll be called on"—

the whole meeting, as Zack Caverly said, was soon put in the "weaving way"; the great yellow eyes began to roll in a sort of subdued ecstasy, the black faces beamed contentment, and woolly heads rocked in keeping with the lilt of the music.

It was not long before a tall, glossy black negro, with small, piercing eyes and thick lips, rose, and with a look of mingled humour and cynicism, began to speak.

"Breddern an' sistern," he said; "some o' you done hearn w'at de preacher ober in de white camp said 'bout dis yer slavery biznuz, an' I wuz askin' to myself ez I sot an' heared you all singin' an' gettin' happy—which is better fer de coloured folks, to be boun' in dis wurrul an' free in de nex', er te be free in dis wurrul an' boun' after you am dead?"

He licked his lips and eyed the congregation for a moment before proceeding.

"I ain't got time to stan' heah an' answer no questions 'bout de rights an' de wrongs ob de coloured folks, but I 'low dar's some folks in dis meetin' wat's run away fr'm der mastahs an' ain't in no hurry to go back. But which am it better to do— cross ober Jordan inter Canaan, er cross de State line inter Canada? I's gwine to make de observation 'bout de black snake w'at change his skin, kase some ob you settin' heah to-day done gone and made de change an' ain't noways better off.

"Dar wuz a black snake w'at lef' home an' gin ter wander roun', but de sun gittin' sorter hot he say ter hissef, 'I reckin hit's 'bout time fer to shed dis heah skin, hit gittin' too hot to carry'; so he des slip hit off, an' he done felt he gwine ter fly instead er crawl on de groun'. When de night come on de wedder done git mighty cole, an' fo' long he come 'cross a skin a rattlesnake des shuck hissef out'n. Mist' black snake say ter hissef, 'I des 'bout slip in dar an' keep warm'; but he ain't no sooner slip in dan 'long come a white man wid a big stick an' he say, 'I don't nebber kill no black snakes, but I kill all de rattle-snakes I ebber come 'cross,' and wid dat he up an' kill de black snake fust lick.

"Now, breddern, dis heah ain't no sermon. I'se speakin' in w'at dey calls de paraboils; dat's de meanin' ob de observation fer de coloured folks, an' dat is—don't nebber change yo' 'ligion, an' don't nebber run away fr'm yo' masters."

Despair took possession of the runaways who were sitting listening, and during the proceedings that followed one of the fugitives sought counsel of Isaac Snedeker, who was attending the camp-meeting and who had arranged that a number of run-aways were to gather here, this being considered the safest plan that could be devised to accomplish their liberation.

The sensation created by the negro's story was such that for the space of half an hour no preaching, nor singing, nor exhort-ing would move the congregation; but after a vigorous effort on the part of the preacher and exhorters a movement of revival became apparent at the farthest end of the meeting, seeing which one of the exhorters pointed over the heads of the people, and, with an angry look, cried out:

"Muster up dem mo'ners dar! Prone 'em up, Brudder Dixon. Brudder Luke Henry, mourn up dem w'ats a-pantin' an' faintin' down dar in de furder aisle. Sis' Jones, whar's yo' singin'-voice? You ain't been out las' night a-imitatin' dem squinch-owls, is you? Now, help 'long dar! I 'low we goin' keep Satan fr'm clippin' yo' wings by de Lord's help dis day."

The meeting of the coloured people proceeded in due order, and by the time it came to an end the afternoon service began in the main camp. The people sat and listened but did not respond, and some of the leaders were haunted by a presenti-ment of failure. To make matters worse, the drunken rowdies beyond the camp began to harass the preachers from the rear, near the creek. Under the influence of cheap, fiery whisky some of them acted like madmen, and a plan was concocted to duck Azariah James in the creek in the evening, after the last service.

The evening meeting began early and lasted till late. At its close another consultation was held among the preachers. Once more it was declared necessary to go out and plead for grace and power to bring about a revival. Uriah Busby advised his wife to invite Elihu Gest and Azariah James over to the wagon to take a "cold check, ez brother Gest looks clean washed out en Brother James caved in, after that long sermon o' his'n."

"A cold check!" exclaimed Serena; "you better b'lieve they want somethin' else besides hard boiled eggs en bread en butter. I'll fix 'em up some real strong coffee, steamin' hot. I kin boil the water in a jiffy in that new kittle we brought 'long; en I calc'late *we'll* take a nip o' somethin' er nuther ez long ez we're 'bout it, fer I feel a mite caved in myself, en I reckin ye all do. I declare to goodness, Uriah, I ain't see ye look so floppy sence the comet scare!"

The two invited guests came, and Mrs. Busby spread a cloth on the ground and was about to prepare the meal with the hot coffee when suddenly the Load-Bearer interposed:

"Jes' wait a while, Sister Busby. 'Tain't no use—I cain't wrastle with the sperit on a full stommick. I ain't never hed no prayers answered that a-way. We've got te go out yander en pray, en if ever I felt the need of it it's right now."

"The meetin' wus sorter cold, en thet's a fac'," said Uriah Busby.

"It war lukewarm; thet's the wust thing a man kin say, for it shows thet the people feel comfortable-like in thar sins."

"It's a pity Pete Cartwright's too feeble to be here," remarked Serena, "fer if he wuz he'd put 'em into hot water quicker'n lightnin'. A lot o' them folks don't want preachin' half so much ez brimstone; some preachers carry it in their pockets like, en jes' throw it over the people."

The preachers were gone about a quarter of an hour and then returned to the Busby wagon and partook of refreshments. The Load-Bearer's face was beaming with contentment.

"I feel like our prayers hev been heerd at the throne o' grace," he said, as he seated himself on the ground and took the coffee Mrs. Busby offered him in a large tin cup; "en this is the fust time I've hed the feelin' since the meetin' opened. Te-morrer's the day."

"It most allers is," remarked Uriah.

"Thet's so," added Mrs. Busby; "it takes two or three days fer a meetin' like this te git het through en through."

"I hev noticed more'n oncet how Sunday kin be favoured by

an outpourin' o' the Sperit; en if Sunday passes 'thout a shakin' o' dry bones thar ain't much hope left fer any protracted meetin'."

"Thet's a fac', Brother Gest," remarked Azariah James; "Sunday's the holy day in more ways 'n one. What's done hez te be done, en will be done te-morrer."

"Here comes Brother Snedeker!"

"Law me!" exclaimed Serena. "I've been wonderin' what hed become o' ye."

"And I have been hunting for you all," he said, coming up to the circle. "There are a good many rowdies and cut-throats on the outskirts of the camp, and it looks as if they were hatching mischief; they have been drinking hard all the evening and are still at it."

"Air thar any slave-drivers among 'em?" asked Uriah.

"Not that I know of, but they are all enemies of this meeting, and they are being encouraged by the whisky-drinkers and pro-slavery Christians."

"But we ain't been disturbed in the meetin's yet, that's one good thing."

"No, but there's been fighting out round the whisky-wagons every time the people assemble for preaching. We are forming a company to protect the preachers and the services to-morrow. We've got to get at least a hundred men enrolled as watchmen, and another hundred who will swear to up and help if the watchmen prove insufficient."

"I ain't got no special fears noways," said Elihu Gest; "that is, not now."

"But ye hed before ye went out te wrastle," said Uriah Busby.

"I tell you what it is, brethren," said Isaac Snedeker, "I shall not be able to remain at the camp longer than to-morrow midnight. I have three or four loads of runaways to look after, and you, Brother Gest, will have to take a party of ten. Brother James will be allotted about the same number, and I'll take as many as my wagon will hold."

"I reckon," said the Load-Bearer, "we'll hev te fix te git clear o' the camp by Sunday night, fust thing after preachin' closes."

"Here comes Squire Higgins!" exclaimed Serena; "sumthin's th' matter!"

"We want all hands over by the preachers' tent," he said hurriedly; "there's going to be trouble."

The Squire carried a stout hickory stick, and advised all the others to arm themselves with the same kind of weapon.

Most of the campers were asleep by this time, but as we approached the spot indicated excited talk could be heard and groups of men gathered as if in consultation.

The preachers' tent stood behind the public platform, midway between it and the creek, and here stood the wagons, buggies, and rockaways of the preachers and elders. The ruffians began by imitating the crowing of cocks, the squealing of pigs, the shouting of "convicted" sinners, the mewing of cats; and while one band was engaged in holding the attention of the preachers, another began to move off one of the buggies to roll it over the bank into the creek, which was ten feet deep at this place.

Elder Johnson's buggy was already wheeled to within a few feet of the bank; two of the rowdies were about to let it fall into the water when Isaac Snedeker brought his hickory stick down on the back of the leader with such force that a cry of pain went up from the culprit. The buggy was abandoned, but, in the meantime, Azariah James had been seized from behind by two powerful ruffians and was being led to the creek to be thrown in. He went without offering the slightest resistance; but just as they reached the bank the muscular preacher turned nimbly, and bobbing up and down twice, in the twinkling of an eye, he flung into the creek first one, then the other of his would-be duckers. While this was going on another carriage was being rolled towards the water, about twenty yards away. This band was headed by the two Wagner boys, who, sufficiently intoxicated to be reckless of danger, were pulling the buggy by the shafts; but while they were pulling it in front others were pushing from behind, and when they came to the brink over went the buggy and the two brothers into the creek! Mingled shouts of victory and derision went up, and it was some time before the younger of the two got out of the water and climbed, half drowned, up the bank.

Several knock-down fights were going on in the vicinity, and amidst the general uproar no one had time to think of the lifeless body of the other brother, now lying in the creek.

Azariah James, Elder Johnson, Isaac Snedeker, and their assistants had given the ringleaders a severe drubbing, stripped them of their weapons and driven them, like so many sheep, in every direction.

Azariah James and Isaac Snedeker now formed a party to attack the vendors of whisky, which they did at the break of day, driving them from the place after pouring out the whisky on the ground.

Not a cloud was to be seen when the sun rose that Sunday morning. The smoke from the breakfast fires curled slowly up through the trees, and the odour of burning leaves and dry twigs perfumed the air with delicious fragrance. The day was warm; people felt it was good to be alive, and many expressed a wish that life would always be just like this.

Elihu Gest was right when he predicted that nothing much would come of the morning service. Serena Busby said the only two things the people did with spirit was eating and singing. Alone, of all the leaders in the camp, the Load-Bearer took a joyful view of the religious situation. The others were growing more and more pessimistic.

"The people air plumb sot in the sins o' the flesh," was what Elder Johnson said when he left the platform after the morning service; but Elihu Gest went so far as to whistle with "good feelin's," so that many of the preachers began to regard him as somewhat *suspect* in earnestness. The proceedings at the afternoon meeting were little more than a repetition of the preceding service; Elihu Gest, however, was nowhere to be seen and Uriah Busby guessed he was "away summars wrastlin' fer extry power."

The night settled down on the camp clear, calm, and beautiful; the people gathered in their places before the great platform and altar palings a full half-hour before the time fixed for the opening exercises, and the number present exceeded that of any meeting yet held.

However, services did not begin for some little time after the hour fixed, as the body of the drowned man was not discovered in the creek till now, and the preachers were engaged in consultation behind the big tent.

As the evening wore on the air became close and sultry, and a feeling of lethargy bore down on the people. Someone had advised the singing of several hymns as the best mode of getting the congregation into working order, and hymn after hymn was sung while a tall, long-haired leader stood beating time with his outstretched arm, waving to and fro with an eccentric lilt of the body, up and down. The platform was now filled with the preachers and exhorters, and in some manner the whole front and all the surrounding camp seemed metamorphosed. Something extraordinary had happened. Yet it was not possible to say what.

A storm was approaching; but those who were engaged in singing paid little heed to the rumbling of thunder. A few minutes more and a squall descended over the camp and a vivid flash sent a thrill through the assembly. The crash was followed by a hurricane of shifting light that swept down closer and closer over the camp. The lightning seemed to spring from the ground, the air, the woods, the camp itself, and it seemed as if objects moved in keeping with the quick sheets of fire that came as bolts from the heavens. Only a few lights were left in the lanterns, and there was something spectral about the vast concourse swaying like grizzled phantoms on the brink of a yawning abyss.

Just before the hurricane passed away a dazzling bolt struck the big elm beside the platform. It fell in a blue-white zig-zag, and to many of the more superstitious it resembled nothing so much as a fiery serpent poured from a vial of wrath overhead, for it split the elm in two, the peal of thunder and the cleaving timber mingling in one terrific report.

A great shout arose from the people near the tree, and the commotion in that part of the meeting had hardly subsided when a voice was heard as one calling from the shores of Tartarus.

Elihu Gest stood on the platform facing the assembly, and a new meaning was added to the confusion and the ghostly candle-light. A picture of peculiar fascination was now presented to the wondering and half-dazed people. Arrayed behind the Load-Bearer, in a jagged semi-circle that stretched from one end of the platform to the other, sat all the preachers and exhorters. Witnesses who had once mourned as penitents before the altar now marshalled to make others mourn, as fixed and motionless as statues hewn from syenite; for there was about them something of the mien of Egyptian bas-reliefs seated at the door separating life and death. Some were bearded and grimly entrenched behind a hairy mask; others, in their long, pointed goatees, sharpened the picture; while others again, clean-shaven, and peering straight before them, presented a death-like pallor, at once frail and frightful, suggesting the keynote of the incommensurable symphony of human emotions now about to begin.

A deep, apprehensive solemnity pervaded every portion of the congregation when the Load-Bearer shouted, in tones that penetrated to the far end of the camp: "You are being weighed in the balance! Tophet is yawning for the unregenerate!"

A sensation as if the ground had begun to move and float spread through the multitude; and when, a little later, he cried: "You're hangin' to the hinges of Time by a hair!" all doubts vanished. Heads began to droop, bodies swayed from side to side, and then, one by one, in couples, in groups, everywhere in the meeting, people fell to the ground, while stifled groans and loud lamentations issued from hundreds of throats at once.

The mourners at the altar were now several rows deep, but still the crowd staggered forward. The camp resembled a coast strewn with the dead and dying after a great wreck, and a murmuring tumult alternately rose and fell like that from a moaning wind and a surging sea.

The night of nights had come! It seemed as if hundreds were in the throes of death and would never rise, so that a mingling of pity and dread filled those who had long since professed religion; for the strange union of material and spiritual forces, the upturned faces, the gaping mouths, the gasping sighs, the clenched hands, the sudden falling away of all wordly props, the swift descent from the mountain of vanity to the vale of sorrows rendered, for a moment, even the helpers and exhorters speechless; but, as Elihu Gest finished, the exhorters on the platform rose and scattered, each to a particular work, some descending amongst the people, some addressing them from the stand.

All the camp lights were now burning. In the midst of the greatest confusion Squire Higgins stood up where he could be seen, and called out: "Is Sister Kezia Jordan present?"

The people at that corner of the meeting rose from their seats. The Load-Bearer and Azariah James were lifting someone on to the corner of the platform. Again Squire Higgins stood up and called out Mrs. Jordan's name, and the word was passed from one end of the camp to the other. "Sister Jordan! where is Sister Jordan?" All preaching and exhorting ceased. An awful silence settled over the meeting, for there, on the platform, lay all that was left of Alek Jordan, who had been killed under the big elm when a portion of the tree had fallen.

At last Mrs. Jordan appeared at the bottom of the steps, at the left. She looked as if she might be walking in her sleep, and Martha Higgins was leading her by the arm. They mounted the steps slowly. At the top Elihu Gest and Azariah James stood waiting. On the platform a transformation had occurred. Seated again in a long semi-circle were the stern, statuesque figures, the faces more solemn and anxious, more strained and yearning than ever; and as Kezia Jordan passed along the platform and approached the remains the Load-Bearer turned as if suddenly inspired, and addressed her with the words: "The Lord giveth and the Lord taketh away," and all the preachers finished the sentence with him: "Blessed be the name of the Lord."

Mrs. Jordan now stood full in the lantern light, and her pallor was plainly visible. She bent over the body, then rose and whispered some words to Elihu Gest. He turned, and facing the multitude announced as loud as he could speak that Sister Jordan accepted this great affliction in a spirit of faith and resignation, and with her hand across her forehead, her eyes half-closed, like one who had been dazed by a sudden and bewildering vision, Kezia Jordan was led away by Martha Higgins and the Load-Bearer down the steps.

Prayers and exhortations followed, and the shouting, the hurrying to and fro, gave place to a feeling it would be impossible to describe.

And now, far down on the outskirts of the congregation, a voice was heard, high, shrill, and broken, which caused the people to turn in their seats and riveted every eye to a spot where a tall figure advanced, dimly visible, up the middle aisle. Out of the woods and the night the apparition seemed to have come, and with tottering steps, hair dishevelled, face trembling and distorted, the once unbending form of Minerva Wagner staggered towards the mourners' bench, the colour gone from her rugged face, the indomitable will from her proud, grey eyes, all her strength departed.

She had just left the body of her son.

"Take me, take me, in all my misery!" she cried out. "I'm an old woman in despair! I'm a stricken woman! Pray for me!"

She turned twice in a sort of whirl, and cast a look of unutterable woe on the people on either side, who, seized with feelings of awe and dismay at the sight before them, could scarcely realise what was happening. She staggered on, now assisted by friendly hands, and, when she arrived at the altar, fell in a swoon among the long rows of mourners.

All night the revival went on, and the next day, and the next; but on the same Sunday night, as the Load-Bearer left the camp grounds, and heard the multitude singing:

> "The year of jubilee has come,
> Return ye ransomed sinners home"—

he waves his hand and cried: "Let 'em mourn, let 'em mourn; jedgment ain't far off!"

CHAPTER *13*

The Pioneer of the
Sangamon Country

ONE evening a well-dressed stranger called at the Log-House and asked my father for hospitality for the night. He proved to be a lawyer from the southern part of the State, who was on his way north on horseback.

Socrates was already there with one of his friends, a rather distant neighbour.

Coffee was made twice in a large pot, and the cups used were of the largest kind, even for those days. Yet, somehow, there was a feeling that so much stimulant was just the thing for that particular evening, for Socrates and his friend had already told us several stories of the earlier days in the South-west, and the stranger was evidently being wound up for a recital of something extraordinary in his life.

I had not yet seen such a character. Rather tall, inclined to thinness, but with a large, bony frame, with broad, angular shoulders, his long, dark face and piercing black eyes were set off by a rough, pointed goatee which seemed to sprout from his chin spontaneously like a weapon and a warning. And yet, with all the seeming hardness, this stranger must have been a lover of Nature and a sort of undeveloped poet.

When at last we rose from the supper-table a half-circle was formed around the hearth, and the stranger settled himself, and, little by little, began to move into the mysterious past, yet not so mysterious for him as for us, the listeners.

"You see," he said, in answer to some questions put by my father, "Most of the settlers hereabouts in those days came from Virginia, Kentucky, and Tennessee. I came in from west of the Blue Ridge; and Western Virginia thirty or forty years ago was about like Illinois is now."

"Consid'ably mixed," remarked Socrates.

"Yes, sir, and for that reason we had all sorts of people willing to stay, and all sorts willing to make tracks for parts unknown. You've heard of the old-time Regulators, I reckon? Wal, I was at the first meeting of the kind that ever took place in this country, and to tell ye how it happened I must go back to the war of 1812, when old Captain Roberts was living in West Virginia with his beautiful and wayward daughter, who was the cause of more trouble in that and other families than was ever heard of in any history outside these domains. She was most beautiful, she was so, and I can tell ye all here now that I never saw her equal in cool, fascinating ways, and in looks that 'ud make some o' the young men hereabouts follow to where the 'willows are weepin' night and day,' as Pete Cartwright has it. She had what a man down in my section calls the 'wild-cat eye,' that is, they were glassy and fiery one minute, and dove-like an' winnin' the next. She had that pride and independence that was natural to the women-folk of her section. I saw her at times when she was most too haughty and overbearin' for her folks to abide with, an' then again I've seen her as skittish and troublin' as a kitten with a mouse, and just as sassy as a chipmunk in April. It was my belief then, an' it is now, that Vicky Roberts was plumb turned in her head by bein' flattered an' spoiled, she bein' the only child; and it looked like a foreordination of events as far as she was concerned.

"Now, Vicky Roberts was courted by two young men, cousins, Hank Cutler and Jack Stone. And that, gentlemen, meant trouble from the word Go; an' what made things worse was the singular disposition of Stone, who was a young man of few words, an' somewhat quiet, an' given to serious thinking, with a clear head, an' with more brains than some folks would be willing to allow. Against Stone come in Hank Cutler, with a cunnin' disposition an' considerably given to underhand dealings, with a head as muddled an' wayward as could be.

"The rivalry of these two was like the meetin' of the clear waters of the Ohio with the muddy Mississippi. Cutler was as reckless as any young man could be in those days, with no conscience to speak of, and to get the gal he was willing to sell his soul an' take the consequences. He was tall an' right smart in his dress, an' calculated to win over any gal by his looks an' manners, bein' of that particular stamp that catches some women, as spiders catch flies, before they know it. Anyhow,

Cutler an' Stone were in for it from the start, an' no time was lost either way.

"When Vicky Roberts saw how things were opening up she kind o' hesitated, not knowing which to choose, an' bein' more an' more flattered in her feelings she kept both of 'em jumpin' on the string, not stopping to think of the steel trap she was settin' for herself, an' perhaps noways caring, either. Some said she preferred Hank Cutler, others again were dead sure she was in love with Jack Stone. But when old man Cutler up an' died Hank was obliged to cross the Blue Ridge on important business in the Old Dominion, and during his absence the real trouble began. Before he left Vicky Roberts made him believe, or he made himself believe, that she was all right on his side, but as soon as he was out of sight Stone took advantage of the occasion by paying more and more attention to Vicky Roberts. Her parents made no objection; in fact, they favoured Stone, he being the most gentlemanly of the two and the most steady, an' it didn't take more'n a few weeks after Hank Cutler's departure to make Vicky Roberts forget him and consent to marry Jack Stone.

"But there was no minister to perform the ceremony. What was to be done? Time was most precious, seeing that Cutler might arrive home before the Methodist minister, then on his circuit, would come that way. They decided to send for a justice of the peace, named Williams, to unite them in marriage. Now, Williams had been out of office for a good while, but everyone declared him fully qualified to perform the ceremony an' make it valid in the eyes of the law. An' so Jack Stone an' Vicky Roberts were married in all haste to repent in all leisure; and scarcely had they become man and wife than here comes home Hank Cutler!

"Cutler didn't let on he was anyways afflicted by what had happened. He attended the reception an' congratulated the bride an' appeared cool an' took things easy like; but his head was filled with sinister plans. He waited his chance to see Vicky when the people were leaving. The opportunity came, an' he says to her: 'Look here, Vicky, do you know your marriage isn't legal? You ain't married according to law.'

"Vicky Stone blushed and at the same time looked Hank Cutler straight in the eye. Then, after a little, she said: 'Hank, how do you know I ain't?'

" 'I know you ain't,' says he; 'that justice o' the peace is disqualified by law, his commission has run out. You ain't married, Vicky, an' if you have children they'll be bastards, an' Jack Stone knows it!'

"She sat down in a chair right where she was standin', all flustered and ashamed like, but Cutler kept on: 'You think it all over, an' when you want to free yourself I'll be ready.'

"When Stone returned to the house his wife asked him plump an' straight: 'Jack Stone, are you dead sure we're married according to law?' But after he had explained matters an' put the seal of certainty on the facts she kept silent, appearing sort o' strange an' gloomy, and attending to her duties without saying much to anyone. And right here comes one of those queer dealin's that, as Pete Cartwright says, gives the devil his chance, and this is how it happened: At the very time that Cutler come back from the Old Dominion the Governor of Virginia had issued a proclamation about the war that had just broke out between Great Britain and the United States. There was a loud call for volunteers; now was the time for the young men to show their mettle. There was sharp rivalry as to who would show the most daring, and in the midst of the boasting and confusion some folks lost their heads, and one o' them was Stone.

"Cutler had already become a soldier, and for no other reason than to lay a trap for Stone. Hank Cutler never looked so dashing as he did on the day he joined the army. He walked about bragging of the things he intended to do in the war and casting odium on the young men who feared for their skins and stayed at home; and meeting Stone on the street where there was a crowd gathered talking about the war Cutler said to the people: 'I'll be hanged if I don't fight for my country first and get married after'; and then he declared that a young man who was tied to a young gal's apron-strings warn't worth his rations nohow, and more of the same kind. He strutted about like a peacock and making about as much noise, until Jack Stone hardly knew whether he was standing on his head or on his heels, and well nigh distracted, knowing as he did that Cutler was mighty favoured in the eyes of Vicky Roberts before her marriage.

"At last Stone could stand it no longer. He signed his name as a volunteer for six months. That same evening there was a dispute between Stone an' his wife. She demanded to know how he could bring himself to join the army only a few days after their marriage. She wanted to know how she would now look in the eyes of the world, an' she told him she might better be a widow. And not only that, but she took it into her head that Stone had never loved her an' was now enrolling himself as a volunteer to escape the responsibility of the marriage relation. During this particular time Hank Cutler had put in his best licks to help on the rupture. He had spoken to Stone's wife just long enough to put a bumble-bee in her bonnet that would keep buzzin' day an' night, without rest. The more Jack Stone tried to explain his actions the more his wife resented his explanations. When he spoke of fighting for his country she looked suspicious, an' every time he spoke of returning from the war in a few months her face grew more set an' distrustful, nor would she speak to him any more.

"All this time Cutler and Stone were conferring together on matters concerning the war, Stone little suspecting the deep designs of his rival and enemy. One afternoon, towards the last of the summer, as the sun was setting behind the old Virginia hills, an' the birds flying low through the underbrush, an' all Nature drowsing in the peaceful calm, an' the old trees castin' their shadows along the descending slopes, Vicky Stone met Hank Cutler a mile from her house, the meeting lasting about twenty minutes. There was where Cutler worked the mischief-world-without-end, an' there was where she made up her mind not to let the parson perform a legal ceremony of marriage when he returned, as he was about to do in a few days.

"When she got back to the house there was some talk of the parson's arrival, but she refused to entertain the idea of a second marriage now, an', besides, Stone himself didn't think it necessary, so the matter ended.

"The whole country was up in arms. The Indians had joined the British. Cutler and Stone belonged to a company of spies in the army, commanded by General Harrison, in the West, and in the discharge of their duty as spies they enjoyed the privilege of wandering about pretty freely; an' more than this, General Harrison appointed Cutler to seek out the whereabouts o' General Hopkins, who was on his way north from Kentucky. Cutler was only too anxious for an occasion such as this, an' some folks say he asked for the job. Anyhow, he succeeded in finding General Hopkins, an' transacting the business in hand, but he never returned to the camp of General Harrison; neither was he seen in

any other camp of the army. At the time they were expecting
his return to Harrison's army in the north-west Cutler was
making tracks for home. By day he was exerting his wits to
avoid meetin' soldiers, by night he was put to it to steer clear of
Indians.

"It was a long an' dangerous journey, an' it meant hidin' a
good part o' the time, sleepin' out in all sorts o' weather; and
the hardships he endured proved his frenzy for Vicky Roberts,
now Stone's legitimate wife. In the army he was given up for
dead, being killed by Indians on his way back to camp, as everyone supposed.

"But Hank Cutler was never so 'live and in fightin' trim. His
war experiences had done nothing else than whet his appetite
for dare-devil scrapes and still more adventure, and I must allow
things were all on his side so far. The devil always wins the first
stakes.

"But where was Jack Stone all this time? Yes, sir, ye may
well ask that. He was with the army, hundreds o' miles away,
an' when Harrison took it into his head to discharge Stone an'
other volunteers before the close o' the war he, too, made tracks
for home.

"It was one o' those beautiful melting days in Indian summer,
when heaven meets earth an' settles right down over everything,
minglin' all things in Nature an' human nature in one bond of
harmony, as it were, an' makin' folks feel as if it was a mighty
good thing to be livin' an' breathin', to say nothing about love,
which is more in most cases than anything else a man can think
of—it was on such a day at high noon that Jack Stone come
steppin' along as lithe as could be up the slope leadin' to his
house, an' walking straight to the door opened it an' stepped in.
Vicky Stone was nowhere to be seen. He thought he heard
footsteps overhead, an' called out; she would be down directly;
perhaps she was fixin' on some nice ribbons an' things to receive
him in. Growing impatient, he passed up the narrow stairway.
The room was vacant. He stood musing for a minute, then came
downstairs again. The whole place had a deserted look. He hurried to consult with Captain Roberts, but the Captain looked
like one in mourning.

" 'I'm looking for my wife,' he says to the Captain.

" 'An' I've been looking for my daughter for some time,' was
the answer.

"The two men stood an' stared at each other. Then Stone says: 'How long has she been gone an' who did she leave with?'

" 'About a month, but I know nothing about her going. All I can tell ye is that she has left here an' left for good.'

"Stone's wife had gone away; no soul in the place knew where to. The neighbours did their best to pacify him, but nothing did any good. He walked about like a man that had been dazed, not knowing what to do. He was seen to go back into his empty house, where he stayed for some time; then he walked out as a man would walk who had taken a drop too much. He began to load his rifle, an' after that he lit out down the hill an' across the valley. He hadn't been gone many minutes when his house began to blaze and before he got across the creek it fell in a heap o' ruins. He had set it afire himself.

"Years passed. The war with Great Britain was over; the wars with the Indians were over, but where was Hank Cutler? Wal, I'm comin' to it as fast as ever I can; but I reckon it took some time for him to play his cards after the deal was made, an' without discountin' nothing it'll take some time to unravel the yarn plumb to the last skein.

"Cutler had made arrangements to meet Vicky Stone after sundown not far from her house. You see he got there safe an' sound, and you see how Jack Stone come back an' found his wife gone; and now in your mind's eye, if you'll just think steady enough about it, you can see Hank Cutler an' Vicky Stone floatin' down the Ohio on a raft they found tied to the bank at the point where they struck the river. The current bein' rapid they got to Cincinnati without too much trouble, and there they stayed till their first child was born, when their wanderin's began in good earnest.

"There's where I saw them about six months after their arrival. It seemed like I never set eyes on a young woman with so much colour in her cheeks an' such a sparkle in her eye, an' there was a look of pride an' defiance in her face that would make a man halt and think twice before takin' liberties with such a proud character. But Cutler, though mighty handsome, and bent on leadin' a life of independence far removed from his old home in Virginia, began to show traces of care an' dissipation. She looked as if she feared nothin' on earth; he looked worried at times, and eyed every stranger that came his way, fearin' to enter into conversation.

"Then one day they left for parts unknown. Her beauty had caused a regular sensation in that section, an' it set tongues a-waggin' 'bout who she could be. An' it must be said that there was somethin' in the looks, dress, an' bearin' o' Cutler that interested more'n one woman thereabouts, so that both attracted attention wherever they were seen.

"But Cutler was conscious of danger. He wanted to get where the settlers were few an' far between. On his second move he made for Indiana, but didn't stop long on that halt. He soon started on the third journey, farther west, an' only stopped when he got to the Wabash, thinkin' the place lonely enough to escape; but after stayin' here several years he got scared, an' suddenly pullin' up stakes, he hurried on with all speed to the rich an' wonderful Sangamon country, which, at that time, was a real paradise of meadow-prairie, woods an' wild flowers, where whole armies might hide in the tall grass in certain sections, an' all the robbers on the face of the earth could find both food an' shelter with the least trouble an' expense; for the land was full o' wild game, an' the groves an' thickets were like so many ready-made habitations. You see, in those days each settler that pulled up stakes over in Indiana to come out here in Illinois had to follow his nose."

"An' the whisky in them days did put a red light on some noses," remarked Socrates.

"It did so," continued the lawyer, "but Hank Cutler was too young to be affected that way. The settlers that came to these regions 'long about 1819 or '20 wandered on pretty much by instinct, an' I've known cases where they gave the lead to the horses an' let the reins dangle."

"A blind hoss or a yaller dog—anythin' that'll walk before a two-legged creetur," interrupted Socrates again.

"Wal, they just took a westerly direction an' let things slide, an' some of 'em struck it rich while others struck it poor by halting before they come to the right place. Now Cutler never halted till he struck it right. He had got clean away from civilisation. He was the very first pioneer in this section of the Sangamon country. In the covered wagon that moved slowly into the peaceful an' lonely haven of rest, much as a sailing boat would drift with a sluggish current, there came, besides Cutler an' his erring victim, two little children—one, a baby born in the wagon after they had set out from the valley o' the Wabash, the other born the year before. The child born in Cincinnati had died some time ago. It was now plainly visible that Vicky Stone's beauty was doomed. Her eyes were growing heavy, her complexion was fading, her whole face was taking on an expression of worry an' care. For her the beautiful rolling prairies an' the rich bottoms of the Illinois River was not a paradise but a valley o' shadows; and as for Cutler, he was sufferin' from hard drinking an' a scared, remorseful conscience—an' yet it ain't hardly likely that Cutler had feelin's enough for remorse. What he did feel was the presence near by of a batch o' squatters that come into the country a little after he got there, an' they had drove stakes not more'n two miles off.

"It was Cutler's habit to keep a good look-out after sunset, an' as he scarcely slept at night this come easy enough, but the life of excitement an' suspense, with every shadow turned into a phantom, was wearin' him out. He looked almost middle-aged now, an' his face showed lines of fatigue; his eyes had lost that look of darin' an' confidence that made him a favourite with the gals back East. He had got about as far as his tether would allow, an' he began to feel the pull in dead earnest. An' now, worse than all, no sooner had he got settled in the most secluded an' lovely spot he could find, in a place now called Cutler's Grove, an' not very far from this house neither, than a reg'lar wave of immigration set in from Kentucky an' Indiana. The newspapers of the cities on the Upper Ohio, an' of Saint Louis, began to give accounts of the rich lands of the Sangamon country, an' Cutler found himself once more surrounded by settlers, scattered here an' there, an' among them others, like himself, ready for any villainy.

"Cutler was on the point of moving once more, but this time his victim objected, saying she was worn out with anxiety an' the rough life he had led her.

"Down towards the river, about three miles away, some new arrivals from Missouri had opened a small store, where whisky was sold an' freely imbibed. It was kept by outlaws an' frequented by men like Hank Cutler; and Cutler himself made this place the headquarters for adventures an' expeditions of a daring an' desperate nature. He now left home for days together, an' Vicky Stone had little if any means o' findin' out where he was or what he was doing. Cutler was by nature more of a leader than the desperadoes who kept this store, an' that is why he naturally took the lead in most of the robberies committed thereabouts.

"Vicky Stone, left by herself for days an' nights, with only dogs an' two little children for companions, had plenty of time for sorrow an' weepin'; but it looked to me then, an' it looks to me now, as if Providence was kind of settin' of him up right in this new garden of Eden to tempt him in the right way, for there was no forbidden apples here in those days—"

"Speakin' o' apples," interrupted Socrates, with his round face all aglow, "speakin' o' apples, allers make me think of ole Ezry Sparr, thet use ter live down thar near Crow's Nest, jest afore ye come te the bend in the river. He hed a real cute way o' treatin' the parsons en circuit-riders thet come along thar. He had a small apple orchard; 'bout the fust orchard ever planted in these parts, I reckon, en his cider war sweet when the crop war good, but hard en stunnin' when apples war skase; en one season when thar warn't much of a crop te speak of along come Azariah James and preacher Dew a-hossback.

"They war a-makin' fer the Conference over te Mount Carmel, en bein' ez thirsty ez fishes out o' water they called fer all the cider they could drink, which war consid'able, the day bein' hot en the roads dusty. Old Ezry Sparr stepped round ez perlite ez could be, but 'peared like he war extry long in fetchin' the cider, en when it war sot on the table it war gone afore anyone hed time te tell whether it war hard, er whether it war saft, er whether it war calc'lated te put 'em in the weavin' way ez the sayin' is.

"Arter a while, preacher Dew sez: 'Wal, Brother James, what d'ye think o' thet thar cider?'

" 'Thet's jes' what I war a-goin' to ask you,' he sez; 'it beats all I ever see.'

" ' 'Tain't the seein' of it,' sez t'other, 'we didn't take no time; en besides, 'tain't allers wisdom te fumble 'bout the mouth of a gift hoss, seein' ez Ezry Sparr don't never charge preachers fer what they drink.'

" 'I 'low ye're right,' sez preacher James, 'but I reckon it's time te ride on; it takes a heap of ridin' to settle real hard cider.'

"Preacher Dew asked ole Sparr te p'int out the way te Crow's Nest, ez they war aimin' te reach the Conference afore nightfall.

" 'Straight on,' sez Sparr; 'but on yer way ye'll hev te pass through what the circuit-riders call the land o' Nod, en ye'll strike it over yander whar ye see thet p'int o' timber.'

" 'The land o' Nod?' sez Brother Dew. 'I ain't never heerd o' no sech a place in this section.'

" 'Very likely ye never did,' rej'ined ole Sparr; 'but I'll be bound ye'll know it when ye git thar.'

" 'Be thar a sign-post?'

" 'Thar ain't no need o' one. Jes' keep yer eye on this man,' he sez, puttin' his hand on preacher James's shoulder, en sorter smilin', 'he looks like he'll do fer a sign-post, at least ez fur ez ye'll go this time.'

"They rode off at a good canter, but they hedn't been out long afore preacher James sez: 'Looky here, Brother Dew, don't ye think we'd better walk our hosses? 'Pears like thet cider's workin' up, en it looks like it'll pop the cork if we keep on joggin' like this.'

" 'Wal,' sez t'other, 'I'm mighty anxious te reach that p'int o' timber en find out jes' what ole man Sparr did mean by the land o' Nod.'

"They rode on, en ez they come te the woods preacher Dew reined up, en lookin' at Azariah James he see him nod his head, then straighten up, en nod ag'in; then Brother Dew hollered out: 'I'll be hanged ef I ain't jes' seen the sign-post! Brother James, we'll git down right here en sleep off thet stunnin' liquor ole Sparr filled us up on.'

"They hitched up en slept in the woods all night, en when they got te the Conference preacher Dew took fer his tex': 'Tetch not, taste not, handle not, 'ceptin' when ye're dead sure o' yer apples.' "

A hearty laugh followed, after which the lawyer continued his story.

CHAPTER *14*

The Regulators

"WAL, as I was saying, Cutler was hard at work playing out his last deal. One fall he an' the three brothers who kept the whisky-store made it up between them to rob a store down where Springfield stands to-day. It had been opened by a man from Kentucky who had come up the river by way of Saint Louis, an' for that day an' time his goods were as tempting as anything could be, an' what he had appeared to most o' the settlers like a banquet o' good things, although it was only sugar, coffee, tobacco an' such like he kept.

"Cutler and his companions made a survey of the land, decided on a route, waited for a night when there was no moon, and then set out on the expedition of plunder. Two of the brothers rode horseback, while the third drove a fast team with Hank Cutler. After riskin' their lives they managed to slip away, having robbed the store of everything they could carry; but coming back home they lost their way in the dark an' had to pass by the house of a man who recognised them.

"Now, when the three brothers were arrested Cutler was not suspected. This gave him a chance to bluff the justice o' the peace and the whole community by passing himself off as a lawyer, which was easy, seeing that the justice o' the peace knew as much of the law as a sheep knows o' the ways o' panthers an' wolves. The stolen things were hid away in Cutler's Grove, but when the trial come on more'n one of us had cause to scratch our head an' wonder what would become of us. Ye see, Cutler had been to college in Virginia an' could spout enough Latin to make the justice o' the peace ashamed of his ignorance, an' so he sat there not knowin' what he was about or what proceedin's to take in the matter; and I don't reckon there ever was a game played like it in this country before nor since.

It was just like little children playin' at law. But Cutler had directed the three brothers just what to say an' how to act; an' when the examination took place everyone came who could get there. It was live or die for all of us in those days. If the robbers got clear the danger for all good citizens would be greater than ever. Excitement ran high, an' every man brought his rifle an' a dirk. The place was so crowded that I had to edge myself in as best I could till I got to where I could see the prisoners fair an' square. There must have been as many dogs in the crowd as there was people, an' the snapping an' snarling more than once drowned the mealy voice of the justice, who looked scared and fearsome. But the settlers kept their mouths shut, an' looked an' listened as they would had it been the Day of Judgment itself.

"The three brothers were brought in under guard, an' the examination commenced.

" 'Jim Ferris,' says the justice, 'I want to know if you can tell us where you were on the night that store was robbed.'

"He was addressing the oldest of the brothers, who stood with his hands in his pockets looking for all the world like a cross between a weasel an' a human devil.

" 'Where was I?' he answered, in a loud, piercing voice that made the poor justice flinch in his seat; 'where was I? Where folks that's worked hard all day feel like they want to be—in bed, asleep.'

" 'In your own house?'

" 'Where else d'ye reckon I'd be?'

" 'Joe Ferris,' he says, addressing the next brother, 'can ye tell this Court where ye were on the night o' the robbery?'

" 'With my brothers, at home in my own house.'

"The justice o' the peace looked like he was trembling in his boots, an' his voice was descendin' more an' more to a scared whisper. An' Cutler, seeing how the land lay, sprang forward about the time the third brother's turn came, an' lookin' the justice in the eye with one o' them mesmerising glances of his, he just toppled him over for good an' all by declaring offhand, an' with a mighty flourish of spunk, that he was with the brothers on that night till late, an' it would be more than human power for any man to leave home at midnight, go so far, an' get home again by morning.

"I was standing right where I could see most of the settlers' faces, an' I was watching to see just how they were taking the queer an' unheard-of proceedin's. There was old man Sawyer and his two big six-footer sons that had just moved up from Tennessee; his big, square face was like a bear trap that had closed up by havin' a chipmunk run over it, an' his mouth fixed so tight that it looked like a crowbar couldn't get between it. As for his eyes, they were for all the world just like the eyes of a chiny cat, fixed an' starin'; an' seein' him an' the others like Andy Scott and Jim Biswell just as set an' wonder-struck, I couldn't take my eyes off 'em.

"The justice, all flustered an' broke up by Cutler's bold looks and confident speech, up and says: 'The prisoners are now discharged!'

"Ye could have heard a butterfly come in the room! Old Sawyer's jaw dropped clean open, showin' his long teeth, an' his tongue was halfway out as if he was catchin' his breath like.

"At last the crowd began to move. One o' the Sawyer boys let his rifle fall plumb across the paws of a big dog layin' on the floor beside him. An awful howl went up, in which all the other dogs joined, an' 'twixt the dogs, the robbers, an' the honest settlers, it was confusion worse confounded.

"In the midst of the din Cutler an' the three Ferris brothers slipped off home.

"When the crowd was disappearing, three or four, like old man Sawyer an' Jim Biswell, set to work to confer about the best means for mutual protection. Sawyer proposed to form a society to rid the country of desperadoes, for there was a deep suspicion that Cutler was the ringleader, and the law, as it stood, was powerless.

"There was a small meetin' held, but nothing important was decided on. As time wore on Cutler seemed to be getting the advantage of the Ferris brothers in business matters, for he opened out a store that took the shine off all the others in that section, at the same time keepin' in with his ole friends, the Ferrises. Business was so good that Hank Cutler did nothing but store-trading an' selling, gettin' most all his goods direct from Saint Louis by boat, an' his store soon got to be the leading meetin'-place for idle an' suspicious characters.

"Now, it was noticed that Cutler spent considerable of his time visiting down by the river bottom, where it was rumoured that a man from the South had settled on bottom land. This

man was possessed of more money in cash than any of the other
settlers, for it seemed he had a large sum locked up an' stored
away; an' as there were no banks to put money in he was
obliged to hide it as best he could right on his diggin's.

"It wasn't long before Cutler was joined in his visits to this
man by two of the Ferris brothers. The aim was for Cutler to
have all the help he could get to carry out his plans for the
biggest robbery yet undertaken in the Sangamon country.

"During their visits to the bottom Cutler an' his companions
informed themselves of the new settler's intentions. They found
out that he would soon be making a journey to Saint Louis by
boat, an' that in his absence he would leave in his cabin valuables to a considerable extent.

"When Cutler found out all he wanted to know, and more, he
came home one day in hot haste an' prepared to sell out all he
possessed except his horses an' a few things he had to keep for
future use. The next day he made known the announcement of
the sale—his cabin, an' all the contents of his store was for sale,
except a stock of whiskey which he could not part with. Things
were going for a mere song, as they say, an' you can believe me,
his sudden selling out an' departure created a commotion among
the settlers, an' all sorts o' rumours. While the sale was proceeding Cutler was actin' mighty strange. He stayed at home nights,
he kept silent, an' grew more an' more gloomy an' sullen. Towards the last he was in such a hurry to sell out that he almost
gave things away, and for miles people hurried in to get the
unheard-of bargains that were going.

"The honest folks heaved a sigh of relief when they saw these
things, and looked forward to a time of peace after Cutler's
departure. When the day of departure arrived it was noticed that
two of the Ferris brothers went with him, an' this looked kind
o' queer, but Cutler laughed away suspicion as he so often did
before, and made like he was only going off on a pleasure excursion.

"He set out about noon on a beautiful day in the early
spring, and moving as fast as the horses would go he crossed the
Illinois River, an' coming to an abandoned cabin on MacKee's
creek towards the dusk of the evening, stopped there and fixed
to take up his residence as long as it suited his intentions an'
plans.

"Yes, sir, you better believe the long-sufferin' settlers back on the other side o' the river received this news with feelin's anything but gay an' feastive. Cutler hadn't moved more'n ten miles further west. It was noticed that the two Ferris boys didn't return, but stayed away, an' it was hoped they had lit out for good; but they were busy rehearsing their parts an' getting ready for a big haul.

"One night Cutler an' his two accomplices dressed themselves up as Indians, with faces painted red an' white, an' made for the bottom where the rich settler lived. The owner was away at Saint Louis, leaving his home in charge of his wife, his son, aged about eighteen, an' a young daughter. All of a sudden they were terrified by the visit of the robbers, who knew exactly where to look for the hidden valuables. There was no resistance offered. Cutler an' his companions took what they wanted, an' in five minutes decamped with the booty—a large sum of money, in fact all the rich settler possessed in cash.

"The very next day the news was brought to the settlement by a messenger on horseback. There was a hurried secret meeting. The greatest precaution was necessary in order to insure success, for the oldest Ferris was still at his store, and every movement of honest folks was watched, an' everything would be reported to Cutler an' the others.

"It took two or three days to get the notice of the meetin' circulated among those most interested. The messages had to be sent to an' fro by stealth in roundabout ways, and finally the meetin'-place was fixed at Jim Biswell's cabin, it being surrounded mostly by hazel bushes, with two roads leading to the back hid by a thick growth o' tall saplings.

"The appointment was for the early morning, as it was thought that Jim Ferris an' his spies would not be likely to be on the look-out at that time, an' when all had arrived the meetin' was called to order by ole man Sawyer, who up an' says: 'Friends, I reckon ye all know what we are here for. Ye've heard the news of the last robbery.'

" 'Yes, yes, we all know, an' we want to act,' cried several voices.

" 'Then let's proceed to business,' said the first speaker. 'I propose friend Biswell here to occupy the chair durin' the proceedin's.'

"Jim Biswell, being chosen, made them a speech.

" 'Ye all know,' he said, 'what the Rangers were during the

time of the Indian wars an' depredations, an' that they were
formed for the purpose o' clearin' the Western countries of wandering bands of evil-doers. But the days o' the Rangers is past,
an' now the time is ripe for something to take the place o' those
organised fighters on horseback. The time has come for each
settlement to stand on its own legs. Friends, ye've seen how the
justice let off the Ferris gang, an' how the law, as such, works
out to favour the men with the greatest cunning an' the most
reckless daring. Now, we ain't got no mounted Rangers to give
us good law an' good deeds, an' I propose right here to fit out a
company of Regulators to do our work an' rid this settlement
an' the neighbourhood of all robbers an' desperadoes, an' that in
the quickest time possible.'

" 'Ye're right,' said ole man Sawyer, 'for the next thing we'll
know murder will take the place o' robbery.'

" 'An' we might far better be murdered,' said Jim Biswell,
'than to have all the money we possess taken from us, an' nothin' left to start work on.'

" 'Ye're right,' spoke up several voices.

"Up to this time Andy Scott had been sitting there as still an'
unpretendin' as you please, an' there was nothing about his
looks to attract much notice, except he had but one eye, an' the
other was kind o' droopin' an' heavy, which gave him the ap-
peaance of a man who had seen considerable service an' was
now set in his mind on taking things just as easy as the law
would allow, an' a little easier than the Cutler gang were disposed to permit at that particular time. Wal, Andy Scott took
the corn-cob pipe out of his mouth, spat on the floor, squared
up, an' says: 'I've been a Ranger myself, an' fit Indians an'
chased robbers all over Indianny an' Kentucky, an' I b'lieve I'm
good for any fightin' these here diggin's can scare up, without
wantin' to brag. I'm willin' to follow, or I'm willin' to lead; I
don't care a shuck which it is—I'm ready. All I want to see is
this here settlement cleared o' varmints like Cutler an' Ferris, an'
the quicker the better.'

"You better believe one-eyed Scott began to look like a leader, an' Jim Biswell put the question: 'What do you reckon is the
best way to go about dealin' with this band?'

" 'Give 'em all the rope they're after,' he says. 'I propose to
form a company o' volunteers right here an' now, to regulate

matters an' carry out the law accordin' to the wishes of all honest folks in this section.'

"The majority of voices were in favour of Andy Scott's proposition, and the chairman proceeded to ask for volunteers. The two Sawyer boys, Jim Biswell, Andy Scott, his sixteen-year-old son, myself, an' six others put down their names as willing to take immediate action, and the meetin' next set to work to elect a leader. And this was not so easy.

"There was at the meetin' a man they called Major, who had been one of the most outspoken against the Cutler band. Someone proposed Andy Scott as captain; but Scott, fearing to take precedence of a man who had been an officer in the war, named the Major, an' this proposition was carried; a committee was formed to arrange an' organise. The volunteers bound themselves by oath to carry out a stated an' determined line of action to rid the country of all evil-doers. A paper was signed by the chairman, the committee, and all the volunteers.

"There was another secret meeting; some doubted the Major's capacity to lead in such an undertaking because he was known to be a man considerably given to talk. Finally things come to a head by an arrangement for all to meet at sundown the next day in a dense thicket near the cross-roads, and from there make straight for the other side o' the river to Cutler's house on the creek. We arrived at the meetin'-place in good time, but found no Major. We waited, an' still our appointed captain failed to appear. We waited for more'n an hour, but the fact was the brave Major was at home having supper with his wife, but pretending to be too sick to come to the meetin'-place. The Major was scared, an' soon after he pulled up stakes an' left for parts unknown, bein' ashamed to face the people. Wal, no one could tell just what to do next. All the volunteers were willing an' ready to move on an' face the desperadoes, come what may, but there was no captain. While we were talking matters over one o' the Sawyer boys said he saw something movin' in the woods to the left; we raised our rifles and stood waiting, but nothing more was seen or heard of a suspicious nature, an' we all laid it to young Sawyer's imagination an' proceeded to settle who should be our leader. Andy Scott was chosen. But Scott was not a boaster, nor a man who wanted to lead in anything. He was an up-an'-down fighter, an' brave as a lion, but only wanted to follow a good captain, an' most o' the volunteers were young an' inexperienced men. It begin to look as if the expedition to the robbers' roost must be abandoned for want of a leader, when out jumped a man from the bushes and cried out: 'Hold, friends! I've heard all you've said. I understand you want a leader. I too have been robbed by the villain you're looking for. I want to be your captain an' assume all responsibility in this proceeding if you'll let me have that honour an' satisfaction.'

"Andy Scott then spoke up, an' says: 'I believe you're the man I see down by the Ohio not more'n six months ago, an' you went by the name of the Wild Hunter?'

" 'Yes,' chimed in Jim Biswell, 'I've heard o' you more'n once, an' it 'pears like I recognise you from the description they give o' your dress, your cap in particular, which seems to be made o' panther skin.'

"He had a half-wild expression that made some of us stand back somewhat, not knowin' into what scrapes he might take us; but his body was as nimble as a deer, an' his whole appearance was calculated to win over our confidence in the long run. He had on a buckskin hunting shirt, deerskin leggin's, an' moccasins on his feet. His step was as lithe as a panther's, an' it was no wonder he come so near us without makin' his presence actually known. He carried a long knife, an' his rifle was one of the finest anywhere to be seen. He stood eyeing our company as cool as a cucumber, with his hands folded across the muzzle of his gun.

" 'You're right, friends,' he says. 'I've been in the southern part of this country and I've been called by some the Wild Hunter, but I don't intend to settle for long in this section. I want to find out where Cutler is, an' I don't care much who goes with me. If I knew how to get there I'd start alone. I must an' will find him. I've been hunting him long enough. A rude fate directed me to this spot just at this eventful time.

" 'You see,' he continued, looking at every one of us as if he could see plumb through us, 'I've been to Cutler's store, but I was three days too late. He had sold out an' left, an' I was now looking for some signs whereby I might reach him, as they told me he had halted about ten miles off.'

" 'Are you intendin' to settle hereabouts?' asked Andy Scott.

" 'My business is with Cutler, and not with anyone in the settlement nor with any interests in this section o' the country, but if you'll take me for your captain we'll be off without delay.'

"There was some talk as to the risks of accepting a stranger, but at last Andy Scott up an' says: 'Looky here, boys, I ain't afeared to follow no man, an' I reckon this here company's got as much spunk as I have. This stranger looks to me dead on the square. There ain't nothin' in names, but I'd like to ask the stranger his name just to have something to call him by.'

" 'Wal,' says the hunter, with a desperate look, 'since ye seem willing to call me your leader, you can allude to me as Captain Stone. I've been nine years in search of Hank Cutler!'

"It was now dark, an' we had miles of trackless wilderness to wander through. When we came to a clearing we made rapid progress, but when we came to water an' thick woods we got lost more'n once.

"Stone stepped along as light as a young buck. We talked in whispers. There seemed to be some guidin' power assisting Stone to sense out the way straight an' clear in spite of almost insurmountable obstacles. He took us knee-deep through water, he tore through underbrush an' thicket, he almost ran in places where it was level an' the ground clear. But when it came to the river we halted. It began to look as if we could never get across, and we lost precious time in making several unsuccessful attempts at crossing. It seemed just like a dream when we found ourselves on the other side making dead-sure tracks for MacKee's creek, which we struck about half-past eleven. Here we took a turn, an' going straight north for about half an hour all at once we come dead in sight o' Cutler's cabin. There it stood in the clearing, as lonely an' as solemn as a horned owl on a forsaken barn door. An' it was midnight at that! I can tell ye it gave me shivers down my back when I saw it. I've been all over this country as far as settlers have got, an' I've seen as much as most, but I hadn't ever seen or felt anything to equal the looks o' that cabin standing there in the clearing. It was unearthly. There was just light enough to see some things pretty plain, though the moon was droppin' below the trees behind the cabin, an' after movin' a little closer Andy Scott allowed he could make out there was smoke coming from the chimney.

" 'But they're asleep,' says Jim Biswell; 'there ain't no light in the house.'

" 'It don't make no difference,' he replied; 'light or no light we've got to go slow, for I'm dead certain they ain't more'n had time to go to bed.'

"Scarcely had he uttered the words, when the door opened and a blazing light streamed out as far as the wood line. A little more and the light would have struck us where we stood, but, as luck would have it, we were standing right where we could see clear across the room, from the open door plumb to the chimney-place. In another second we could see someone moving about. Then we could see two; and just as we were beginnin' to wonder how many there were inside, the whole band became visible walkin' about.

" 'Whoop-ee!' whispered Biswell, 'they're all there.'

"We stood an' counted 'em—Cutler, Jim Ferris, and his two brothers. They were going an' coming from the fireplace, burning up papers an' other stuff that they took from the last house they robbed. They were destroying the evidence.

" 'Let's make for 'em!'

"Andy Scott spoke so loud, it seemed like the robbers must hear him an' get a start on us.

"Captain Stone waved his hand.

" 'Wait an' watch here,' he said, 'till I go forward a little closer.'

"Another big blaze rose up in the chimney; we could plainly see the men sorting, counting, an' dividing piles of coin. A table stood at one side, an' on it was a whisky-bottle. When the counting an' dividing was over, Cutler poured out for all to drink, an' we could hear the words:

" 'Fill up, boys, we can all afford it after the last haul!'

"Captain Stone had now got within a few yards of the cabin. Yes, sir, we were all mighty excited. We could scarcely keep from making a dash for that open door; and it seemed like Stone was listening a long time to hear just what was bein' said, but he was only gone a few minutes. When he returned he gave us orders to follow close at his heels an' wait for the word of command, whatever that might be, an' we all set to wonderin' just what his intentions were as to the capturin' o' Cutler. It was clear he didn't want us to run up an' shoot now that we had got to the place an' had a dead spot on every member o' the band. Stone had worked out what to do. That man could see ahead; he knew exactly how things would turn up; an' he was the least excited of us all.

" 'Follow me, comrades,' he said in a whisper, and we crept up till we were close enough to hear every word spoken in the cabin.

"Cutler an' his gang were finishing off the last of the whisky. Cutler said: 'It's time to get some sleep; we've got to be away from here by sunrise, for we've got the biggest ride before us we ever done. We've got to get clean away till we get into the Indian country, north-west o' here.'

"But Jim Ferris opened another bottle o' whisky an' set it on the table an' began to pour out, an' with that they all set round the fire with their feet sprawled before 'em as careless an' shiftless as ye ever see.

"Stone was now right before the door. He was waiting for Cutler to stand up. The very minute he did so the captain, with eyes like a wild cat, made one bound inside.

" 'Stand there till I kill ye!' he hollered out, his voice hoarse with nine years of pent-up fury.

"Cutler stood like he was petrified. He was gapin' at Stone with a ghastly look when Stone sent a bullet through his heart. He fell in a dead heap. We made a rush for the Ferris gang, who were so taken aback an' filled with liquor that no resistance was made. An awful scream came from above, an' down rushed Vicky Stone.

"Lord a' mercy! I can see her now, with her hair all loose, an' her eyes wild with despair, a-bendin' over the body an' makin' out to listen for signs o' life, an' shoutin': 'Is he dead, is he dead? Have you killed him?'

"Stone stood a moment gazing at the haggard features of the once beautiful Vicky Roberts, then pulled her away from the body, an' getting her over where the light shone plumb in his face he jerked off his big panther cap, an' lookin' at her, asked: 'Have you ever seen me before?'

"A terrible scream was all the answer she gave, and the unhappy woman fell in a swoon on the floor.

" 'It is enough!' he said. 'I reckon judgment has been delivered as far as we have got'; and with that he fixed to leave the cabin and was soon lost in the darkness.

"We buried Cutler in the woods, and this was the first grave of a white man in these parts. We warned the Ferris brothers to quit this section, giving them ten days to clear out, but at the end of that time we went with Andy Scott as captain of the

Regulators to Cutler's Grove an' found the brothers still there. They defied us. We burned the cabin, bound the three desperadoes, took 'em to the river several hours distant, made a rough raft o' water logs, forced the brothers on to it an' then pushed it out to float down stream with nothing but the clothes on their backs. We told them to return meant certain death.

"Vicky Stone made her way back to Virginia, where I have always heard it said that Stone came to see her once a year regular an' never stayed more'n about ten minutes.

"On his twelfth yearly visit he saw her die; but no one ever knew what passed between them in that last solemn hour.

"Jack Stone followed her to the grave, and after the burial took his gun and walked away, and was never again seen or heard of.

"An' now, sir," our visitor concluded, "you have heard the story of how the first company of Regulators came to be formed, an' who it was that filled the first grave in these Western wilds."

CHAPTER 15

Alton and the Mississippi

MY FIRST good view of the Mississippi was from the bluffs behind the city of Alton.

The prairie we had left was full of birds, insects, flowers, and animals, but now from the great river and the scenery all about there issued forth something suggestive of silence and destiny. In the west rosy clouds floated like scattered wings in an emerald sky, while on the Missouri side a virgin forest shone in all the russet and gold of a Western autumn. There was something bewildering in the never-ending flow of the silent waters from unknown sources in remote Minnesota to the far-away shores of the Gulf of Mexico, primitive, savage, majestic in its loneliness, laving banks of islands fringed with the long tresses of willow and wild grape, through what seemed to me a country of perpetual adventure and romantic change. With its noiseless, stealthy current, and in harmony with all the surroundings, there came over the mind a newly awakened sadness like that produced by vague, faint music arriving in the night.

It was much the same with the prairie, with the difference that, while the wind moved the tall grass in wave-like undulations, here a vast space of water was moving in a flat, compact body without waves, in one fixed and endless direction, and all the hopes, fears, and affections of the world could vanish in this current towards the gulf of oblivion and leave not a memento behind. It was the place where philosophers might sit and ponder on the mystery of time and eternity.

Down a few miles below, to the south, just above the mouth of the Missouri, there was an island covered with foliage, situated in mid-stream, which to me was a place full of mysterious charm. I used to sit gazing in that direction, trying to imagine how things looked in the wonderful meeting-place of the two

161

great rivers. From the bluffs back of the town I could see for miles, but my favourite place to sit was just above our house, on the outskirts, looking south, with nothing to mar the wild, primitive charm of river and wood, for in this spot the town itself was invisible. There were days when I sat for hours on this bluff; the supreme moments came with the passing of boats, such as the *War Eagle*, the *City of Louisiana*, or the *Post Boy*, down the Mississippi in full mid-stream. The *War Eagle* was a side-wheeler plying between St. Louis and Keokuk, the *Post Boy* was a stern-wheeler plying between St. Louis, Alton, and towns on the Illinois River. When a boat made the return journey down stream it put the last touch of enchantment to the face of the waters. It filled me with visions of distant worlds as it skimmed the smooth surface, the smoke from the chimneys leaving a long, scattered trail, the white steam puffing out of the 'scape-pipes in rhythmic movement, the paddle-wheels throwing out thick showers as the beautiful apparition sped like a dream southward. Around it gathered all the illusions natural to ignorance and inexperience. It departed down the river like some vision floating away on the stream of adventure into regions to me unknown and unheard-of. Other boats came and went, each with a wild, inarticulate charm, but when I heard the long, low sonorous whistle of some new and strange arrival the effect was such that I went about in a sort of ecstasy and my mouth was sealed for the rest of that day.

These boat whistles were musical and suggestive beyond anything I have ever heard since; they gave to the river region something poetic and mystical; they were the voices that broke the silence and haunted the shores of the great valley, and the effect of these sounds while the boat loomed slowly up the Mississippi in the deepening dusk gave me a *frisson* of the supernatural. Out of what curious world was the boat now emerging? From what land of adventure had it found its way thus far? On the nights when I saw the fitful lights far down the black gulf and heard the thrilling sounds of whistle and puffing engines, sleep was a thing not to be thought of, and I lay awake thinking and wondering.

About two miles from the town there was a place where boys used to band together to "go in swimming," and in this spot I took my first swimming lesson. One day I swam a little too far from the bank and found it hard work to escape from the powerful Mississippi current. Here at this particular spot there was a delicious shaded creek where we fished for perch and bass, and farther on, in the woods, we went in search of paw-paw trees and came across flying squirrels, strange birds, and huge flocks of wild pigeons. These were the woods of enchantment, by the borders of the Father of Waters, in the soft, warm autumn days when health and unadulterated joy made life worth living.

Rafts and drift logs were other things that added romance to the Mississippi, the raft especially, it being an object that floated without emitting any sound. It looked frail and phantomesque, in keeping with the strange shores and virgin forests, the people handling it giving the impression of men arriving from some shipwreck on distant seas.

Alton gave me hundreds of new sensations, but the town itself did not interest me so much as the boats at landing-time, the heaving of the big gang-plank by bands of black, burly negroes, the fearful oaths of the semi-savage mates of the genus slave-driver, beings of a class apart, whole continents of civilisation separating them and *us*, the bustle and hurry of passengers coming off or going on, the timid, languorous air of some of the country people with heavy carpet-bags, the sharp, keen faces of old-timers and professional gamblers, the interminable line of negro boat-hands, coming and going like great black bumble-bees from a floating hive which emitted steam and smelt of tar and spices, the profoundly suggestive air of cosmopolitanism whiffed out from the deck in bales of cotton, barrels of sugar, rum, molasses, tobacco, and sacks of grain that made the stoutest negroes stagger like drunken men, a fresh volley of curses smiting them when they appeared about to fall—all this filled me with amazement. I held my breath the first time I heard the mate hurl volley after volley of oaths at the perspiring negroes, hustling helter-skelter to get the work done within a given time. I saw the black man actually at work. Hundreds of times, then and later, on the levee at St. Louis, I stood and watched these black deck-hands, and singling out someone weaker than the others I wondered how he would manage to carry his load up or down the gang-plank.

One day a group of idle negroes were standing watching the departure of the *War Eagle*, when I overheard some observations touching the profession of a Mississippi mate.

"Don' you set dar en talk te me 'bout dat *War Eagle* mate bein' 'tickler," said the oldest of the negroes. "You's too young yit; wait till you git on one o' dem boats w'at goes furder down de ribber en den you likely see summin w'at make you 'member dar's a debble w'at hold a mo'gage on po' weak niggers. If you 'low dis mate am full o' p'izen don' you nebber go 'way fr'm heah; if yo' shanks am ekil te ca'yin' a load up dat gang-plank 'thout stoppin' de bref in yo' wind-pipe den I say keep on right whar you is. Talk te me 'bout cussin'! You ain't nebber heared none yit! Dat mate down on de *Belle o' Memphis* he fling a tail o' brimstone behin' dem niggers w'at fill de air wid blue sparks, dat he do, en one o' de hands he fin' it so hot on de gang-plank he toppled ober in de ribber te cool hisself off; yes, sah, he toppled ober jes' te 'scape de red-hot cussin' o' dat mate. Nudder time one o' de hands he 'low he gettin' de rumatiz in his shoulder-blade, en 'low he 'bliged te stop ca'yin' barrels en passels on his back, but fust thing he know he fin' hisself comin 'up de gang-plank on de *Belle o' Memphis* mos' doubled up under one o' dem big loads, en he 'gin to puff en blow, en right dar de mate he broke loose en he 'gin te let off steam, en he cussed dat tremblin' nigger till de rumatiz fin' it 'greeable te change fr'm de upper story te de heels, en dat ole nigger don' nebber feel it no mo' in de shouldah-j'ints. Yes, sah, you heah me!"

The buildings and stores of Alton and the general aspect of the whole place impressed me with a sense of age. There was about it something mature, settled, old-fashioned; but I discovered many years later that all the river towns were dreamy and sleepy except those in the far north.

Here I went to the public school, but I cannot remember having learnt a single thing worth knowing except perhaps Longfellow's "Psalm of Life," which the whole school, boys and girls, repeated in chorus every morning at the opening. This was a "Yankee" school, the principal, Mrs. Lee, and the class-room teacher, Mrs. Crane, being from New England. One old saw out of the geography I remember to this day: when Mrs. Lee put the question to the brightest girl in the school, "What did the Mexican soldiers do when they first heard the sound of the American cannons?" she gave her golden curls a shake and bawled out the answer, "They thought it was thunder and lightning and fled from them."

Her name was Rosa Coffin; and the name, her fearless manner, her smartness, and the Mexican War, all combined to stamp this little incident on my memory.

Going to this school must have been part of the great subconscious scheme of romance in my life; it had to be. It was a pleasant waste of time. What I enjoyed most about it was the sight of hundreds of swallows or martins inhabiting holes in the banks of the new street cut through the hill over which I had to pass before I could reach the school-house. This was to me a never-ending charm.

In Alton my parents were communicants at Christ Church Episcopal. The service was to me very curious and solemn, the severe face of the bearded rector, Dr. MacMasters, exactly fitting the rough stone walls of the church and the dim sepulchral atmosphere of the edifice within. My parents sometimes went to hear Dr. Taylor preach at the Presbyterian Church, and here I heard a new set of hymns, but to my thinking—and I think so still—they lacked the sentiment, originality, and simplicity of the old Methodist hymns of the prairie. The fact is, this Alton and everything in it was a chip off the old block of New England and European conventions. Looking back at it now, I cannot see any difference between it and Boston or London, excepting in size and geographical situation.

We were living in a large old house on the southern outskirts which had once been occupied by nuns who had a private school there. It faced the great high-road leading out into the prairies, and we could see from the windows the wagons and buggies arriving from the country far beyond. This residence was the halfway house between the Log-House and the one we were to occupy in St. Louis; and it was for me well that it was so, for in this way the change from the open prairie to the cosmopolitan metropolis of Missouri was made gradually.

One day our attention was attracted to the number of people coming down the hill in wagons and on horseback, and while watching them two figures that looked familiar approached, jogging along on steeds that looked tired. The men had about them something odd, almost fantastic. As they passed the house we recognised Azariah James and Elihu Gest. In less than half an hour along came Isaac Snedeker, then other familiar faces. But what did it mean? All the old outspoken Abolitionists from up-country, with some of the Pro-Slavery people, were filing past. When my father was asked what was the matter, he only said: "To-morrow is the great day!"

CHAPTER 16

Abraham Lincoln

IT WAS the 15th day of October, 1858. Crowds were pouring into Alton. For some days people had been arriving by the steam-packets from up and down the river, the up-boats from St. Louis bringing visitors with long, black hair, goatees, and stolid, Indian-like faces, slave-owners, and slave-dealers, from the human marts of Missouri and Kentucky; the northern visitors arriving by boat or rail, Abolitionists and Republicans, with a cast of features distinctly different from the types coming from the south.

They came from villages, townships, the prairies, from all the adjoining counties, from across the Mississippi, from far-away cities, from representative societies North and South, from congressional committees in the East, from leading journals of all political parties, and from every religious denomination within hundreds of miles, filling the broad space in front of the Town Hall, eager to see and hear the now famous debaters—the popular Stephen A. Douglas, United States Senator, nicknamed the "Little Giant," and plain Abraham Lincoln, nicknamed the "Rail-Splitter."

The great debate had begun on the 21st of August at another town, and to-day the long-discussed subject would be brought to a close. Douglas stood for the doctrine that slavery was nationalised by the Constitution, that Congress had no authority to prevent its introduction in the new Territories like Kansas and Nebraska, and that the people of each State could alone decide whether they should be slave States or free. Lincoln opposed the introduction of slavery into the new Territories.

On this memorable day the "irrepressible conflict" predicted by Seward actually began, and it was bruited about that Lincoln would be mobbed or assassinated if he repeated here the words he used in some of his speeches delivered in the northern part of the State. From the surging sea of faces thousands of anxious eyes gazed upward at the group of politicians on the balcony like wrecked mariners scanning the horizon for the smallest sign of a white sail of hope.

This final debate resembled a duel between two men-of-war, the pick of a great fleet, all but these two sunk or abandoned in other waters, facing each other in the open, the Little Giant hurling at his opponent, from his flagship of slavery, the deadliest missiles, Lincoln calmly waiting to sink his antagonist by one simple broadsider. Alton had seen nothing so exciting since the assassination of Lovejoy, the fearless Abolitionist, many years before.

In the earlier discussions Douglas seemed to have the advantage. A past-master in tact and audacity, skilled in the art of rhetorical skirmishing, he had no equal on the "stump," while in the Senate he was feared by the most brilliant debaters for his ready wit and his dashing eloquence.

Regarded in the light of historical experience, reasoned about in the light of spiritual reality, and from the point of view that nothing can happen by chance, it seems as if Lincoln and Douglas were predestined to meet side by side in this discussion, and unless I dwell in detail on the mental and physical contrast the speakers presented it would be impossible to give an adequate idea of the startling difference in the two temperaments: Douglas—short, plump, and petulant; Lincoln—long, gaunt, and self-possessed; the one white-haired and florid, the other black-haired and swarthy; the one educated and polished, the other unlettered and primitive. Douglas had the assurance of a man of authority, Lincoln had moments of deep mental depression, often bordering on melancholy, yet controlled by a fixed, and, I may say, predestined will, for it can no longer be doubted that without the marvellous blend of humour and stolid patience so conspicuous in his character, Lincoln's genius would have turned to madness after the defeat of the Northern Army at Bull-Run, and the world would have had something like a repetition of Napoleon's fate after the burning of Moscow. Lincoln's humour was the balance-pole of his genius that enabled him to cross the most giddy heights without losing his head. Judge Douglas opened the debate in a sonorous voice plainly heard throughout the assembly, and with a look of mingled defiance and confidence he marshalled his facts and deduced his arguments. To the vigour of his attack there was added the prestige of the Senate Chamber, and for some moments it looked as if he would carry the majority with him, a large portion of the crowd being Pro-Slavery men, while many others were "on the fence" waiting to be persuaded.

At last, after a great oratorical effort, he brought his speech to a close amidst the shouts and yells of thousands of admirers.

And now Abraham Lincoln, the man who, in 1830, undertook to split for Mrs. Nancy Miller four hundred rails for every yard of brown jean dyed with walnut bark that would be required to make him a pair of trousers, the flatboatman, local stump-speaker and country lawyer, rose from his seat, stretched his long, bony limbs upward as if to get them into working order, and stood like some solitary pine on a lonely summit, very tall, very dark, very gaunt, and very rugged, his swarthy features stamped with a sad serenity, and the instant he began to speak the ungainly mouth lost its heaviness, the half-listless eyes attained a wondrous power, and the people stood bewildered and breathless under the natural magic of the strangest, most original personality known to the English-speaking world since Robert Burns. There were other very tall and dark men in the heterogeneous assembly, but not one who resembled the speaker. Every movement of his long, muscular frame denoted inflexible earnestness, and a something issued forth, elemental and mystical, that told what the man had been, what he was, and what he would do in the future. There were moments when he seemed all legs and feet, and again he appeared all head and neck; yet every look of the deep-set eyes, every movement of the prominent jaw, every wave of the hard-gripping hand, produced an impression, and before he had spoken twenty minutes the conviction took possession of thousands that here was the prophetic man of the present and the political saviour of the future. Judges of human nature saw at a glance that a man so ungainly, so natural, so earnest, and so forcible, had no place in his mental economy for the thing called vanity.

Douglas had been theatrical and scholarly, but this tall, homely man was creating by his very looks what the brilliant lawyer and experienced Senator had failed to make people see and feel. The Little Giant had assumed striking attitudes, played tricks with his flowing white hair, mimicking the airs of authority, with patronising allusions; but these affectations, usually so effective when he addressed an audience alone, went for nothing when brought face to face with realities. Lincoln had no genius for gesture and no desire to produce a sensation. The failure of Senator Douglas to bring conviction to critical minds was caused by three things: a lack of logical sequence in argument, a lack of intuitional judgment, and a vanity that was caused by too much intellect and too little heart. Douglas had been arrogant and vehement, Lincoln was now logical and penetrating. The Little Giant was a living picture of ostentatious vanity; from every feature of Lincoln's face there radiated the calm, inherent strength that always accompanies power. He relied on no props. With a pride sufficient to protect his mind and a will sufficient to defend his body, he drank water when Douglas, with all his wit and rhetoric, could begin or end nothing without stimulants. Here, then, was one man out of all the millions who believed in himself, who did not consult with others about what to say, who never for a moment respected the opinion of men who preached a lie. My old friend, Don Piatt, in his personal impressions of Lincoln, whom he knew well and greatly esteemed, declares him to be the homeliest man he ever saw; but serene confidence and self-poise can never be ugly. What thrilled the people who stood before Abraham Lincoln on that day was the sight of a being who, in all his actions and habits, resembled themselves, gentle as he was strong, fearless as he was honest, who towered above them all in that psychic radiance that penetrates in some mysterious way every fibre of the hearer's consciousness.

The enthusiasm created by Douglas was wrought out of smart epigram thrusts and a facile, superficial eloquence. He was a match for the politicians born within the confines of his own intellectual circle: witty, brilliant, cunning, and shallow, his weight in the political balance was purely materialistic; his scales of justice tipped to the side of cotton, slavery, and popular passions, while the man who faced him now brought to the assembly cold logic in place of wit, frankness in place of cunning, reasoned will and judgment in place of chicanery and sophistry. Lincoln's presence infused into the mixed and uncertain throng something spiritual and supernormal. His looks, his words, his voice, his attitude, were like a magical essence dropped into the seething cauldron of politics, reacting against the foam, calming the surface and letting the people see to the bottom. It did not take him long.

"Is it not a false statesmanship," he asked, "that undertakes to build up a system of policy upon the basis of caring nothing about the very thing that everybody does care the most about? Judge Douglas may say he cares not whether slavery is voted up or down, but he must have a choice between a right thing and a wrong thing. He contends that whatever community wants slaves has a right to have them. So they have, if it is not a wrong; but if it is a wrong he cannot say people have a right to do wrong. He says that upon the score of equality slaves should be allowed to go into a new Territory like other property. This is strictly logical if there is no difference between it and other property. If it and other property are equal his argument is entirely logical; but if you insist that one is wrong and the other right there is no use to institute a comparison between right and wrong."

This was the broadsider. The great duel on the high seas of politics was over. The Douglas ship of State Sovereignty was sinking. The debate was a triumph that would send Lincoln to Washington as President in a little more than two years from that date.

People were fascinated by the gaunt figure in long, loose garments, that seemed like a "huge skeleton in clothes," attracted by the homely face, and mystified, yet proud of the fact that a simple denizen of their own soil should wield so much power.

When Lincoln sat down Douglas made one last feeble attempt at an answer; but Lincoln, in reply to a spectator who manifested some apprehension as to the outcome, rose, and spreading out his great arms at full length, like a condor about to take wind, exclaimed, with humorous indifference: "Oh! let him go it!" These were the last words he uttered in the greatest debate of the *ante-bellum* days.

The victor bundled up his papers and withdrew, the assembly shouting: "Hurrah for Abe Lincoln as next President!" "Bully for old Abe!" "Lincoln for ever!" etc., etc. Excited crowds followed him about, reporters caught his slightest word, and by night time the bar-rooms, hotels, street corners, and prominent stores were filled with his admirers, fairly intoxicated with the exciting triumph of the day.

CHAPTER *17*

St. Louis: Society and the Churches

IN THE late autumn of 1859 we were settled in St. Louis, and for me, at least, the real stress and movement of life began.

Alton, as I said before, was the halfway house between the open prairie and the cosmopolitan city on the Mississippi, the great Emporium of the West, as it was called at that time. The weather was cold and gloomy, the air full of smoke, the houses old and dingy; there was not the faintest suggestion of anything bright or cheerful.

St. Louis looked old, perhaps, because its spirit was old; its character was fixed, like that of a person long used to fixed modes and habits, conventional and contented. There was no hurry and bustling. Things had always progressed slowly because of the atmosphere of Southern lethargy and luxury, the ease and nonchalance in which so many of the ruling classes of St. Louis had been born and bred. Without slavery the city would have worn a very different aspect.

Society in St. Louis was the outcome of two things: the institution of slavery, and the fact that the majority of the leading citizens were church-going Episcopalians; yet it required all sorts and conditions of people to compose a cosmopolitan city, and St. Louis had them—thousands of free-thinking Germans opposed to thousands of German Catholics; thousands of Irish, almost to a man faithful Catholics; the descendants of old French families from Louisiana, mostly Catholics; Scotch and American Presbyterians, Unitarians, Congregationalists, but not many Methodists.

In the commercial world the Yankees ruled; but the old, slow, languid, proud, hospitable founders of St. Louis, and its social leaders, were the owners of slaves, and they formed the majority of the members of the Episcopal Church.

171

In St. Louis this church was at the head of fashion and social exclusiveness, and the code of honour was that of Virginia, Maryland, Kentucky, and the Far South. The Europeans who emigrated to America at that time could not grasp the facts in relation to this proud, aristocratic class. It was slavery that came as a barrier. People from the Eastern States, as well as people from Europe, had white servants; the old St. Louisians were never served by white people. Yet all went well in society as a whole. The Germans lived apart, principally in the northern and southern portions of the city; the French kept to their old customs and traditions; the Irish, as a class, lived apart, and in case of illness they would send for a doctor who was an Irishman.

My parents became communicants of Trinity Episcopal Church in Washington Avenue. The different churches in St. Louis were to me like different people. I studied them as I would a rare flower or a curious picture. Our Sundays were portioned off as follows: At nine in the morning I went with my eldest sister to Sunday-school at Trinity, where she had a class of very young people, and where I sat under Henry Simmons, a young man who, later, became a wealthy and influential citizen, and who, for all I know, may still be living. As soon as Sunday-school was over the church began to fill for the morning service. At one o'clock we went home for a cold luncheon, my mother permitting no cooking to be done on Sunday, after which I started again with my sister to attend an afternoon school at Dr. Anderson's Presbyterian Church, on Sixth and Locust Streets. My sister taught another class here, and no sooner was this school over than we hurried away to the southwestern part of the town for another Sunday-school at a Presbyterian Church where Mr. Wood was the leader.

We had only time to return to the house for another cold meal, when again we set out for Trinity Church, my parents always attending both morning and evening services to hear Dr. Hutchinson preach in his simple way, without a gesture, without an idea, without the faintest suggestion of any deep emotion or reviving influence. The old order might have gone on till the present for all that this good man's sermons did to change anyone or anything. As I remember it, the congregation here was typically exclusive and conventional; ceremonious to the point of bowing with extreme deference and courtly politeness when a lady was being ushered to a seat in the softly-cushioned pews, the congregation rising and sitting down like a company of well-drilled soldiers, no one turning to look about, no sensational incident ever occurring to mar the unity of the whole.

Three persons in this congregation stand out clearly defined to my vision, even at this distance: there was a young man named William H. Thomson, the head of Trinity Sunday-school, who, elegant in his dress, manner, and figure, used to bow his beautiful wife into her pew as if she were a royal princess attending some formal Court function; there was a distinguished citizen named D. A. January, tall, stiff-necked, with an eagle eye and a powerful head, he, too, conducting a beautiful wife to her pew with a courtly, imperious air; and my father, towering some inches above the tallest, the most imposing of them all, as straight as a statue, inflexible as a steel rod.

It would seem that such an assembly were destined to sit Sunday after Sunday without a thrill of emotion, but there were moments during the service when music came to make up for the lack of eloquence and power in the preaching. Yes, we had music! And, of all things in the world, operatic music. We sat under the spell of a paid choir; we were charmed by the incomparable voice of the gifted Annie Dean, and there were times when the listeners must have lost sight of rector, pulpit, vestments, everything, in the delightful sensations produced by the four gifted singers of this choir. Nor was this all the sensation Sunday had to offer. If inside the church the ear was charmed with lovely voices, outside, when the congregation was dismissed, there was a feast for the eyes in the lovely faces of the women, dressed in the latest Parisian fashions. All the churches were full on a Sunday, and when the people streamed out, long, stately lines of beauty passed through the central part of the town; and as we came to Pine Street we met the major portion of St. George's congregation coming up the street, and these, intermingling with people from Christ's Church, made the streets glow with delicate colours and that Southern type of beauty that made St. Louis famous long before the great War of Secession.

Well do I remember one Sunday in 1860, when the soft airs of an early spring wandered up from the west, transforming the streets, the people, their looks, their dress, while, bathed in limpid sunshine, the brilliant procession from the churches filled the streets; and from the throng of elegant women there came now and again a passing whiff from the orange-groves of Louisiana; and from old family prayer-books with golden clasps, saturated with the faint odour of old rose-leaves, there emanated an overpowering sense of the frailty of wealth, the inutility of fashion, the fatality of beauty, which in some mysterious manner came with a presentiment of languid decay and predestined calamity. It was a delightful promenade around a paradise of ease and contentment, where luxurious growths hid the vapours of the volcano under their feet. In what state of mind would aristocratic St. Louis find itself in another year? In the meantime I saw and heard all I could without asking any questions of anyone.

First, I had a deep desire to see the inside of that, to me, solemn and mystical edifice that stands on Ninth Street, near Washington Avenue. How many times I had passed its great, bulky doors without going in! How calm and sleepy it stood in the hot summer days, how dark and gloomy when the days were cold and smoke hung over the town; but my souvenirs of old St. Louis are of warm, genial airs, of long, dreamy springs and splendid autumns; and admidst the tranquil hush of all that neighbourhood the old Jesuit Church of St. Xavier stood like a block removed from the Mexico of Montezuma, plunged in the shadows of a mystical something which I could not fathom. It had an aspect all its own. Beside it all the other churches looked very modern and very simple. It faced the street without any architectural pretension, as if to say: "My power is within; on my façade is the alphabet; within you will find the language, the music, the myrrh, and the mystery!" It had the quality and illusion of very old lace once worn by grandees at great Courts, and handed down from princes to personalities, and from personalities to humble priests. It was placid as a still, deep lake shut in by mountains, and all about it there was an air that seemed to say: "Nothing matters; the world is a shadow."

The bells of St. Xavier sounded like no other bells in old St. Louis. I could hear them distinctly where we lived, and I remember three, the far-reaching boom of the deeper bell carrying with it a suggestion of peremptory mournfulness, an impression of something fixed and permanent in a city of fleeting illusions.

At last, one day, early in the year, I was sauntering by the church when my attention was directed to the crowds hurrying towards its doors. All ages and conditions of people were represented in the gathering, with hardly a glimmer of fashion visible, the people mostly of the humbler classes, emigrants from the old country, still moved by the memories of tragic scenes— women in black, women with pale, pinched faces, haunted yet by the hunger and the horror of the Irish famine, mounting the church steps as if to a Calvary of devotion, all bodily fatigue forgotten for the moment. Such were the people I saw pouring through the doors of the leading Jesuit Church of North America. I stood and gazed at all these earnest, wistful faces and half an hour must have elapsed before the impulse seized me to pass the threshold of the mysterious edifice and see and hear for myself. I slipped in, holding my breath for fear someone would ask me what I was doing there, and I was gradually pushed forward by the ever-increasing masses of worshippers until I stood in a throng nearly halfway up the left aisle. Absent were the tall, graceful lilies, the wandering whiffs from pressed rose-leaves of the ultra-refined worshippers of Trinity; absent the conventional dignity and pomp of wealth, and in their places appeared the inviolable sorrows of deep and prolonged tribulation, the voiceless gestures of the weary in exile, the sombre hues, deepened by the pervading gloom of the massive church, and the dusky faces of negro worshippers scattered through the assembly like black beads on a pall of mourning.

All the pews in the galleries and in the main body of the church were filled, the aisles were filled, a crowd stood packed under the choir. I felt as if some unseen presence was about to descend on the altar, and all at once I was startled by a peal from the organ and choir, and a procession of priests entered the chancel.

There was a maze of soft, flickering lights and glistening vestments, and I thought of the contrast between this and the scene of the camp-meeting; and although Trinity Church was only two blocks distant, what a contrast between the service there and this ceremony at St. Xavier's! I was in another world. Here were symbolical mysteries, accompanied by Mozart's music, with stately movements in harmony with the beauty of the rhythmic sounds; and faces, figures, colours, lights, glittering vestments, were presently merged in a cloud of vapoury incense, rising in puffs toward the galleries, descending slowly, imperceptibly, until objects in front seemed enveloped in a soft, transparent haze, out of which came strange odours of the Orient.

A priest now mounted the steps to the pulpit, and all eyes were riveted there. His hair was black, his face very dark, his glance quick and magnetic, his voice and message imperative.

Father Garaché—for he was the preacher—was a man who had something to say and knew how to express himself. He seemed to eye everyone individually, now to the right, now to the left, now straight before him; and the congregation, rapt in awe and fear, sat rigid under his terrible denunciations of the wicked and his fearful descriptions of Purgatory.

After that, when the preacher stepped down from the pulpit, he looked like one returning from a long and weary walk through a wilderness of tombs; and the music of the organ came as something magical to invite the half-freed spirit back to the house of flesh and a world of apparent realities.

Here I looked about me at the worshippers. In a pew just beyond where I stood I thought I saw someone whose figure seemed uncomfortably familiar. Could it be possible? Yes, no—yes, it was he—the fat, round back and neck of Mr. O'Kieff, the class-room teacher of Benton School, who had beaten me on the hand with his ruler only two days before.

I pitied him; for somehow he seemed even more contrite and miserable than the poor woman in black sitting near him, weak and weary as they looked, and I said to myself: "The next time he beats me on the hand I shall think, 'I am happier than you, and I can afford it,' "

There are persons who oppress the imagination with a feeling of mortality at the very time when a sense of immortality is supposed to dominate all the other feelings. How heavy and material, I thought to myself, would poor O'Kieff's coffin be, and how light that of the frail widow in mourning sitting next him. All these humble women, pale, shrunken, filled with the fire of devotion, they looked to me more than half spirit already, only waiting the slightest breath to waft them away, soul and body, to regions of eternal repose; and they gave to the church, the mass, the symbols, the music, the assembly, the final gesture of resignation when, at the supreme moment, there was a sound of a mystic bell in the chancel; then a rustling of garments, as of innumerable wings settling down to rest, and the whole concourse sank to the floor on their knees. A tall priest stood up in front of the altar with the Host held high before him; an immeasurable solemnity brooded over the multitude of bowed heads, and there was a mingling of prayers and pity and sorrow for dear ones left behind in the old country, and the heart seemed to have reached the nadir of worldly resignation. Again the bell sounded; and there arose over all the congregation, from the serried ranks of bent bodies, supplicating whispers, almost inaudible, muffled sighs that might have been groans but for the frail, faint voices emitting them, and short, quick phrases, as if the last scene had been reached, and the last shadow was passing on the dial of time, and desire had become futile and all action useless.

I know not how or why, but the sight of all these people coming out of the church, down the steps—a slow, mystical stream of human hopes, emotions, and sorrows—affected me even more than anything I had seen within. As I stood outside and watched the descent of that throng, the sad expression on the faces of many of the elderly people impressed me profoundly. Attending mass at this church was indeed a serious matter, and the majority would return to humble homes where there would be souvenirs of the old country, and sighs, and affectionate allusions to the absent.

Little did I then dream that I should one day sing my first solo before the public at high mass in the choir of St. Xavier's!

CHAPTER *18*

The Great Fair

THE memorable October of 1860 had arrived, the forerunner of the fateful days of November: an October laden with the wild fragrance of Missouri fields, with the last of the flowers of wood and prairie scattered here and there, and ancient oaks and elms guarding the high-roads leading into the country. And there were the peaceful farmhouses in the environs of the city, lying embedded in foliage just beginning to change from green into purple, and a something in the air that was not spring and hardly cool enough for autumn, yet, at the hour of noon, radiant with a touch of summer, when everything seemed wrapped for the moment in a dreamy languor, with the wonderful agricultural fair-grounds, resembling one of Claude's most visionary landscapes.

Two things made the fair of this autumn stand out detached from all the preceding ones: it was the last gathering under the old political and social order, and the Prince of Wales was coming to St. Louis with the special purpose of seeing the immense amphitheatre and the far-famed trotting races.

I went with my father early on the morning of the Prince's visit, and passing out beyond the city limits, where the road was black with people, came to the splendid expanse of sward and wood and placid waters where we were soon swallowed up on the dense crowd representing every trade and profession in the city and State: farmers, jockeys, horse-dealers, cattle-breeders, city merchants, officers, bishops, Southern planters, gamblers, river-captains, pilots; and there were dignified matrons attended by their beautiful daughters who represented all the leading churches of the city, each in charge of a booth where all sorts of fancy articles were sold for the benefit of the different charitable institutions. Such a sight could be witnessed nowhere else in the world.

The Prince of Wales arrived on the grounds in a carriage drawn by four black horses. In the same carriage sat Lord Lyons, the British Ambassador, and the Duke of Newcastle; and as soon as the royal party appeared in the crowd it was surrounded, or rather mobbed, by a band of shouting boys who grasped the spokes of the wheels and helped the carriage along.

The Prince looked serious and somewhat bored; and no wonder. Nevertheless, he was repaid for having to pass through this mob when he took his seat in the amphitheatre and where for more than three hours he was entertained by a brilliant display of trotting matches. Nowhere else had the royal party witnessed such a concourse of people amidst such surroundings.

While my father was greatly taken with the trotting matches and the fine display of fat cattle, I was interested in the crowd itself, the first real mob I had ever seen. And what a mixture of sensations—the struggling masses of people on the outside of the amphitheatre, the gawks from the backwoods, the heavy, listless gait of some, the quick, smart movements of others, the open-mouthed amazement, the cynical cunning of the confidence men, the vendors of drinks, the queer noises, the dust, the smell, the confusion of aims, the clash of interests, the voices of strange, wandering singers, the sound of guitars—so sad, so serene in this bedlam of bewildering emotions—the glimpse of the Chinese pagoda rising from the centre of the arena like a pagan symbol in a feverish dream, the shouts from a hundred thousand throats as the trotting favourites measure noses in the last round on the greatest day in the history of the fair!

Who had time to think of the approaching elections, the rumours of war?

I returned home that evening moved by the simple melody sung by the three young singers with their guitars; and all through the years that followed I heard, and still hear, the words that seemed to be born with the music.

> "Shall we never more behold thee,
> Never hear thy gentle voice again?
> When the Spring-time comes, gentle Annie,
> And the wild flowers are scattered o'er the plain."

A few weeks later the fair was forgotten in the political excitement of the hour. Election day was at hand. A new President was to be chosen.

CHAPTER *19*

The Planters' House

THE Planters' House! What did it not represent in the history of the Far West in the early days! To me it was St. Louis itself. This famous hotel typified life on the Mississippi, life on the prairies, life in the cotton-fields, life in the cosmopolitan city. It stood for wealth, fashion, adventure, ease, romance—all the dreams of the new life of the Great West. It was the one fixed point where people met to gossip, discuss politics, and talk business. It was the universal rendezvous for the Mississippi Valley. Here the North met the South, the East met the West. It looked like nothing else in the hotel world, but it always seemed to me it was intended more for pilots, river-captains, romantic explorers, far-seeing speculators, and daring gamblers.

It was here the goatee type was seen in all its perfection. On some of the chins the tufts of hard, pointed hair gave a cork-screw look to the dark faces, which somehow harmonised well with the eternal quaffing of mint-juleps, sherry-cobblers and gin-cocktails.

An hour spent in the Planters' House just before the great election was an experience never to be forgotten. All who did not want to shoot or be shot steered a clear course in some other direction, for here, in the bar and lobbies, were the true "fire-eaters" to be met, and while some had already killed their man, others were looking for a man to kill.

The fire-eaters were of two kinds: those who said little but did much, and those who drank much, talked much, and brandished pistols freely. Besides these there was an independent third party, namely, the listeners. Those were the wise, silent ones. They were, perhaps, the most interesting because they were amusing. The wise, silent listener would be smoking a big El Sol cigar, which gave him something to "chaw" on; and during the fearful oaths and invectives poured forth by the fire-eater the unfortunate victim would find his huge cigar not only smoked but "chawed" down to the very stump. Thus, without knowing it, he would be chewing and smoking at the same time. How innocent and bland he sometimes appeared while in the clutches of a down-river bowie-knife man. The fire-eater could hardly be mistaken for any other type. It was the keen, glossy eye of a snake under strong, dark eyebrows, sometimes thick and shaggy, sometimes thin and arched; and if the latter, the whole aspect of the face was fashioned in harmony with the clear-cut eyebrow, penetrating as a black steel point, above a piercing black eye. A pair of such eyes once fixed on a lounger bent on keeping peace, and his case was settled. But the silent listener at once took refuge behind a vocabulary of stock phrases. After a few drinks the political desperado would feel himself beginning to "b'ile over," and looked about him for someone to blow off steam on. There would be the man of peace at the bar who feels that one drink is quite enough and wishes to take a seat in an arm-chair or lean against the wall of the bar-room, take it easy, and just look and listen; but a fire-eater, just in from the bloody borders of Kansas, has spotted him; he forces him to have another drink, and begins:

"Sorter dull in St. Louis! I reckon things will liven up by election day."

The silent man with a fixed vocabulary answers:

"I reckon they will."

"Looky heah," continues the desperado, placing a hard, lanky hand on the shoulder of his victim, "I've put day-light through more'n one Abolitionist out there in Kansas, an' I'll be hanged if I don't do the same for the fust man here who says he's a-goin' te vote fer that miserable skunk, Abe Lincoln."

"Yes, sah."

"I reckon the Planters' House is all sound on the Little Giant, good ole Steve Douglas."

"I reckon she air."

"Now you look like a fair, square, up and down Douglas man, an' solid on the nigger question."

"I reckon I be."

"I kin pick out the skulkin' Yankee cowards in a crowd any day; ye kin tell 'em by their sleek ways an' their innocent looks, eh?"

"I reckon you can, sah."

At this juncture up stalks another fire-eater, eyes glaring, hair long and loose, his big felt hat set back on his head, and, fixing his ferret gaze on the silent man, shouts:

"Hurrah fer Fremont! I fit under John C. Fremont! You're a Fremont man, I know ye air. Come on, have a drink with me, gov-nah," and up he drags the wretched victim to the crowded bar, and there, trembling like a canary-bird in a cage between two rattlesnakes, the man of peace and silence has just wit enough left to answer with assumed assurance: "Yes, sah; I reckon ye're right, sah."

But the scene has not ended.

The Kansas fire-eater, who is now fairly on the war-path and itching for a scalp, turns suddenly on the man of peace and shouts:

"Looky heah, stranger, you told me just now you was fer Douglas! What do you mean by harrowin' the feelin's of an honest man? If there's anything I despise worse'n a Yankee it's a turn-coat. Yes, sir-ree, a turn-coat! Set there a-tellin' me how clean broke up ye air on Steve Douglas, an' now ye're drinkin' that stranger's whisky an' tellin' him ye're plumb gone on Fremont! Is that there a fair fight?"

By this time the silent man is saying his prayers, also in silence—scared, white in the face, not knowing what to do or what to say, afraid to move, his stock phrases worse than puerile, with just life enough left to hear his heart thumping and not enough strength left in his arm to raise his glass to his lips.

"If I thought you was a turn-coat I tell ye what it is, stranger, I'd let ye have this right through yer gizzard," and out he whips a dirk, pointed and deadly, a fearful gleam whirling in a circle as he brandishes the cold steel over his head with a wicked twist of the shoulder.

But the Fremont man, now beginning to feel the whisky working, stands at the other side of the man of silence. He, too, is armed, but with a revolver.

"See here, pard!" he cries, "suppose we fight it out right now, an' let the gov'nah here hold the stakes, as ye might say."

The gov'nah? Good heavens! He means the wise, silent man, the innocent, neutral lamb, the chewer of peaceful cuds and mumbler of joint-stock phrases.

But listen. You can almost hear what he is thinking. He is

saying to himself: "When rogues fall out the honest come by their own"; and at the first sign of hostilities down he dips and, like a yellow dog, wriggles his way through the crowd to the door and "slides out."

The bar-room, corridors, and halls are now filled with excited men under the influence of drink and half wild with suppressed passion. Some, with bloodshot eyes, pass in and out as if seeking someone to devour; the place begins to steam with the heat, and to cool the heated blood more iced mint-juleps are disposed of, and yet more, until heads begin to reel, quarrels arise from mere nothings, and amidst a chorus of howls and imprecations the Yankees, the "Dutch," and sometimes the Irish are denounced as "low white trash," cowards, and traitors.

In such crowds, about that time, might have been seen the auctioneer of human flesh, the professional slave-seller, the boldest, most abandoned of them all, because the law was on his side. Erebus had spewed him up from the nethermost corners—a pollution to the polluted, a creature without wit, humour, or feeling; a menace to civilisation and a curse to patriotism.

The Planters' House was the magnet-stone that attracted not only the country "moss-backs," but the city millionaire, the poor man out of work and the busy man with too much work; and here, with the others, came Captain U. S. Grant, plain, unassuming Mr. Grant, as he was usually called, and if not the plainest man hereabouts, certainly one of the most discouraged and disappointed. He was often to be seen lounging about the public rooms waiting for something to turn up. The future commander-in-chief of the Army belonged to the silent ones, but one whose wit had been sharpened by a vast worldly experience and profound knowledge of human nature, and his silence was not a sign of lethargy and stupidity, but of knowledge and wisdom. I can see him now sitting in an arm-chair, smoking an El Sol cigar and waiting with an air of extreme patience and resignation. But waiting for what? Did he himself know? Why was he in St. Louis at all, since everything he attempted proved a business failure, from hauling cord-wood into town from the log-house he had built for his family out on the Gravois Road, and selling it, one load at a time, to the opening of a real estate office for the buying and letting of houses? Everything he now touched failed; and yet, when the critical hour arrived, this plain, silent man, this business failure, was on hand to offer his services to General Lyon at the United States Arsenal.

My father often talked with Mr. Grant about the price of town lots and the rent of certain houses.

Captain Grant had been all through the Mexican War, and had served nine years in the United States Army, and had seen service in California. He had seen life as few had seen it, yet there he was, one of the most discouraged men to be met with anywhere in the Mississippi Valley.

How different the visits to the Planters' House of Major W. T. Sherman! When this future commander-in-chief came it was not to lounge about, for he was too busy. He too had seen service in California. He declared he had come to settle down in St. Louis as an ordinary business man. Major Sherman lived only four blocks from us, on Locust Street, and Willie Sherman I knew very well.

Whenever I wanted something like an excursion I would take a ride on a Fifth Street car and go for miles in a northerly or southerly direction. Major Sherman, as President of the Fifth Street car line, was often to be seen going to his office in North St. Louis in one of these cars. One day three future generals happened to be riding in the same car together—Grant, the hero of Vicksburg; Sherman, of the great march through Georgia; and Grierson, of the famous raid through Mississippi.

CHAPTER *20*

The Torch-Light Procession

THE last torch-light procession in St. Louis, before the presidential election, was forming and about to begin its long march through the principal avenues and streets. Fremont, Douglas, and Lincoln were among the number of aspirants to the Presidency. I remember it as occurring just before the sixth of November, the great day of decision, the flames from thousands of torches lending a glow of warmth to the chill feeling in the autumn air. My father, being a Lincoln enthusiast, was hard at work winning adherents to the Republican cause. None but the women and children were idle, and all took sides.

My impression of this winding file of men was that it had entered the city from some strange, distant country—that it had, in some way, come up from the river, and that the host of men with torches were bringing with them an element of bitter strife, of combat, final and fatal. I stood in the dense crowd on the side-walk, and as the followers of the different candidates passed with their various emblems I was struck with the difference between the Lincoln men and the others. About the latter there was something spasmodic, excitable, almost hysterical, the weakness of their favourites coming out in their own shouts and actions, in the expression of the faces, in the hang-dog look of the bodies; and it was not surprising, for on the part of Lincoln's opponents there was that huge coil of the black serpent, Slavery, to drag with them, and the effort was already plainly visible on every face and every figure. Besides this, there was every indication that many of Lincoln's opponents were under the influence of drink, while the friends of the Rail-Splitter walked with calm bodies and cool heads, shouting with a will, fixed, determined, with the consciousness of power and pre-ordained victory.

On it went, winding, winding, in and out, the flickering lights passing like a fiery dragon as far as one could see, the whole city receiving a symbolical visitation by fire, a baptismal warning of what was coming within the short space of a year from that hour.

At last the day of election came and the city woke in a sort of dream. People hardly knew what they were doing: the tension of the past few weeks had been more than many could bear. Thousands walked to the poll in a half-dazed condition, with barely sufficient will power to cast a vote. Haggard faces were to be seen, men who had not slept soundly for weeks; for the triumph of the Abolition Party, the election of Abraham Lincoln, meant the freeing of the slaves and the ruin of thousands of slave-owners.

The seventh of November arrived, heavy with fatality; there were rumours, impossible rumours, that the tall, gaunt Rail-Splitter up there at Springfield, Illinois, was elected. Yet none but the Republicans dared believe it. The thing sounded too much like the closing of a period, the passing of a cycle, the winding-up of an age of dreaming.

The eighth of November arrived, and the dreadful rumours were repeated, this time louder, with more presistency, with something depressing added to fear; but when the ninth was ushered in and the rumours were turning to acclamations of victory, a feeling of consternation took possession of all who owned slaves.

What to do? The question was asked on either side; but there was no immediate solution of a difficulty so unheard-of, so unique. Wait and see what the Republicans will do when their idol, Abraham Lincoln, is inaugurated as President on the fourth of March next.

In April of the next year, 1861, about a month after Lincoln had entered the White House at Washington, I was sitting at my desk in the Benton School. The windows were open and I noticed a strange flag fluttering about in the yard below. Presently, up went the flag to the top of a pole, high enough to be seen by people in the street. It was the first display in St. Louis of a Secession flag.

During the raising of this flag Mr. Gilfillan, the principal of Benton School, was nervous and angry; he walked about the room darting fierce looks at certain of the pupils. The burly

O'Kieff, in his class-room, at the recital of lessons, gave us extra hard beatings with his ruler.

When I left the school-house I met excited groups of men discussing the significance of the hoisting of such a flag. Everyone looked anxious and worried; things were coming to a head —thunder-clouds were gathering; but the lightning was reserved for the tenth of May.

At this time we were living on Pine and Ninth Streets, in the heart of the "fire-eating" district, only three blocks from the headquarters of the Rebel Club, which was also on Pine Street.

Up to the present things were going on in the usual way, and to the eyes of a stranger St. Louis, which was even at this time the storm-centre of the War, wore its habitual, sleepy aspect, more sleepy during the warm spring months, perhaps, than at any other time of the year—at least, it always seemed so to me; and while a few far-seeing men, like Grant and Sherman, could see the storm coming, many of the Southern people, especially the young men, looked at the situation much as they would at a trotting match at the fair grounds—the blue ribbon would be carried off by a racer from Kentucky. Others thought there would be a short tussle with a few Northern Abolitionists, when things would settle down again in the old way; no matter what happened, the courage—both moral and physical—would all be on the side of the South. It was not conceivable that a Government headed by Lincoln could fight anyone or anything.

Some days passed. With the taking of Fort Sumter by the Rebels at Charlestown, South Carolina, President Lincoln called for volunteers to put down the rebellion. Five regiments, composed mainly of German citizens of St. Louis, were soon got together and were to be seen marching towards the National Arsenal in the southern part of the city. Could it be possible? Were these foreigners taking sides with the North? Were these shuffling, heavy, stupid-looking men, incapable of marching in order, setting out to fight someone? People in the streets looked on amazed. Even the friends of the North could hardly believe their eyes. As for the Southerners who saw the queer regiments pass, jeers and jokes greeted the "Hessians," as these Germans were called; and the word "Hessian" became from that day a word of contempt among Southern people in St. Louis.

These troops did not march so much as shuffle along; and I can see them now, for never since that time have I seen troops in any part of the world at all like them. I was instantly struck by the look of detachment on their faces, the machine-like movements of their bodies, the long, shuffling, dogged step, and, somehow, I thought they looked hungry withal, and perhaps they were, and I received an impression as of a quick impact of something silently fatal, bewildering, crushed, ghastly. Were these Germans stoics? Or were they what they looked, simply apathetic? Were they hiding their feelings under a mask of indifference, or were they simply human automatons? Mystery.

CHAPTER 21

Camp Jackson

WHAT a day for the young bloods of St. Louis! We stood on Twelfth Street and watched the gathering of the aristocratic clans, so to speak—the sons of wealthy Southern families, Secessionists and Rebels, even now, forming in line here, Monday, the sixth of May, by order of the Governor of the State. Many of them I knew personally; some of them were members of Bible-classes at the different Sunday-schools I attended; and I noticed in particular young Hutchinson, the son of the rector of Trinity Church.

All the different companies were here, some of them in handsome uniforms; but the brilliant appearance of the Dragoons put every other company in the shade. Could anything equal this gathering for harmony of colour, the beauty of youth, aristocratic breeding, clannish pride, courage, audacity, contempt of the Northern Abolitionist? Out they marched, in regular order, headed by military music, to Camp Jackson, where, by Governor Jackson's command, the "boys" were to pitch their tents and engage in drill for a short season. In other words, they were to prepare to defend the State against any attack of Lincoln's volunteers. Open secession was freely talked of, and the Hessians and the Yankees were to be annihilated at the mere sight of such an imposing array of blood, colour, and military tactics.

The camp was pitched in Lindell Grove, just outside the city, a place I knew well as a picnic-ground for Sunday-school gatherings in summer-time. Here all was forgotten save youthful vanity, impossible ambitions, flirtation; and life, as it looked in this fashionable rendezvous, was something worth living. The ladies came in hundreds, to see or to be seen, and every tent was well supplied with all the delicacies of the season. War, if there was to be a war, would be a splendid pageant, headed by a military band; and the members of Company A, the Washington Guards, the Missouri Guards, the Laclede Guards, and the others, would only have to show themselves to make the weak-kneed Hessians and Negro-worshippers turn and run for their lives.

The greatest national tragedies have always begun by a comedy. And this comedy went on exactly four days. On the 9th of May crowds visited the United States Arsenal, in the southern part of the town, where General Lyon was hastily getting his German regiments in order, and where we met Major Sherman, who had come down on a Fifth Street car with his two boys to see what was going on. In his *Memoirs* General Sherman says:

"Within the Arsenal Wall four regiments of Horse Guards were drawn up in parallel lines, and I saw men distributing cartridges to the boxes. I saw General Lyon running about with his hair in the wind and his pockets full of papers, wild and irregular; but I knew him to be a man of vehement purpose and determined action. I saw, of course, that it meant business, but whether for defence or offence I did not know. The next morning I went up to the railroad office in Bremen, as usual, and heard at every corner of the streets that the "Dutch" were moving on Camp Jackson. People were barricading their houses. I hurried through my business as quickly as I could and got back to my house on Locust Street by twelve o'clock."

By the time Major Sherman got home, General Lyon, with his Hessians, was at Camp Jackson.

On that morning, the 10th of May, my father, who had gone out very early, came home with alarming rumours. Our house, he said, was situated right in the midst of the danger zone. We were likely to catch anything flying about in the shape of bullets, and he had heard that General Lyon was about to order his five German regiments up from the Arsenal to Camp Jackson, and in all probability they would march past our house. The only safe place in our house—which was a "frame" one—would be in the basement, the walls there being of brick; and here we were ready to go at the first sign of danger. Half an hour passed, then an hour, and still no sign of anything unusual. Never had the streets seemed more tranquil. While one member of the family was on the portico looking down Pine Street, I was on the watch looking down Ninth Street. All of a sudden, without so much as the beating of a drum, without the slightest noise, except for the shuffling of so many big, heavy feet, General

Lyon made his appearance at the corner of Ninth and Chestnut Streets, just one block away, riding at the head of a drove of Hessians—for they seemed like so many cattle to me, with, no doubt, some wild bulls among them capable of causing a stampede, no one knew what, all the more menacing because so awkward—and, turning the corner, faced straight up Ninth Street. They would pass our house. I gave alarm, and down came every member of the family into the basement, when the thick outside shutters were closed for fear of bullets. There was a wide crack in one of the shutters, and through this I got a good look at the queerest body of soldiers I ever saw. On they came, shambling up Ninth Street until General Lyon came to Pine Street, when, at the corner of our house, he turned his men up Pine Street in the direction of Camp Jackson; and hardly had he done so when crack! crack! went rifle shots, and we all dipped bodies, squatting in the corners. On they came, regiment after regiment; it seemed as if they would never cease passing. At last, peeping out, I saw the end of the long, shambling line dragging its dogged length off towards the country.

Out flocked the people into Pine Street. Two bullets had struck our house, and just outside a German solider was sitting on the side-walk with his back to the wall. Coming closer we could distinguish where the Minié bullet had penetrated his temple. He was dead. Close by a servant with a pail of water was washing a stream of blood off the side-walk where someone had been killed, and the sight to me was indescribably horrible. My father said this was civil war. We walked on down Pine Street, and at Seventh Street we went over into Olive Street, and then, seeing a crowd, we came to the fruit stand of some Italians. The dead body of the proprietor had just been carried in, and loud wails arose from the wife and children, so suddenly plunged into mourning. All along the line of march there had been firing, both from the ranks of the German volunteers and from individual Rebels; these latter fired into the ranks of the soldiers while hidden behind church pillars or from windows.

Meanwhile, on the Germans trudged to Camp Jackson, spreading consternation among the people everywhere *en route*, while the fashionable throng in Lindell Grove preened their beautiful feathers, like so many birds of paradise in a Garden of Eden.

All at once a rider on a swift horse announced the words: "The Hessians! The Hessians!"

Was it, then, nothing but a dream? Could it be possible that the Yankee General Lyon, a nobody from the Government Arsenal, was tramping up the bend in the road, and in another moment would be descending towards the Grove, with other troops arriving exactly on time by another road, hemming in the whole camp, the gaily-dressed crowd, the sight-seers?

The streets in town being free of soldiers, we went up Locust Street, where we saw Major Sherman, with his son Willie, walking up and down before his house, talking to the neighbours, and "listening for the sound of musketry and cannon in the direction of the Camp."

Major Sherman walked over to Olive Street, beyond Twelfth, and there saw a man running from Camp Jackson, shouting as he ran: "They've surrendered! They've surrendered!"

With this news Major Sherman went with his son as fast as he could to the Camp, while I returned with my father to our house, where developments were awaited with the greatest anxiety. At the Camp Major Sherman and his boy just escaped being killed by throwing themselves on the ground, and several men, women, and children lost their lives in a wild fusillade, owing to the irresponsible actions of a drunken man who had nothing to do with the soldiers of either side.

At last we heard the cry: "Here they come!" The bitter hour had arrived. From Twelfth Street they were marching down Pine Street past our house. The different companies of gay and sanguine young Rebels, now prisoners of war, came marching down between files of the hated and despised Hessians on their way to the Arsenal, right through the heart of the city. Every window on Pine Street was filled with spectators—mothers, sisters, wives, for the men were elsewhere. Imprecations were showered on the "Dutch," handkerchiefs were waved in honour of the prisoners, and when they passed our house we saw young Hutchinson among the number.

They put on a bold front; they were not of the kind to let an incident like this discourage them; for, after all, they proved themselves made of sterner stuff, and hardly one there but would turn up later in the Rebel ranks on the bloody fields of Tennessee and Mississippi.

CHAPTER 22

General Fremont

IN THE summer of 1861 I acted as page to General Fremont, who had succeeded General Harney as military commander in St. Louis, and who occupied Major Brant's new mansion on Choteau Avenue, where he had his headquarters. I wore a dark blue uniform, and my duties consisted in carrying letters, dispatches, etc., from General Fremont to officers in other parts of the house. I saw people of all conditions trying in every way to obtain an interview with the General. One day, on entering the commander's room, I was surprised to see two foreign officers seated in front of his table. I took them to be Germans.

They wore striking uniforms; and the comedy of the whole thing became apparent when people learned that General Fremont had invited them to accompany him home from Europe to give the officers of his army some idea of military tone and style. The leading citizens were indignant. They could not understand such a whim on the part of a democratic leader at a time when action and courage meant everything, personal appearance nothing.

General Sherman, in his *Memoirs*, says:

"McClellan and Fremont were the two men toward whom the country looked as the great Union leaders, and towards them were streaming the newly-raised regiments of infantry and cavalry, and batteries of artillery."

When General Sherman came to St. Louis to see Fremont on urgent business connected with the war, Sherman stopped at the Planters' House, and meeting Mr. R. M. Renick, inquired where he could find General Fremont. Mr. Renick said: "What do you want with General Fremont? You don't suppose he will see such as you?" Then he explained that "Fremont was a great potentate, surrounded by sentries and guards; that he had a more

showy court than any real king; that he kept senators, gover-
nors, and the first citizens dancing attendance for days and
weeks before granting an audience," etc.

Callers came by scores, among them several old scouts and
pioneers who had accompanied Fremont on his Western ex-
ploits. I was as much interested in these men than I was in the
General himself, for they recounted the whole history of Fremont's disastrous expedition from St. Louis to California in
1848. One day several of these men appeared, and the oldest
asked to see the General. They were old friends, they said, and
expected to be admitted to his presence without any trouble;
but they waited a long time, returning day after day, and for
weeks I saw them sauntering along Fourth Street, hanging about
the Planters' House, where they told stories of their thrilling
adventures among the Indians. I saw much of these men and
others in later years, during my sojourns in New Mexico, Arizona, and Utah, who had been with Fremont on his exploring
expeditions, and I always listened with deep interest to all I
could hear about the wild West of the 'Forties and 'Fifties.

Fremont left the Missouri River in October, 1848, on his
fourth expedition to California. He was then thirty-six years of
age. His aim was to make for the Rio Grande, and from that
wild region find a pass through the Rocky Mountains. The route
to the Pacific Coast had never been explored, and Colonel Fremont (as he then was) had no aid from the Government, as in
former adventures. He picked out thirty-three men—hunters,
scouts, muleteers, interpreters, half-breeds, and some Indians,
well tried by him in his former travels through the deserts and
mountains. He had to pick out and test, before buying them, a
hundred and twenty mules. Then he had to look to the selection
of fire-arms, ammunition, bacon, corn-meal, coffee, sugar, blankets and buffalo robes, fur wraps, besides coloured blankets,
beads, and paint as presents to placate the Indians and gain their
friendship. Much was needed before they reached the Great Divide and the region of snows. They were making straight for the
hunting-grounds of the man-slaying Apaches and Comanches, the
crafty Kioways, the fierce Utahs and Arapahoes, the Navahoes,
and the other tribes roaming the plains and hills at that particular season.

There were the Sioux and the Omahas, who might be met
with either on the war-path or on some hunting expedition.

They followed along up the Kansas River, and soon began to see signs of that moving life that made the prairies of the Kansas region the happy hunting-grounds of the Far West of those early days.

Colonel Fremont now sent on a small band of scouts twelve hours in advance of his company. The scouts were sent out with the fleetest horses and were on the look-out for Indians. They came to a place where it looked as if the country was dotted with sage-brush, but as they proceeded they discovered buffaloes instead of sage-brush. The animals were moving slowly down from the north, a wilderness of black forms.

They could not discover through a spy-glass any end to the herd. At times small, compact groups grazed together; then the animals became more scattered, but there was always an unbroken line somewhere visible. In an hour's time the herd became thicker, and they soon began to traverse the main portion. The earth was now black with buffalo, and the aspect of the moving animals began to look dangerous; the scouts feared a stampede, surrounded as they were on all sides with savage-looking beasts. The number was computed at many hundreds of thousands.

The party moved with caution, not intending to do any killing till they got to the edge of the herd. Suddenly a commotion was visible among the animals where there was a slight rise in the prairie. At that point they were on the gallop, while a mile or two away the herd was stampeding. The Indians had arrived. The scouts stopped and made ready. Two dangers faced them: the stampede and the savage Sioux, now galloping their horses along-side of the finest bison and pouring their arrows into the flying bulls. No one seemed to know from what direction the Indians had arrived, but just at that spot there was a break in the herd which left an open space through which the Sioux made the attack. They had, no doubt, been waiting in hiding somewhere in the prairie. They were killing for winter supplies, both for meat and buffalo robes, and at first they were probably too much concerned with the hunt to trouble themselves about the white men. Part of the main herd was making straight for the scouts, while another portion had headed off to the left, and yet a third broke in an easterly direction, and the whites were at a loss to find a reason for so curious a thing among the buffaloes, when to their amazement they saw what they understood to be second band of Indians coming, as it were, out of the ground. This band separated into two parts, their aim being to drive the herd in a given direction. The scouts proclaimed them Comanches, as these rode Mexican mustangs and had the crafty art of creeping along, hiding behind their animals or low bushes or slight elevations of the ground and then suddenly making their presence both seen and felt.

It looked now as if the Indians of both bands and the stampeding buffaloes would sweep down and surround the scouting party. All they could do was to wait, all eyes fixed on the manoeuvres of the Indians. The buffalo that had been divided and scattered by the Comanches were running helter-skelter in three divisions, chased by the fleetest and most cunning of the bands, uttering a quick, sharp yell. By this time the buffalo everywhere had caught the panic. All raised their heads and started on the run, followed by the animals coming down in the main stream from where the Comanches began the chase.

A small band of Comanches had now to deal with two bulls, probably infuriated by arrows. They had turned on their pursuers and were charging among them, and while this was going on the Sioux had approached the scouting party on the other side, the buffalo fleeing before them in another stream. The time had come for the Indians to stop the chase and attend to the white men.

The whole scene had taken but a short time, hardly long enough for anyone to realise fully what was happening.

The scattered Comanches assembled in one group for a pow-wow. The Sioux, on their side, had never scattered, but had come to a stand, leaving a large number of dead buffalo strewn along the line of chase. One of the scouts, called Lame-Bear, a renegade Comanche spy, who knew a little Spanish and some English, now gave his opinion of the situation by signs and words as follows: Both bands of Indians had come out on a hunting expedition as well as for adventure; they had met here by chance; but the Comanches, still more cunning than the Sioux, when they discovered the white men, formed a plan to stampede the buffalo. In the confusion they would attack the white men, but the superior numbers of the Sioux caused them to change their plan. Now they were holding a council of war; in another moment the whole thing would be decided; there would be a "lifting of scalps."

Lame-Bear had hardly spoken the last word when the Comanches set out with a great war-whoop straight for the Sioux, who were sitting as still as stone images on their horses. The Comanches swept on like demons, unconscious of their own inferior numbers.

"Look!" cried Lame-Bear, "the buffalo!"

It was a fresh stampede from the north. The vacant space separating the Comanches and the Sioux was threatened by this new mass of frightened animals, coming down in a stream that would pass right in front of the band of Sioux, driven, no doubt, by another band farther north. Seeing this, the intrepid Comanches redoubled their efforts to reach their rivals, and at the moment the first buffalo reached the line a hail of arrows poured from the two bands and several Comanches fell. In another second a horse fell under a Sioux, then several warriors. The space had now become fairly blocked with buffalo, and, maddened by the smell of blood, they bellowed and jumped about as they passed close to the Sioux, who were now forced to desist, while the Comanches, caught in the stampede, were compelled to gallop along with the herd to escape destruction.

The scouts began to move on, when the Comanches veered round to the south at a safe distance from their guns.

CHAPTER 23

The Dance of Death

AFTER travelling between four and five hundred miles out from the Missouri, Fremont's expedition struck the pow-wow grounds on the Kansas River, the camping-place where the famous hunter and scout, old Fitzpatrick, had in charge some thousand of Indians.

At that time this scout was acting as Government Indian Agent. His special business was to deal with the savages in such a manner that they would, at least for a time, leave the white emigrants unmolested while on their way across the plains and mountains to California. Fremont expected to meet here some hundreds of Indians, mainly chiefs and leading warriors, instead of which he encountered whole tribes gathered from the Far West, South, and South-west. He calculated on staying here some little time to find out all he could, both from the whites and the Indians, who could give him important information and all the latest mountain news brought in from scouts and hunters from the West.

Before the establishment of this agency, hundreds of emigrants had been murdered and their scalps taken; but old Fitzpatrick, as cunning as any Apache, knew all the weak and strong points of the Indians, and could pacify them at small cost either to himself or the Government. He knew the magic power residing in coloured beads, red and yellow blankets, paint, and such trifles, when dealing with them. Yet, in spite of all this, the Indians were fooling him.

Whole tribes of sleek, well-fed savages, arrayed in feathers, brilliant blankets, paint, and all the finery of needlework and fantastic neck and head gear, greeted Colonel Fremont's arrival, gazing in grim silence and weird dignity at the white men, their mules and their weapons. There were one or two tribes new to

Fremont's scouts. There was old Flying-Horse, chief of an intrepid band of Southern Apaches, with a great flight of eagle feathers pointing outward from the crown of his long head to the nape of his neck, a stripe of yellow paint running from his forehead right down his nose, across his chin, and down his breast; and two Indians of greater importance than any of the chiefs: the much-dreaded Arappa-Honta, grand enchanter of the Navahoes, and Umbaha-Tan, a great medicine-man and "weaver of spells" of the Utahs.

Queer things were brewing.

That same evening Lame-Bear asked one of Fremont's men to walk out with him where the others could not hear what he had to say. When they got beyond the camp Lame-Bear began in a mixture of Spanish and English: "You see that big Medicine, Umbaha-Tan? He is no friend of Chief Fremont! I have peeped in his wigwam, and know what he is doing. He has made a 'bad fire' in there; to-morrow he will begin his enchantments."

Here Lame-Bear began to turn round and round in imitation of someone who was being dazed and mentally confused, dizzy in the head, not capable of clear thinking.

"Is Umbaha-Tan working against one person or against all our party?" asked the scout.

"The whole party. All will feel his power."

"How is such a thing possible?"

"Because the white men don't understand," he said.

"What will Umbaha-Tan do to-night?" asked the scout.

Lame-Bear gave a slight twist of the head, and, with an expression of weariness, said: "He will perform the ban-ha-ha," which meant the overture of the play, or the creation of the atmosphere.

The guide felt that any words or explanations would be useless, that nothing could change the order of Fate. He himself had his mind made up and knew precisely what to expect.

The moon rose and began to light the plains, and the campfires blazed in the clear, still air; and while Fremont's men were smoking and resting the Indians began to glide about, ghost-like, in the moonlight, by ones and twos at first, coming and going for the most part in absolute silence. Some of them were roasting buffalo, which they did by making a big hole in the ground and cooking the whole carcass, barbecue fashion.

Old Fitzpatrick was asked if he did not think the Indians in the camp were more sullen than usual, but he only said: "I don't see as they act any different from the real Simon-pure article"; and then he went on: "You know how Natur' turns 'em out, I reckon; Natur' manifactures 'em, but she don't finish 'em; when she manifactures a white man she finishes him. An Injin is finished when he hez a top-knot, an' he's polished when he gets his war-paint on; a white man is polished jest as soon as he gets his face washed."

Arappa-Honta, the enchanter, was receiving visitors in his wigwam. He sat cross-legged, on thick cushions of bear and buffalo skins, bolt upright, his body quite still, partly wrapped in a robe of wild-cat skins. The white visitors immediately became conscious of something wonderful in the influence he threw about him of length and distance. Everything about his features was long and thin: long, narrow head, rising far above his eyebrows; long, narrow eyes, veiled and absent; long, thin nose; long spare jaws and chin; and a neck that might have grown in a night, like a mushroom-stalk. The marvellous head was capped with a circle of black feathers, and from the centre of the crown rose three black ostrich-feathers, which must have been brought from St. Louis or Mexico, or stolen from emigrants. His arms were covered with ornaments, while his face was made still more extraordinary by being covered with saffron paint; there was a black streak of paint running from the top of his forehead, down the nose to his bosom. These colours meant that he was getting ready for business; the days of idle dreaming were past.

According to Lame-Bear, Arappa-Honta was getting ready to travel, in spirit.

His body had something of the painted image about it, so still and motionless.

An Indian, with something of the wild animal in his face, placed on the fire, which was burning in the middle of the wigwam, some leaves that raised a thick smoke. Arappa-Honta moved his head a little and breathed deeply; then he prepared his pipe, filled it with some of the leaves and began to smoke. Several of the Indians did the same, after which the white visitors left the wigwam. Hearing muffled sounds coming from the direction of Umbaha-Tan's lodge, they went towards it. Indians were walking about outside, listening; there was not one who did not know the secret meaning of the deep, drum-like sounds coming from the weaver's tent. As the Indians drew nearer they would stop, bow their heads and listen, the same as if they had been white men listening to the sound of earth falling on a coffin. Indians of different tribes came and went, their eyes glistening like black beads in the bright moonlight; they glided past like cats, and listened as if smitten by some unknown power. They seemed to be absent from the spot and enjoying something far away.

Old Fitzpatrick was holding a confab with Colonel Fremont in the commander's tent, with some other scouts and guides, and already there were signs of contradictory evidence and advice concerning the route to be taken and attempts to be made to find passes through the Rocky Mountains.

Up to this time Fremont had appeared pretty confident of his ability to go straight through the mountains without much loss of mules and with but little danger to his men; but now old Fitzpatrick told one story, while the new arrivals from the west told another. Fremont refused to take a decision, and said he would wait a day or two, when fresh news might arrive that would clear up certain doubtful points.

That night the whites lay awake listening to the low, drum-like beatings in Umbaha-Tan's wigwam. Once in a while the unusual notes of a flute-like instrument could be heard coming from the direction of Arappa-Honta's wigwam. These sounds only ceased with the setting of the moon. Lame-Bear said he had a presentiment of impending disaster, and he could see the mountains loom like bastions in the blue distance; bleak, barren, more immovable than the stars, inhospitable as frozen tombs, inviting the last gasp in the still, frozen air; and some of the white men felt a horrible attraction towards the desolate snow-covered region of the Rockies.

The whole camp, white men and Indians, were up early and stirring, some busy with one thing, some with another, while in one of the tents a mail-carrier from Taos, in New Mexico, was being awakened by some of the men who had been deputed to watch him and keep him from what the Indians called the death sleep. He had ridden for some days and nights, making a record journey, and had given strict orders to have his sleep broken after a few hours, as the Indians considered it fatal for a man in that condition of fatigue to sleep twelve hours on a stretch. When he got his eyes wide open he thought he was captured by Indians and going to be bound to a tree and tortured, and he began to shout and rave; but they finally brought him to by dashes of cold water over his head and face.

The news he brought gave Fremont no information that could be used to any advantage.

Lame-Bear came about noon with the news that the Indians were getting ready for a great dance. It was being kept as secret as possible; but, even if the secret leaked out, nothing could stop them, as the dance was to appear like a festival of peace and goodwill.

Early in the afternoon small bands of Indians began to come in with the spoils of the buffalo hunts, and the Comanches encountered on the plains arrived with the scalps of the Sioux slain in the buffalo fight. The sight of fresh scalps, the plentiful supply of buffalo and antelope meat, the perpetual noise of the musical instruments of the different medicine-men, kept the Indians at fever-heat, and for the rest of the day painted faces became more and more plentiful.

Huge barbecues for a buffalo-meat feast were in preparation, and the chiefs became more independent and haughty in demeanour.

About eleven o'clock that evening the Indians emerged from their lodges by hundreds, making tracks for the open prairie south of the camp. At the same time the sound of Indian drums came from various parts, increasing in force until the air vibrated with the queer noises; and the painted faces and arms of many of the savages added something demoniacal to the scene.

When questioned about it, old Fitzpatrick said it meant a buffalo dance; others thought it a dance in honour of the moon; others, again, declared it was a dance in honour of Fremont, and this last explanation was accepted by most of the white men.

Lame-Bear now said that several tribes would hold dances in unity; but the leaders would be the Utah tribe, headed by Umbaha-Tan, and the Southern Apaches, headed by old Arappa-Honta. All the preparations had been made beforehand, and things went as by clockwork. Far out on the plains a long row of flickering lights could be seen. At last the Indians arrived at the dancing-grounds, carrying small torches made of pine knots, and gathered in a huge circle, without noise or confusion, as if each Indian had rehearsed the scene scores of times, and knew the exact position to take.

There was a signal; the whole crowd, to the number of thou-

sands, squatted on the ground, all decorated in their best colours, the flaming reds of the blankets becoming visible in the
glow of the torches, with the bright yellows gleaming among the
crowd out in the clear moonlight. On either side, through the
mass of squatting Indians, there was space enough for horses and
files of dancers to pass. From beyond the circle, on one side,
there came two Indians mounted on Mexican mustangs, with
faces painted in red stripes, meant to be taken as a symbol of
peace to the whites of the camp, but in reality to deceive. They
walked their horses round the circle once, and passed out on the
other side. Two more appeared, with faces painted white and
red, and made the circuit. Lame-Bear said it was meant as a
warning to all the Indians of the sort of thing they would witness, and prepare them for the full display of the medicine-
men's power. These in turn were followed by a group of four
reed-blowers, with bodies half bare and curiously painted. They
were the musical charmers who would put the crowd in the
proper mood. The whistles produced a great and solemn change.
Faces became rapt with wondering awe as the group walked
round and round the ring. Other dancers entered, followed by
mounted Indians. A band of twenty Utahs, disguised as wolves,
appeared, and began to crawl and jump as they slowly passed
round. The wolves snapped and growled as they approached a
figure seated alone on the rim of the charmed circle, and when
they arrived in front of the strange apparition sitting robed in
white and black—for it was the great Medicine, Arappa-Honta, in
a new dress, resembling a demon in the midst of a wild beasts'
inferno—they halted in a line, squatted, and set up a whimpering
and whining which no white man could imitate. This over, they
rose and moved on, limping in imitation of a wounded man or
animal. When halfway round the ring in strode an Indian of
giant frame encased in a full buffalo skin—horns, hide, and tail,
all complete; swaying to and fro, he rolled along till he got in
front of the wolves, and then he began such antics as would
defy description, for it seemed impossible for one man to carry
such a weight and perform such evolutions—such a rising and
falling of the body, such a limbering movement of legs and
head, and when he got as far as Arappa-Honta the buffalo went
on his knees before the great Medicine, and with a smart toss of
the woolly head struck the ground with one of his horns. He
rose from this posture the moment Arappa-Honta touched the

horns with the tip of a long, slender reed; but the buffalo had hardly turned away before he was faced by all the wolves in a line, moving towards him in perfect order three steps forward, then one step in retreat, repeating this again and again till they got to the centre of the circle, all the animals keeping silent. By the time the wolves reached the centre the state of the crowd was such that the noise of a cannon let off would not have caused an Indian to turn his head or raise an eyebrow, for with every step forward and backward it was seen that the charm, whatever it might be, was working out without a hitch. All who had eyes could understand for themselves. The savages sat spellbound, seeing the tide rise and recede, while the lone buffalo stood, his shaggy head rolling from side to side, awaiting the inevitable moment when the wolves would close in and surround him. On they came, the tension of the spectators becoming unendurable as the wolves took the last three steps forward, halting, amidst a chorus of grunts and growls, under the buffalo's nose; but on the instant six Indians on ponies came galloping down to the circle, and, halting, sent a whirlwind of arrows at the body of the buffalo. Every arrow struck where it was aimed; the beast fell, first on his knees, then over on his side; the Indians on horseback rode off, and at the same time the twenty wolves formed in a ring around the prostrate buffalo, moving in a circle, turning round and round, and by the time they had all made the circuit a band of stalwart Indians, encased in the skins of huge grizzlies, erect on their hind legs, came wobbling and capering in. All the drums began to beat, the reed-whistles made a shrill, weird nose, and the big grizzlies, advancing, erect, towards the immovable Arappa-Honta, the real dance, the wonderful Indian ball, now began.

As the grizzlies turned their backs on Arappa-Honta they faced the wolves, arrayed in a line about fifty feet away, and at once the grizzlies began to reel like drunken men, while the wolves suddenly moved forward a few paces, limping, snarling, and now and then giving short jumps.

The big grizzlies now began a slow movement towards the centre, and when about thirty feet apart both lines halted. One of the wolves and one of the largest of the grizzlies parted from the ranks, and stepping forward to within a few feet of each other, a duel of fantastic figures was set going. With this signal a troop of thirty warriors in buffalo skins entered at a brisk trot, and being welcomed by a chorus of howls and savage grunts by all the animals in the arena, a mad quadrille was inaugurated in which all the buffaloes, wolves, and grizzlies joined, each animal doing his best to escape from contact with the others, twisting and evading, by frantic contortions, the wolves, nimble as foxes, passing and re-passing in and out of the whirling mass.

The actors had in a short time assumed a more regular form of dancing, and the wolves were now circulating among the bigger animals in a long serpentine line that entered the crowd at a certain point and progressed in, out, and around like a wriggling snake; and during the time this was going on a marked change was visible on the faces of the onlookers. The Dance of Death had begun. All that had gone before might be taken as overtures and introductions. This was the weaving, the maze of bewilderment, chaos and destruction for the white man. As the wolves wriggled in and out, the buffaloes and grizzlies made desperate efforts to avoid them, but in vain. No sooner did they succeed in avoiding contact with the wolves on one side than they were touched and pushed on the other by wolves skipping and dodging back in a double circle. Quicker and quicker they glided, sometimes on all fours, sometimes standing erect and leaping, for now a buffalo, after wobbling and staggering and making every effort to escape contact with the wolves, reeled and sank to the ground; a wolf leaped over the body, while another, following, stood on the prostrate beast, uttering unearthly yells.

It was the beginning of the end. Buffaloes and grizzlies, all were reeling together in the maze of death. Two grizzlies fell, and the same movements were performed over their bodies. The nearer the victims came to falling the faster and more furious did the action become; it was no longer a question of avoiding the wolves, but simply a question of when the tottering grizzlies and buffaloes would fall dead, while Arappa-Honta sat pointing with his magic reed, now at this animal, now at that.

Down they dropped, one by one, the sounds of the victorious wolves becoming louder and more general. Arappa-Honta rose, and, waving his wand over the arena, a storm of grunts and fierce howls broke out from the Indians and the wolves, now dancing a last ronde over the bodies of the vanquished.

CHAPTER *24*

In the Maze

IT WAS late in November when the expedition reached the small settlement of Pueblo, on the upper Arkansas River, among the foot-hills of the Rockies. Here Fremont took a fresh supply of provisions, and meeting old Bill Williams, a mountain trapper, he engaged him as guide.

It was not long before they came to the snow, and Bill Williams hesitated. He was in doubt as to the passes; but Fremont forced his way on as though possessed by a power he could not control. The difficulties of the position seemed even now more than Fremont and his party could overcome, and yet they were only at the beginning. Most of the passes were packed with snow, and it required ten days to do what in summer-time would have taken two or three.

They pressed on. A great fear was bearing down on some of the men. The guide, Williams, hesitated more and more, while Fremont, not daring to show the slightest sign of discouragement, put on a bold face. He dared not turn back. They were at the threshold, so to speak, where they had plenty of time to contemplate the frozen peaks and passes of desolation, and not a white man, not an Indian, but held his breath when they came to the awful ravine of Rio del Norte.

They had arrived at what seemed the insurmountable barrier. Fremont looked at old Bill Williams, but not a word was spoken. No one could speak. What was the use? How is a man to argue with a chain of frozen rock thousands of feet high?

Fremont took Williams aside, but no one knew what was said during the talk. Williams dared not admit he had blundered, and Fremont dared not turn back, and he decided on the desperate attempt to pass through the snow-packed ravines and dig upward towards the backbone of the Rockies. All hands were encour-

206

aged to make the attempt, and Fremont talked to his men like a comrade. He worked as hard as any, was firm yet kindly in his speech, but fixed on impossible things. They could see how he was driven on and on, against reason, against common sense. No one had any will except to push forward to the heights of isolation. Attempt after attempt was made, the men working like condemned prisoners, making desperate efforts for freedom and life, against a hundred odds, against Fate. They might have battled with the snow to some good purpose, but now they had arrived at the region of storms; the wind blew down from the summits, howled around the crags and through the ravines. Not a man there had ever seen such a winter. No sooner did one storm cease than another set in from the north-east or north-west. The mules, reduced in flesh and strength, dropped off one after another, frozen in their tracks. Still the men worked on as under some fatal spell.

A last attempt was made to reach the watershed. The almost impossible task of stamping a path in the snow was accomplished, and animals and men walked over this with extreme caution, exposed to the icy winds, one mule after another falling, never to rise again. They had reached, by a superhuman effort, the storm-swept summit where the fierce winds kept the ground bare of snow, and a little food could be found for the cattle. Lower down all vegetation was hidden under snow.

They were now face to face with the first great calamity of the expedition, and all hope of saving the mules was at an end. Fremont tried hard to look cheerful, the guides pretended to be hopeful, but all felt the first swift touch of death in the most abandoned part of the Western wilds; all began a secret and silent preparation for the last wrestle with the grim and lonely conqueror. They were in the first grip. Fremont mentioned the name of his old friend and companion in adventure, Kit Carson, and longed for his counsel; but Carson was living in Taos, far away to the south.

They were now more than twelve thousand feet above sea level, and all the mules frozen to death. The first night in the high regions came with a clear sky and a still atmosphere, with the thermometer below zero. The stars looked like silver lamps floating in the air not far above. The howling of hungry wolves came to the ears of some of the men like warnings and prophecies of impending calamities, and kept several of them from sleeping, in spite of the great fatigue they felt. In the morning one of the half-breeds swore he had heard the tom-toms of the medicine-men, and saw Arappa-Honta sitting in his tent. Others declared they had heard queer sounds, but the men were not certain whether they were awake or dreaming at the time. The half-breeds became apprehensive. They considered the expedition as good as doomed, and called to mind the scenes and rumours at the great dance.

Fremont now held a solemn counsel with King and Preuss, two of his right-hand men, and it was decided they should return to the Rio del Norte without delay.

As soon as they arrived at the Rio del Norte Fremont called for volunteers to go to the settlements for mules and provisions to enable the whole of the party to push on to Taos. He picked out four men, naming King as their commander, and the order was to lose no time in sending back provisions to the camp, as there was just enough food to last fourteen days at a pinch.

When King left the camp it was like a party of ghosts walking off in the desolate wastes in search of a refuge.

The ordeal began from the very moment King and his small party vanished from sight and left the larger party on half rations, in weather that was arctic, every day full of suspense, every hour heavy with foreboding. Hardly a night but what one or two of the men heard, or thought they heard, the beating of tom-toms, while in dreams they would see repeated certain movements of the Dance of Death.

The nights became heavier, the days more weary. On the fifth day after King's departure one of the men was frozen stiff, and death entered the camp. It snowed more or less every day.

Fremont was now all but panic-stricken, but he maintained a stiff upper lip, and after waiting sixteen days decided to set out for the settlements himself, with four new men. He now took it for granted that King and his party had been killed by the Indians. Fremont took his old friend, Preuss, with him, a little food, and their blankets. His intention was to make for a place on the Red River some miles north of Taos.

"Now men," he said, before starting, "if I am not back here before your rations are out, or if you don't hear from me by messenger, strike out for yourselves and follow my trail."

Fremont was not long away before he struck a fresh Indian trail. He took this trail, which led in the direction he wished to go. He marched on, and the fifth day came across a lone Indian who was taking a drink from a hole he had made in the ice. The Indian happened to be the son of a Utah Chief and a friend of Fremont's. The Indian became a guide to the party, and furnished them with horses from the tribe living close by, and the next day they all set off again on the dreary march.

They had gone about six miles when Fremont discovered some smoke in a small wood. His courage rose, for now this must certainly be King and his party. It was more than three weeks since they had left the main camp. They hurried towards the spot; that smoke looked so comforting, there in that desert of snow and ice, and it looked as if things would now take a turn for the better. Fremont and his band were soon in the wood face to face with three half-starved men, half-crazed, and so changed he could scarcely recognise them. They were not able to walk. One of them grinned like a bear at bay. Fremont had hard work to get them to talk, but he kept on just as one would with Indians or little children. They had evidently killed a deer, and the bones were lying a little way from the fire where the men were sitting.

"But where's King?" Fremont asked several times.

"Well, you see, King ain't here," stammered one of the men, a little bolder than the others.

"I can see that," replied Fremont; "I want to know where he is, if you can tell me."

"Well," the man stammered, "he *was* here; that is, he came here with us day before yesterday."

"Where did he go?"

"He didn't go no-wheres."

A horrible grin distorted the features of the spokesman.

"You see, he give out when we got here; he starved to death."

A fearful silence settled over the group. Fremont, with a face as white as the snow, gazed in horror at the bones and then at the three pitiable survivors. They had been living off the remains.

By a superhuman effort Fremont managed to take them a march of one hundred and sixty miles, reaching the Red River in ten days.

From the town of Red River he sent back to the twenty-two members of the expedition he had left in the mountains one of his trusty men, Godey, with forty mules and several Mexicans. This band of twenty-two men had waited seven days in camp in the gravest suspense, and then left, going in the direction taken by Fremont and his party. They were now wanderers in a land covered with snow, with no game, no resources, no hope. They were marching, as it were, to their own funeral. Already, before abandoning the camp, Lame-Bear said he saw Arappa-Honta in a dream. He said the party was doomed. Other men were filled with strange presentiments. Some, reduced to mere skeletons, began to see visions.

They set out under a leaden sky, with a bitter wind coming down at their back, the whole face of Nature opposed to any kind of courage or hope, and they were not surprised when only two miles out of camp Lame-Bear turned suddenly about, faced the little band, let his blanket and gun fall, and asked one of the men to shoot him. After going about from one to the other begging to be shot and getting a negative response Lame-Bear turned, and, walking back to the forsaken camp, died there all alone. The others pressed on in a confused maze of thoughts. Death seemed everywhere. It surrounded them, enveloped them, urged them on, and again urged them to fall down in the snow and give up. They had only made ten miles when a man named Jim Wise began to sing and shout; he threw up his arms, looked up at the sky and sank down in the snow. Two Indians, members of the expedition, wrapped the dead man in his blanket and covered him with snow.

They pressed on.

The next day, Carver, one of the strongest men, a hunter known for his prowess, began to see visions. He stopped the company and began to describe things. He called to mind some of the strange scenes at the Indian Agency; he saw the barbecue where the buffalo was roasted whole; he said if the men would sit down in the snow the Indian cooks would attend with dishes of stewed venison, buffalo tongue, prairie-chicken, and many other things for a feast.

Carver's hopeless condition had a deadly effect on some of the men, themselves hovering on the borders of collapse and delirium, but there was nothing to be done but wander on, the merest shadows of a once sturdy band.

The next day Carver walked away into the deep snows and they saw him no more.

The cold was greater now, although at first it did not feel so; and the moon, sinking down behind the Rockies, in the west, left them in the middle of the night, with the stars, the snow, and the awful silence, fearing to sleep. When the morning dawned it brought a sky as blue as sapphire, a crisp, sharp air, in which nothing stirred, in which brilliant sunshine, withering cold, the blue above, and the white pall covering the earth, wrestled together in mocking rivalry, all Nature getting ready for the last scene.

They had been marching but a short time when, right before them, there loomed a mirage of churches and houses, pleasure-grounds, monuments, graveyards, shimmering streams, waterfalls glistening in the sunlight, huge flowers, and white tents pitched on the shores of beautiful lakes, crowds of people appearing and disappearing, exactly as in a dream. Somehow they were gazing at a mirage.

The Indian members of the band broke out in yells of exultation; they shouted, threw up their hands, danced in an ecstasy of joy; for there before them, they said, lay the happy hunting-grounds of the spirit-world.

Haler, who was in command of the little party, brought the company to a halt and began a speech to the men.

"Comrades," he said, "it ain't safe to go on like this. We've got to break up into small bands and scatter. . . . We've got to scatter. I don't expect to survive, but I want to ask you one last favour: don't shoot me, but wait till I die, then you can have my body."

No sooner had he ceased speaking than they began to scatter in small bands, each in a different direction, hoping to meet a rescue party from Red River direction.

It was now only a question of how death would arrive: by being starved or by being frozen; and some of the men did not object to the latter process, as it was painless and quickly over.

The bands started.

At first it was agreed that as soon as a man gave out the others should light a fire and leave him, but soon even this was found impossible. Some were beginning to get snow blind, others were deranged, others were distracted by superstitious notions of disaster whispered about by the Indians; and all at once someone called to mind the scene of the wolves, the buffa-loes, and bears in the great dance they had witnessed, and each man felt himself in a maze.

One of the bands concluded to lie down in the snow and wait for the first man to die. The Indians in this party, after a cannibal feast, began to howl and dance, and the white men, now crazed with suffering, joined in the ghastly chorus of cries, groans, yells, and mumbling imprecations. The party asumed the aspect of a company of demons on the snow, made more ghastly by the powerful moonlight, and the death dance began over again, this time in its livid reality. Two of the men were breathing their last, others were about to fall; some were describing circles, curves, in single or double file, stamping, turning about, jumping up and down, the Indians jabbering in an unknown dialect, their faces becoming more and more distorted.

The orgy of death ended the following day with the arrival of Godey and his Mexicans, who took the survivors to Taos, where Fremont was waiting at the house of his old-time comrade, Kit Carson.

Fremont had lost all his mules, the whole of his outfit, and nearly half his men. Nothing daunted, however, he went to work, organised a new expedition, took a more southerly route, and reached California in the spring of 1849 safe and sound. And I heard an old scout say: "There ain't a bullet can touch him! That man's got what they call a charmed life."

Certainly of all the public men of that time, who led adventuresome and romantic lives, Fremont was the most daring and the most original.

The people of California sent him back to Washington as their Senator.

* * * * *

Many years after my St. Louis experiences I visited General Fremont at San Jose, California. We talked much of the War days, and although an old man, he seemed like one who had never known trouble or disappointment, hale and serene. He passed away at last, peaceably, in his bed, after what seemed indeed a charmed life.

CHAPTER 25

Grierson's Raid

ATTACHED to General Grant's army was General Grierson's*
brigade, consisting of the Sixth and Seventh Illinois Cavalry and
the Second Iowa Cavalry. These men and boys, some of whom I
had known on the prairies near the Log-House, were destined to
engage in the most dangerous and thrilling cavalry raid of the
four years' War. Of this raid Grant wrote: "It was Grierson who
first set the example of what might be done in the interior of
the enemy's country without any base from which to draw supplies"; and of whom Sheridan said: "Grierson was the first to
teach us how to handle cavalry successfully."

On the morning of April 17th, 1863,† General Grierson set
out from the town of La Grange, in Tennessee, at the head of
1,700 men, camping at night in the town of Ripley, in the State
of Mississippi, after a ride of thirty miles. The next day a Rebel
force was encountered in the act of destroying the bridge span-
ning the Tallahatchie River, and after the Rebels were put to
flight Grierson's men restored the bridge to its former condition.

Sunday morning, April 19th, brought many and exciting adventures. Two companies, commanded by Captain Trafton, made
a dash at New Albany and drove the Rebels out of the town,
while two more companies plunged into the woods near by in
search of horses. They soon brought back all they could lead,
and by noon the brigade was again on the march, heading due
south, through the heart of hostile Mississippi.

On the next day Major Love, of the Second Iowa, was put in
command of sixty men from each regiment with orders to return to La Grange with the captured horses. The raiders ad-

*General Grierson was a cousin of the author—Ed.
†"Grierson's Raid," by J. S. C. Abott. *Harper's Magazine*, February, 1865.

vanced towards the south, and camped at night at Clear Springs after a ride of forty miles during the day. Early the next morning the march was resumed, and Colonel Hatch was detailed to break up the railroad near Okeola, but in the perilous attempt he encountered a large force of Rebels, received a serious wound, and his small body of troops was scattered. General Grierson pressed on, and after a hard ride of forty-five miles camped at a point eight miles south of Starkville. The news of Grierson's raid was spreading like wildfire throughout the State. The raiders came without warning, and when they left it was without any clue to their plans; mystery enshrouded their every movement. As they proceeded south the danger of their position increased with every mile, yet General Grierson was determined to enter Baton Rouge at all costs, regardless of all obstacles.

And now the telegraph wires had to be cut along the railroad from Macon. Two men volunteered to carry out this dangerous project, but in spite of their already tried bravery their courage failed them at the last moment. Everyone looked with dismay on a duty which even these trained veterans dared not undertake, and yet the work had to be done. At last a company of the Seventh Illinois was detailed to proceed to the work, with Captain Forbes commanding. With thirty-five men he left the regiment on a ride of fifty miles through a country swarming with Rebels. No one expected to see Captain Forbes and his company again. They directed their course straight for the large town of Macon, but they were forced to turn aside and make for the town of Enterprise on the railroad, and as they came in view of the place they were greeted with the sight of three thousand Rebel soldiers in the process of disembarking from a train of cars. Here Captain Forbes had a flash of inspiration. Without a moment's hesitation he rode forward, bearing a flag of truce, and demanded the instant surrender of the place to General Grierson, whom the Rebels supposed to be close in the rear with a formidable force. The ruse succeeded. Colonel Goodwin, the Rebel commander, asked for an hour in which to consider the proposition. Captain Forbes complied with this request, and put this hour to the best use he knew how in a hard gallop toward the Pearl River with his little band of thirty-five men; and the three thousand scared Rebels in the town of Enterprise were not called on for a more definite reply to the demand for surrender.

In the meantime the Sixth Illinois and the remainder of the Seventh had made, during the day of the 19th and the following night, the most extraordinary march of the whole raid. Coming to the town of Starkville, they destroyed a large Rebel shoe factory, committing a large quantity of leather and several thousand pairs of shoes and hats to the flames. After this they suddenly found themselves surrounded by treacherous swamps and swollen creeks. The spring rains had overflowed every stream. The roads, of which they were utterly ignorant, were like rivers, in many places from three to four feet deep, and yet on they went during the night of the 22nd, jaded men and jaded beasts, without a guide, without a sign-post to direct them, for delay meant death. As they approached Pearl River, they met a small party of Rebel pickets working with superhuman energy, stripping up the planks of the bridge floor and hurling them into the waters below. The pickets being disposed of, the raiders pressed on into the night without a single halt except at the town of Decatur, where they captured and paroled seventy-five prisoners, destroyed two warehouses full of commissary stores, four loads of ammunition, burned the railroad bridges and trestle work, and captured two trains of cars and two locomotives.

At sunrise on the 29th General Grierson's band found themselves on the outshirts of Brookhaven. Here they burned the depôt of the New Orleans and Jackson railroad, their cars and bridges, and paroled two hundred prisoners. The townspeople were panic-stricken until they found that all private property was respected, when they became profuse in their hospitality and the hope that the Union would soon be restored.

General Grierson wrote: "I could have brought away a thousand men with me, men whom I found hiding in the swamps and the forests, where they had been hunted like wild beasts by the conscript officers with bloodhounds."

At last, covered with dust, haggard, and in rags, with a wild fire of delight and pride in their eyes, on May 2nd they galloped into the streets of Baton Rouge. The story of their incredible adventures ran with the echo of their horses' hoofs. The excitement became indescribable. Nothing like it had been known during the War. Less than two thousand men had ridden through the State of Mississippi, encountering every conceivable danger, every known hardship, with thousands of Rebels at their heels.

During the last thirty hours of the raid the intrepid band rode

eighty miles, engaged in three skirmishes, destroyed large quanti-
ties of military stores, burned bridges, swam one river, took
forty-two prisoners, and all without a single halt and without
food.

In this raid General Grierson rode eight hundred miles, with
no guides except rude country maps and a pocket compass,
relying the whole of the way on the country for forage and
provisions. The raiders had cut three railroads, burned nine
bridges, destroyed two locomotives and nearly two hundred cars,
broken up three Rebel camps, captured and paroled one thousand prisoners, and brought into Baton Rouge with them twelve
hundred captured horses.

For twenty-five years subsequent to the Civil War General
Grierson had to deal with the most savage Indian tribes on the
wild plains along the borders of Mexico, and he so conciliated
their confidence that from hostile savages they became his
friends. After being made military commander of that vast territory lying between New Mexico and the Pacific Ocean, which
includes Arizona and Southern California, General Grierson re-
tired in his old age to Jacksonville, Illinois, in the heart of
Lincoln's country, the town from which he went forth to the
Civil War as Colonel of the Sixth Illinois Cavalry, where he lives
a tranquil life, as if he had never known thirty years' military
service of the most dangerous description.

The last time I saw him was at a reception I gave in his
honour during one of my last sojourns in America. He was still
in active service and came to the reception accompanied by his
military staff.

General Grierson, like General Fremont, seemed to possess a
charmed life. Shot at scores of times, I believe he never once
received a wound, and now, past the age of eighty, is still in
good health.

CHAPTER 26

The Valley of Shadows

ONE of my favourite modes of passing idle time was on the levee watching the incoming and outgoing boats. They arrived and departed by scores, for this was the golden age of adventure in the Mississippi Valley.

From the slumbering solitude of Minnesota the mighty stream had drifted for ages before a white man's canoe was seen upon its surface. Then came the shriek of iron whistles, the swirl of puffing machinery, the confusion and clashing of hordes of adventuresome settlers, ushering in a new era and a new world.

The departure of a favourite boat during the *ante-bellum* days made up a picture for the memory of a lifetime. Here came hunters and trappers from the western and northern wilds, men with rifles, pistols, weapons with blades like butcher-knives, fashionably dressed planters returning South, men resembling half-breeds, dark, quick-tempered desperadoes, jovial comrades, professional gamblers, negroes, mulattoes, octoroons.

Indeed, in the sight of certain persons a Mississippi steamboat was a puffing nightmare of profanity and wickedness, while to the reckless adventurer it meant increased activity, a more expansive feeling of life and liberty. Freed from the trammels of sheriff and bloodhounds, desperadoes from every State saw in it a floating paradise of luxury and licence. Once on the bosom of the great river responsibility and worry were forgotten, and the still, small imps of the imagination began to rise with the curling smoke from the chimney-stacks and the rolling swell from the paddle-wheels. The steamboat was a world in itself, unlike anything ever seen or dreamed of—a floating hotel at whose tables friends and foes, preachers and infidels, card-sharpers and merchants, slave-drivers and Abolitionists, planters, politicians, and cut-throats rubbed shoulders and ate together. It served as railway, stage-coach, and tavern; it had the freedom of the back-woods and the *dolce far niente* of the log-cabin, while skilled negro cooks served up corn-bread that melted in the mouth and caused many a passenger to compare it with the coarse hominy and gritty corn-meal of their own rough and primitive homes. Little wonder that the ordinary traveller found the Mississippi boat a haven of rest; that after such meals, after the French coffee or the Kentucky whisky, they would sit in armchairs on the deck, with their feet extended on the railing, their heads thrown back, and puff wreaths of odorous smoke from cigars made in Havana, think of things until now unthinkable, and dream of wonders to come, while the boat floated down with the current through balmy airs, over a surface that touched the high-water mark of two lonely and romantic shores. It was no wonder that at meal-time danger was a thing that no one stopped to consider, in spite of the fact that the steamboat of those days resembled nothing so much as an architectural tinder-box, ready to disappear in a sudden blaze, sink to the bottom by striking a snag, or go to pieces by an explosion.

Fashionable pleasure-parties came and went from and to the Far South, and on the broad expanse of the hurricane deck, under the opal lights of southern skies, beautiful and gracefully robed creoles lent to the aerial promenade something serenely antique and remote, and as the boat swept majestically past the shores of Louisiana, soft airs, wafted from bowers of orange blossoms, fanned the faces of a people without a care, who lived by the day, whose lives seemed a tranquil and luxurious dream.

Down in the "ladies' cabin," at the end of the boat, there were evenings when the place resembled some quaintly designed drawing-room in a fantastic country house, and on certain occasions there would be music and dancing.

A steamboat had three separate worlds. There was the boiler-deck, the nethermost part, what timid minds might call the inferno, peopled by negro deck-hands, slaves, and "poor white trash," from which strange, broken echoes rose and fell, snatches of songs blown up on the night winds mingling with the muffled din of slamming furnace-doors, spitting 'scape-pipes, and whirling paddle-wheels. Then came the saloon-deck, peopled by the men of all social grades travelling "first-class"; lastly, the exclusive portion set apart for ladies.

In warm weather a roaring trade was done at the bar, which

glittered with cut-glass, crystal decanters, silver mirrors, bottles arrayed to attract the eye and tempt the individual taste; and the "barkeeper," ablaze with diamond studs and breast pin, condescended, with cool and deliberate demeanour, to serve his customers who, at certain moments, stood around the counter two rows deep. That part of the saloon near the bar was usually occupied by gamblers engaged in playing for high stakes, and around the tables here scenes of wild and tragic excitement were often enacted.

One day, at the beginning of the war, while standing on the levee close to the water's edge, I heard someone shout: "Hello there, Bub!"

I looked up and saw a tall, angular young man, wearing the uniform of the Union Volunteers. He was looking down at me from the deck of the *City of Alton*, where he stood with other volunteers in blue.

"What are you doing here?" he shouted.

I looked hard at him for some moments before I recognised a young man I had known in Alton, and hardly had I done so when a man standing beside him shouted: "Say, Bub, don't you want to come along with us?"

To my great astonishment, it was Azariah James, who was also a volunteer. The preacher from the prairies and his companions-in-arms were about to enter the strife; talk and preaching were to be put aside for action.

The boat was crowded with soldiers, young men from the country round about the Log-House and the district about Jacksonville. There must have been, at that moment, on the *City of Alton*, a dozen men and boys I had known in Illinois. Here they were, coming down in boat-loads from the prairies, from the cornfields, from the meeting-houses, from the backwoods. In three months' time all these meek-mannered, awkward young men would be turned into weather-beaten soldiers, and in the short space of six months into hard and toughened fighters. Things had changed, and things would change again, as in a night, and to many on this boat, and other boats here on the levee, life would soon cease to pass as in a pleasant dream, and would become a long nightmare of dangers and terrors inconceivable.

In the winter of 1862 a great fleet of steamboats set out from St. Louis to Memphis, Tennessee, to co-operate in General

Grant's surprise movement against Vicksburg, the Rebel strong-hold on the Mississippi. I stood for hours gazing in admiration at the different boats under Government orders to proceed to the South. There was the beautiful *Die Vernon*, destined to embark the Third Kentucky Regiment at Memphis; there was the *Des Arc*, wrapped, as it seemed to me, in an aura of glory, for the officers and escort of General Smith's First Division; there was the *City of Alton* for two Ohio Regiments; the trim, light-going *Hiawatha*; the *Spread Eagle*, skimming the water like a bird, loaded with the One Hundred and Twenty-seventh Illinois; the *Sucker State*, with her characteristic smoke-stacks, suggesting to me the wilderness and prairie; there was the stately *Dakota*, slightly battered about the paddle-box; the powerful *City of Memphis*, whose very name called up delightful souvenirs of the sunny South, embarking two batteries of Missouri Artillery and the Eighth Regiment, with a section of Parrott guns; and the *Omaha*, the *Sioux City*, the *Indiana*; the handsome *Westmore-land*, for Colonel Stuart's Fifty-fifth Illinois from Benton Bar-racks; the *Adriatic*, the *Gladiator*, the *Isabella*, the *Polar Star*, superb among the galaxy of river meteors; and twenty-five more of like build and swiftness.

What a change had come over the river! No more pleasure-trips, no more going and coming for the mere love of travel and change. Most of these boats had been, and would be again, loaded with soldiers sound in wind and limb going down stream to the front, returning with wounded or fever-stricken invalids, or whole troops of Rebel prisoners. The ladies' cabin, the hurri-cane deck, the boiler-deck, saloon, all were full of soldiers; nobody thought of distinctions, there were no vacant spots, and the pilot-house perched on the *Texas* rose clear and white from a sea of soldiers, like a great bird's nest at the top of a forest of animate trunks, and the steps, the railings, the promenade, the rim all round the skylights of the roof, were dotted and hung with men in blue unforms, standing, sitting, lolling, lying down, a knapsack for pillow, chewing tobacco or eating oranges, gazing at the people below, some joking callously, some with pensive faces, homesick already, others in the throes of unconquerable agitation, others longing for the fray, while towering smoke-stacks belched forth rolling pillars of black smoke that spread in trailing clouds far over the water.

The river front was the centre of bustle, noise, and excitement. If the town itself seemed asleep, the long, wide, sloping levee was all life, with hundreds of drays, mules, negroe deck-hands, some of them idle, but many more working as they had never worked, shouting, cursing, the hoarse voices of mates rising above the general din and arriving across the cobble-stones like the ravings of men in delirium, while the soldiers on the steamboats contemplated the movement and uproar going on before them with the mien of so many statues in blue. Groups of idle negroes looked on bewildered, expressing the opinions of whites, picked up here and there. Some of them were free men and they could do as they pleased.

"Ketch me on one o' dem boats!" remarked a burly black; "I done bin down dar an' I know w'at dey gwine do. Dey ain't gwine down dar fer te 'joy deyself lak at a picnic; dey gwine down te Kaintuck an' Vicksburg te play de 'possum an' de coon. Mistah 'Possum he done absquatulate hissef in a big hole by de ribber-bank, an' by-an'-by 'long come Mistah Coon fum St. Louis on one er dem boats, an' he invite de 'possum out, but de 'possum he say 'No, sah!' he declah he gwine ter stay right whar he am. De coon 'monstrate wid de 'possum but de 'possum run roun' by de back do', come up ober de bank an' 'gin te let fly at Mist' Coon settin' dar on de boat in de cool ob de ebenin'. Dat make de coon ask hissef whar all de bumble-bees an' yaller hornets come from—ziz, ziz, boom, whiz! it gittin' stingin' hot on Mistah Coon's boat; de bullets dey fallin' lak hail, one man drop, den nudder, an' nudder; Mist' Coon 'low dar ain't no time fer te tarry, he ring de bell fer de pilot, he ring de bell fer de engineer, he shout fer de fust mate, de mate 'gin te cuss an' howl—de boat let loose fum de levee. No, sah! it ain't good fer de coon's health te come 'sturbin' de 'possum in his hole down dar; dis niggah gwine stay right whar he am."

The spring of 1863 was a period of grave suspense in St. Louis. Would Grant succeed in taking Vicksburg?

On the night of April 16th, a long line of dark objects could be distinguished bearing down stream toward the redoubtable Rebel batteries of Vicksburg. Admiral Porter headed the line in the gunboat *Benton*, followed by the *Tuscumbia*, so far beneath the surface that her black iron sides were almost invisible; then, a little to the right of the ironclad fleet, and hugging the oppo-site shore as much as safety would permit, came the steamboats with ten huge barges in tow laden with corn, freight, and provisions. Would they succeed in running the batteries in the dark? Would the crew of the steamboats stick to their posts? Never, ever to the eyes of the most hardened pilot, had the moving gulf of water appeared so menacing, so black, so hungry for victims. The mighty stream, as the fleet approached Vicksburg, never seemed so wrapped in silence as now, owing to the stillness of the crews and the absence of all unnecessary noise. All was going well. The *Benton* was now opposite the Fort. All at once an awful sound smote the ears of the men on the boats. The Rebel batteries had opened fire. A thunderous roar went up from the *Benton*, whose guns were all ready and only waiting for such a signal. The time had arrived for the testing of nerves, the trial of courage, the last ordeal of shock and terror.

The batteries of the Fort are now belching forth shot that tear across the ironclads with deadly impact, skimming along the surface with a sickening splash so near as to make death fairly palpable. The *Benton* has escaped; she is now beyond the fire range; but here comes the ironclad *Tuscumbia*, now, in her turn, within the range of fire. The steamboat *Forest Queen* is there, too, trying to pass with the *Tuscumbia* as an escort. Something bursts just above the surface of the water, driving steel splinters and bits of iron in every direction. It is the first bomb from the Rebel mortars. One of the steam-pipes of the *Forest Queen* is gone; a moment more, and a ball rips through the hull; quick, the *Tuscumbia* takes the damaged boat in tow, and, with all steam on, heads for the bank. The air is streaked with whirling flashes from the Vicksburg mortars, bombs burst in mid-air, they descend in a hail of sparks and fire, they burst in the water, on the decks, around the pilot-houses; ears are deafened with the roar of Parrott guns, it is impossible to hear the officers' commands; the steamboats rush past with all haste, for a new terror has come. The river is becoming a living inferno. Light is spreading over the town of Vicksburg, where houses are on fire; houses are ablaze on the opposite shore; waves of light rise and fall, and rise again in different places; a cloud of sparks is shooting up from the steamboat *Henry Clay* in mid-stream; the black waters of the Mississippi begain to shimmer with a ghastly glow, the flames lap the board with magical swiftness; the river is bathed in an awful yellow light, through which the bursting shells descend in arches of fire, disclosing the crew of the *Henry Clay* making frantic efforts to escape from the burning hulk. Men are going to the bottom; her pilot, who is floating on a piece of wreck, is picked up by General Sherman, who is there with a yawl, while hard by lucky *Silver Wave* skims along out of the danger zone, escaping with a mere scratch.

On the *Henry Clay* were two boys whom I knew in Alton, and in the yawl with Sherman was Azariah James, and another volunteer we had known in Illinois.

On the 4th of July Vicksburg capitulated, and the Mississippi, became once more free to navigation.

In this same month I went on a visit to the family of the Reverend Samuel Smith, a Presbyterian minister at Alton, and there, on the second day after my arrival, as I was roaming about the levee, I saw a steamboat arrive and a score of passengers come ashore. Among them was a man who was hardly able to walk, and who stopped to look about him as if in search of someone. In a few moments a woman came running down to meet him. The man was Elihu Gest, the Load-Bearer, so changed by illness that at first I did not know him. He had been at the front with an ambulance corps, and, later, acting as nurse in the Overton Military Hospital at Memphis. He was now "invalided home," and his wife had come to meet him with a covered wagon.

When I returned to St. Louis I found my father getting ready to move with the family to Niagara Falls. We left Missouri in August, and arrived at the celebrated watering-place at the height of a brilliant season, with all the great hotels full, with balls two or three times a week at the Cataract House and the International Hotel, so far removed from the War that it seemed as if such a thing was not known. And yet, even here, on the borders of Canada, there was hardly a home that did not have a friend or a relative at the front.

For me, at least, the change from the hot city on the Mississippi to the cool breezes wafted up from the Rapids and the surging cataract was almost too good to be true; and for more than a year, during our stay in that wonderful spot, I wandered about free at all hours, enjoying to the full this new revelation of the beauty of Nature.

So goes the world, for "Time and the Hour runs through the roughest day."